The Personal Is Political

Personal/Public Scholarship

VOLUME 7

Series Editor

Patricia Leavy (*USA*)

The titles published in this series are listed at *brill.com/pepu*

The Personal Is Political

Body Politics in a Trump World

Edited by

Christine Salkin Davis and Jonathan L. Crane

Christine Salkin Davis
Matthew 25:35

BRILL
SENSE

LEIDEN | BOSTON

All chapters in this book have undergone peer review.

Library of Congress Cataloging-in-Publication Data

Names: Davis, Christine S., editor. | Crane, Jonathan Lake, 1959- editor.
Title: The personal is political : body politics in a Trump world / edited by Christine Salkin Davis and Jonathan L. Crane.
Other titles: Body politics in a Trump world
Description: Leiden ; Boston : Brill Sense, [2020] | Series: Personal/Public Scholarship, 2542-9671 ; volume 7 | Includes bibliographical references.
Identifiers: LCCN 2020027156 (print) | LCCN 2020027157 (ebook) | ISBN 9789004436305 (Paperback ; acid-free paper) | ISBN 9789004436312 (Hardback ; acid-free paper) | ISBN 9789004436329 (eBook)
Subjects: LCSH: United States--Politics and government--21st century. | Trump, Donald, 1946---Influence. | Identity politics--United States. | National characteristics, American. | United States--Social conditions--21st century.
Classification: LCC E912 .P47 2020 (print) | LCC E912 (ebook) | DDC 973.933092--dc23
LC record available at https://lccn.loc.gov/2020027156
LC ebook record available at https://lccn.loc.gov/2020027157

ISSN 2542-9671
ISBN 978-90-04-43630-5 (paperback)
ISBN 978-90-04-43631-2 (hardback)
ISBN 978-90-04-43632-9 (e-book)

This book is printed on acid-free paper and produced in a sustainable manner.

ADVANCE PRAISE FOR
THE PERSONAL IS POLITICAL: BODY POLITICS IN A TRUMP WORLD

"A compelling collection of chilling personal narratives that reveal, resist, and, ultimately, raise the awareness, understanding, empathy, hope, and social justice activism needed to end the discrimination, marginalization, and oppression experienced by diverse bodies during the Trump era."
– Lawrence R. Frey, National Communication Association Distinguished Scholar, Professor, University of Colorado Boulder

"Davis and Crane have edited a broad range of experience across contexts, identities, and issues. In the 'Trump World,' we have reached the time when our words and their meaning are viscerally located *and experienced* in our bodies, and this book escorts readers through a tour of these loci. As readers, we are challenged to stay present through the discomfort of evidence of political dismembering described and expressed through bodies impacted during the era and rabid discourse of Donald J. Trump. The book dares us to move beyond discursive tropes about the personal nature of the political, while we are faced with the affective proof in our own responsive bodies as we read this collection of narratives. It forces us to face how politics painfully impact us through the vulnerable body when hegemonic oppression is given voice through someone like Trump."
– Sarah Amira de la Garza, Associate Professor and Southwest Borderlands Scholar, Arizona State University

"As I write, darkness has descended upon our nation, as yet another African American man has been executed by police sworn to serve and protect our citizens. Widespread protests have erupted in response, all in the midst of a deadly pandemic. President Trump's predictably bellicose response has been to *threaten* citizens exercising First Amendment rights. Into our divided, discordant world, this book shines a welcome new light, offering new ways of thinking about the origins and potential trajectories of this strange moment in our history. Here's hoping that some thoughtful narratives and counter-narratives can help, in some small way, to save us from ourselves."
– Christopher N. Poulos, Professor, University of North Carolina Greensboro

To Jonah

CONTENTS

ACKNOWLEDGEMENTS

We would like to thank our spouses, families, colleagues, and friends, who are surely ready for this book to be finished. Thank you for your love and support.

We also wish to acknowledge Graduate Research Assistants Karly Bynum and Heather Stegner for their patient assistance with transcription and formatting, and attention to millions of details. We truly could not have done this book without your help.

Thank you to our chapter contributors, their study participants, and to our anonymous interviewees whose voices are heard in the Dialogues. We appreciate your candor and thoughtfulness, your sharing of stories and vulnerability.

Thank you to everyone in the resistance as they fight for social, racial, and economic justice.

DEDICATION

This book is dedicated to Jonah, who represents the potential good in the world and all the vulnerable people we are duty-bound to protect. It is also dedicated to the people we love, with whom we live and work, and to everyone who aspires to a more just future. This is written in the hope we will do better.

> The act of telling the story is itself an action, a chance in a tilt toward the future. I still believe in truth, and facts. I still believe that the telling reinforces those things. I believe that in the telling, there is hope (Bernstein, 2020, p. 413)

REFERENCE

Bernstein, A. (2020). *The American oligarchs: The Kushners, The Trumps, and the marriage of money and power.* New York, NY: Norton.

KIMBERLY DARK

PROLOGUE

Driving Home, in Reverse

INTRODUCTION

This is an autoethnographic essay about increased anxiety in the wake of Trump's election and presidency – my own, of course, but also the anxiety those who voted for him must've been feeling under the threat of a woman nearly being elected president. It's an essay about how the body keeps score and makes sense of things when the mind fails – or is maybe just too slow – and a response is warranted. It's about how we persist, despite incomprehensibility and lack of control, sometimes able to get help and learn the lessons the body teaches, sometimes unable, waiting. This essay in three parts begins at the end of 2017 and moves backward, not just to the beginning of that year, but to other moments in time that may provide transferrable meaning, comprehensible memories of survival, and similar feelings of peril.

> For myself, "survivor" contains its other meaning: one who must bear witness for those who foundered; try to tell how and why it was that they, also worthy of life, did not survive. And pass on ways of survival; and tell our chancy luck, our special circumstances. (Olsen, 2014, p. 39)

December 2017

Just. Can't. Do. It.

Like a cat going into a bath twists this way and that. You want to push? Someone gets hurt. Better I pull off the freeway and not push it. Like a dog that thinks it can't walk on linoleum and just won't go. I can't make my foot press the gas pedal down.

Ohio in October was the beginning of the end. A bridge popped up out of nowhere. I was already having trouble staying above 50 mph on the freeway and there it was. Everyone was going at least 65 and I slowed to about 20 in bumper-to-bumper traffic, flicked on the hazards. I actually thought it'd

DOI:10.1163/9789004436329_001

be easier to drive over the edge of the bridge than to stay with that feeling. “No,” I said to myself aloud. “No, you are going to get to this university and do the event. You are going to have dinner with students and make it to the Cleveland airport tomorrow. You are going to see your son in Chicago. That’s all you have to do. Go see your son and your grandson ….” My own voice talking in the car, convincingly, got me across.

And then I just couldn’t do it anymore. No more driving on freeways. What had been difficult for more than a year became impossible.

That night, near midnight, I let the GPS guide me down every small road in Ohio from Oxford to Cleveland. Across a small bridge, I drove alone. After that, no more bridges either. And, anywhere I could see an embankment to the right, I couldn’t do it. Or really, any long left-turning road. No. Not that either. I thought the therapy in spring was helping, but it wasn’t helping enough. I thought maybe the ho’oponopono would have an ancillary effect.

September 2017

Mostly, he laughs and listens and stops me when I say something useful. “Hey wait a minute!” He yells, bright eyed. “Take a deep breath, say that part again.” After I do, he says excitedly, as though listening to a good story, “Okay, what else?”

I have come for a ho’oponopono session because the worry I have for my son and my mother are preventing me from sleeping. Ho’oponopono is the process of making things right. You don’t need someone’s permission or participation to make things right. The people with whom you want to make things right don’t even need to be alive. You can do it all by yourself.

Say this:
I’m sorry.
Please forgive me.
Thank you.
I love you.

You can do ho’oponopono with the help of a kahuna, a guide. I am crying all the time and I can’t sleep and driving with others on the road has become so hard. I live in Hawaii, where ho’oponopono is the indigenous way of helping. I often work on the mainland where freeways abound. I know I need help.

My mother is losing her memory and may not have enough money to make it through the rest of her days. She is incorrigible and won't accept any help from me that would make any kind of sense. She won't move into the downstairs apartment at my house. She won't give up her Lexus and her giant poodle's visits to the fancy groomer twice a month. She voted for Trump and thinks everything should be okay now that he won. She's losing her memory and knows that something is wrong. She can't afford her mortgage and needs to move out of her house. I don't even know her full financial situation. I can't help her because she won't allow it.

My son has a good job, better than most. He has health insurance and a modest pension. He works for a university but, he reminds me, his adjusted income is less than mine was when I was his age, with less education and a job with lower status. He reminds me of this because he thinks I judge him poorly. He is 27 with $100,000.00 in debt. His father and I paid for his Bachelor's degree, but he took out loans for the masters degree. He hears judgment in everything I say and he is constantly anxious about providing for his family. His partner looked for work for two years. For now, their son knows a middle-class lifestyle but what does that even mean anymore? He is taking medication for the anxiety. When they finally split up and he moves into a two-bedroom apartment he can ill-afford, I wonder if he should've gotten a studio. An adult and a child can live in a studio apartment, I reason silently. Maybe I am judging his decisions in addition to judging the economic circumstances my nation has created. I cannot help him and I cannot sleep at night. He takes anxiety medication and rants on the internet about how cisgender white men have ruined everyone's life. He is a cisgender white man, painfully woke.

"You gonna light a candle for your mother and one for your son. You're gonna ask God to take care of them because you've done all you can do." I nod, tears streaking my face. Near the end of the session, the kahuna says, "How're you feeling? Anything physical I can help with?" I shrug, but he looks expectantly. "You gotta rash?" he finally asks, as though I've forgotten, which I have. The rash seemed so minor in comparison to the worry for my son and my mother.

"I do." I said matter of factly. "In my armpit. Since the election."

"Right," he says, as though that was the answer he was looking for. He jumps up and goes to the kitchen, comes back with a mason jar full of bright yellow creamy liquid and a giant avocado. "Take a sip of that," he says. I do and he watches my face. "Is it good?" he says. I nod. "Good! You take a jar of this, turmeric, sea salt, coconut milk. And you drink it in one day, with a whole avocado. You gonna feel some things move!"

My eyes widen and he laughs again. "No gotta be weird about it. Just have some avocado on toast in the morning, on a salad at lunch. Pau. You ate a whole avocado. Don't have to sit there with a spoon and eat it all at once!" He laughs uproariously. "You gotta tree with fruit at home?" I nod. "Great!" He exclaims, "you don't need my avocado. That'll take care of the rash, but not the president. Need more than avocados for that!" I nod sadly. Somehow, we didn't even talk about the driving.

February 2017

It happened once before. I just couldn't bring myself to accelerate on the freeway. The cars were closing in. My hands went numb and my vision tunneled. What the hell? I used to drive cross-country, sixteen hours a day on the freeway, no problem. Suddenly, I couldn't do freeways and bridges.

That's how the body is: totally in charge. I can forget this fact, act like it isn't true and sometimes that ruse takes hold for a while. I'd say in my mind, just accelerate and pass this car. My numb hands and unresponsive pedal-foot would reply, bow down before the body, foolish thinker. You may be chatty, but you're not in charge.

It happened to my father a few years before his death. He couldn't go on the freeway, even as a passenger. Once a large man, his body had shrunk. His hands and knee joints seemed enormous against his shrinking limbs.

We never spoke of it directly, but I saw his fear. He'd get in the car for me to take him to the doctor and he'd immediately tell me which route to take. No freeways. I'd just shrug and say sure, but suddenly, when he died, I couldn't drive on the freeway either. I didn't put it together on my own but my friend remembered his fear and said, "grief comes out in strange ways." I hadn't thought of it, but somehow that felt right.

Now it's back. I can't stand anyone driving next to me over 30 miles an hour. After my father died, I struggled with that driving anxiety for about a year and then, poof, it was gone. I felt fine again, like nothing was ever wrong. Halfway through 2016, when Donald Trump was on every TV in every public place, the sound of his voice in every broadcast, I suddenly couldn't drive in traffic again. My father died more than six years ago, but when the anxiety came back, I knew it wasn't him. It was Donald.

Why do people keep handing him a microphone? Why does the news keep showing up at his events? That's what I kept wondering, when I'd see him. When he received the Republican nomination, it still didn't make sense. And then it did. Something I had not taken the time to understand had blindsided me. And now, I become frightened in a part of me that the chatty mind can't control. The body and the mind are communicating below the radar of my awareness. Who are all those people in those cars? I don't know them. They could do anything at any moment. None of us are safe. Somehow I know, in my flesh, that the rise of Donald Trump's popularity was driving my inability to drive.

To be clear, I am still driving. I'm not stalled and sweating in the driveway. I have to drive to a university and teach three days a week after all. I have to. An hour each way and no reliable public transportation or carpools to be had. I've searched online, asked friends. So I drive. I'm just slow, unsafe. I need to stay in the far right lane where no one can get to the right of me. Sometimes I get off the road and breathe, cry, rest. I arrive everywhere in a sheen of perspiration, my chest aching and my body withered with exhaustion. I breathe through it. When I can switch the channel in my mind to thinking "we're all just moving in the same direction together" or even "life is a grand mystery and mostly we're fine," it gets better. Until it gets worse again.

It's not like I didn't understand that racism has always been a profound motivator in politics. Or sexism or homophobia. People become afraid that they aren't getting as much as they deserve. Indeed, they're not getting as much as the culture promises. Fear drives the ballot. Keep the immigrants away. White men and white families should get theirs first. It's an undercurrent in the body, even when the mind can't quite articulate the pull. As soon as he had the nomination, I felt the possibility of election and I remained watchful, ever watchful of what was whizzing by on either side of me.

My son was born during the height of the AIDS crisis. Politicians were threatening concentration camps for gay people and I was afraid my son could be taken from me and his father because of our queerness. A distant fear, but a fear nonetheless. His dad and I, though we were both queer, were married to each other. On paper, we looked like a "normal" family and that gave me some small comfort. Still, as a writer and human rights activist, it would've been easy enough to target us if it had come to that. Thankfully, it didn't come to that. I don't recall any body-anxiety back then. I don't recall any rash or difficulty sleeping or driving.

Oh yeah, the rash. I've never had skin problems. At first I thought it was a rash, but it was a yeast infection. Cortisol released into the body at high levels when I drive can apparently reduce immune functioning and elevate blood sugar. That often causes candida overgrowth. Yeast infection.

At an academic conference in November, right after the election, a woman spoke on this topic during an ad hoc meeting in which a group of feminist scholars were discussing responses to the election. This woman urged self-care. And when she mentioned candida overgrowth, I wasn't the only one in the room nodding knowingly.

The body remembers and makes associations. Now that I recall, now that my mind recalls, I can tell you I had yeast infections as a young adolescent, right before I broke away from my incest-supporting home.

Notice how I word that? My incest experience was not just about a thing my step-father did to me in private. I lived in an incest-supporting culture that was organized around my incest-supporting home. The body keeps score. I left that home in order to make a new life, a counter-cultural life to supplant the one I had been given. My repertoire for living and learning is large and still, the body retains everything in a tight weave. Nothing escapes the understanding of skin and muscle. I am starting to see, by which I mean feel, that there is something wonderful about this cumulative wisdom, even though I can't get to work well-rested these days. Something's happening that feels too familiar. And yet, I am not young. I am capable. I am knowledgeable. I don't have clear language for this driving problem yet, but I know the body has taken care of me before.

When I was thirteen, my step-father would sometimes take me to the country club where he played golf and the men there seemed to know something about me. At least they thought they did. I didn't look like a child and a lot can be assumed about someone young who doesn't look like a child. A girl who looks like a woman draws assumptions like flies. The rash, the sleeplessness – that feeling again, like being at the country club with my step-father, and realizing suddenly that everyone's in on the joke about my lack of worth. Blindsided.

Hillary Clinton almost won. Some say she did, because of the popular vote, but that's not how we choose a president. I went online to see what I could find about the electoral college voters and most were already Trump supporters. There would be no overthrow of the system. The fact of her near win, the assumption on shows like *Saturday Night Live*, that she had already won because of her superior experience and clear plans, fueled a sexism that lives in our bodies, not only in our minds and mouths.

It's not that America's sexism is stronger than its racism. It's just more hidden. Most people live in two-gender households, work in two-gender jobs. We are constantly in semi-civil contact, rigid rules in place to ensure the functioning of social and familial systems so that the weft and the warp of our national fabric can hold together. Whether fashioned of slave cotton or immigrant silk or the hats and ties Trump imports from China, the fabric of oppression won't easily unravel or be torn asunder. Despite what we believe about ourselves as "loving women" or "not being racist" we are participating in the system as it is, as it has always been.

Most Americans still live in segregated neighbourhoods, attend racially segregated schools, so it's easier to create stories about Others that don't require a lot fancy machinery in the mind to close the weave. This is a problem, to be sure. Our isolation causes stories of the Other to go unchallenged. Police brutality based on race is more readily ignored than police brutality based on gender. In hiring practices, similarly, racial discrimination trumps gender discrimination. Race is a problematic construction, albeit a different problem from the one we face with gender.

Hillary Clinton was the most qualified person for the job of President and yet, still a woman. Allowing any woman to win such an election would've confirmed the domination by "intellectuals" and "professionals" of "working" people, of "regular" people in America. "Even their women are entitled to dominate us; even their women are in on the joke about our subjugation." Americans don't hate rich men; they've succeeded at the game. But intellectuals who have some kind of special knowledge, some kind of inside jokes? Smart women? I'm sure more than a few folks got that yeast rash just from watching her on television.

We are not supposed to hear women talk in public of policies and wars and what they will do with the mantle of power. We are also not supposed to hear men say the kind of things that Trump was heard on tape boasting about grabbing, about entitlement, about women's intimate anatomy. We are in such denial about how it feels to have heard these things, that whichever words felt most threatening went straight to our bodies for deciphering, not to our minds. Sure, we tried to sort out what those words-made-public meant. And then we chose sides. Is it dangerous for people to choose sides as a way to feel safe? Of course it is.

My country has been hostile toward me before – supporting the incest of my family home, threatening to incarcerate me as a disease-carrier and unfit parent. I've often thought about these as a sociologist, impersonally. Governments and systems are my focus. Suddenly, as people laugh along with Trump's buffoonery and cast their ballots in favour of his "new and different," I can feel how the government is us. The culture is us. The people who have imperilled me this time are driving right alongside me on the road. Logically, incest is so much more personal than an election, but no. The animal fear driving the choices of everyone I meet on the street is somehow communicating with the animal fear moistening my own body. It may not be a majority that elected Donald Trump – the groper, the liar, the kind of guy who makes the rape joke with a drink in his hand. Millions voted for him. And I'm as terrified as they are.

November 2016

I fear the highway. And yet I drive. I see the people in their cars, hurtling along on autopilot, thinking about their jobs, their families, singing with the radio. Each of us stewards a vehicle that could cause havoc and death if we make a wrong move and others do not react defensively with due haste. Mobility is freedom. Freeways connect places that would otherwise seem far from each other. My god, I think as I drive on the freeway, these people could do anything.

Paolo Freire discussed the fear of freedom in people who might otherwise consider themselves awakened. I find myself pondering this possibility in myself:

> As Hegel testifies: 'It is solely by risking life that freedom is obtained … the individual who has not staked his or her life may, no doubt, be recognized as a Person; but he or she has not attained the truth of this recognition as an independent self-consciousness.' (Freire, 1970, p. 36)

It's easy for me to consider the voting behaviours of those who want to protect their status, their investments, what they believe they've earned. Fearful cowards, I can call them, ignorant of their unearned privileges. As reports emerged, post-election, of more Trump signs on lawns than before the vote, I thought about 'independent self-consciousness.' Fear breeds duplicity. The truth is, I know this all too well within my own soft system, my tensing muscles and breathing chest. I am still on the road, yet bound by the cloak of the status quo, belted in by the strap of fear. "Fear of freedom, of which its possessor is not necessarily aware, makes him see ghosts" (Freire, 1970, p. 36). My father is sitting right beside me, one hand on the car door as if he could steady it. He became so small and frail in his old age. A big man all his life. A big man with big hands and a thick head of hair. He didn't see this small man coming, hair lost, skin like paper, eyes darting with fear and issuing orders about which route to take.

CONCLUSION

We do not have the power we thought we had. Blindsided. Whatever credentials or appearances or money or talk of freedom and work for liberation we possess will not bring us safety. How do I become more radical, more clear, more able? The body is preparing me by showing me my fear. At first, I got in the car and drove anyway. I took the body's response to that wilful behaviour like a beating, but I told myself I had no choice. Then I couldn't do it anymore. I am now paying a driver to deliver me to class. I will teach online this fall.

I am learning and earning the freedom to participate with all of those unknown weavers of the national fabric in the cars beside me. All, nameless drivers whom I must take on as colleagues as we bring to consciousness the cultural pains we've mostly carried in our bodies, have carried in other people's bodies, isolated in the powerful weave of the patria that we claim is not us, but it is us. It is us. Even when we can't accelerate, can't control the flow of traffic, can't see what's coming next. We must do our best. To keep moving forward.

Right now, I am still moving in reverse. Take me back to the time when things felt possible. All of it is in my body. I have to believe this. Early childhood held possibility. Then came the years of trauma that I almost didn't survive. I've lost limbs and grown anew like the axolotl. I've done it. My body knows the experience of surviving, then thriving. Right now, I have to trust that it's all there in my body. I feel like something two-dimensional these days. I get in the car and it's either yes or no. I am binary. But I remember that I can re-animate, become 3D with just the right turn, the right breath. I will open out like peace cranes from what seemed like flat paper. I just don't remember how.

Take me back to the time before, when I drove cross-country with no troubles. Sometimes 16 hours in a day, back in the 80s when I lived in my truck and it was the Reagan administration then. The AIDS epidemic. My friends were dying and then I had a baby. Would they take my baby? I felt like my country was really truly trying to kill me. The car meant freedom then. The way dusk looked, coming over a ridge, coming over a bridge, a painted desert laid out around the road felt like a blanket welcoming me to peaceful slumber. You got this. I'd say to myself. You got this. It all felt like freedom when I was moving. I can't move now, but I remember.

If the body keeps the score, then it's all in here. Somehow, I can go back by going forward. I can go forward by going back. The kahuna says that the ancestors and the generations to come all know what they're doing when they arrive in my body in the present moment. I can call them in.

It was all bravado back when I was still on the road during the first year of Trump. Somehow I could story myself through it. Maybe I still can, but not alone. The ghost of my father is with me. My mother and everyone else who voted for him is with me. My son and his middle-class expectations, his whiteness and his anguish for all that his embodiment represents – he is with me. The foot that won't press the gas pedal now is the same foot that knew how to drive away from trouble before. We can't see what's just over the edge, what's ahead as the road curves. Life is a great mystery. That's for damned sure.

REFERENCES

Freire, P. (1970). *Pedagogy of the oppressed.* London/New York, NY: Continuum International Publishing Group.

Olsen, T. (2014). *Silences.* New York, NY: The Feminist Press at CUNY.

CHRISTINE SALKIN DAVIS AND JONATHAN L. CRANE

DIALOGUE 1

I ring the doorbell and raise my eyebrows at Jon standing next to me.

"Remember," I say, "you promised to help me stay calm."

"I'll kick you under the table if you get argumentative," he says, smiling.

I do not feel reassured. We are here to interview several old friends of mine, exercise and church buddies for several years, people I have not seen much since the 2016 election. Although I don't know for sure how these friends voted, I believe they are supporters of the Trump presidency. My distress at the election and what our country has become under this administration has been so strong, I haven't known how to face them or what to say to them. I've always had great respect for these friends, but I can't understand their political beliefs, nor can I understand how people whose opinion I value so much can be so far away from me politically. I hate conflict so I've avoided the conversation entirely. I would still like to avoid it, but Jon and I felt this dialogue was crucial to the book, to give voice to Trump supporters, to re-humanize the Other side of the political divide. I'm hoping this will be a good first step toward healing the breach this election has caused with friends. I feel my heart pounding in my chest as I wait for Andrea[1] to answer the bell.

As I stand there, I look around at her suburban brick home, her manicured lawn, and the sun dappling the fall leaves with spangles of light.

Andrea opens the door and greets us with a big smile and hug. "Come on in! Larry and Elizabeth are already here!"

We follow Andrea to her living room and we all spend a minute catching up on exercise regimens and redecorating. Elizabeth used to jog religiously with my husband and me. Andrea just redid her living room and I admire her decorating taste. I take a deep breath. It's time to start. I hope our friendship survives.

"So," I say, "we're interested in listening to your thoughts about Trump, before and after the election. We're not asking you to disclose who you voted for, unless you want to. But I know you are generally politically conservative."

DOI:10.1163/9789004436329_002

Elizabeth leans forward. "Okay. Well, I'll start out by saying, I did vote for Trump."

"Have you always voted for Republicans?" I ask the question to the group.

Andrea chuckles. "Well, in my younger years, I leaned more Democrat. I'm not ultra conservative."

"I voted for Bill Clinton for his two terms," Elizabeth says, shaking her head. "I voted for Ronald Reagan for his two terms. I voted George Bush for two terms."

"So it wasn't a given that you would vote for Trump, just because he was the Republican nominee," I say.

"That's true," says Elizabeth.

Andrea nods. "My vote for Trump was more of not wanting Hillary. More than wanting Trump."

"Can you say a bit more about that? Like, what about Hillary were you against?"

"Well," says Andrea nervously.

"We promise we won't judge," I say, hoping I can keep that promise.

"One thing that turned me off to Hillary Clinton," Elizabeth says, "and I have always wanted there to be a woman president of the United States, but there were two things she lied about, she lied about not having pneumonia, and her private email servers."

Andrea and Larry nod.

Elizabeth says. "You know, the first time Obama ran for President, I voted for him. But I wasn't so happy with the second part of his administration and I thought that Hillary would have been a continuation of that. I thought we needed a change."

"What kind of change?"

"I hate to use broad descriptions like too much left or too much right," Andrea says, sitting forward, nervously laughing again. "I hate to say it, I don't know, I guess I should just relax, and just say what I want to say."

"Just say it," Larry says. "You're among friends."

I notice that she's as reluctant to have this conversation as I am.

"Go ahead," I encourage, "you're going to say it eventually." I remember that when we were jogging, we used to be able to talk about anything, including politics.

"Yeah," Jon says. "you are part of a really interesting group that voted for Obama the previous election, and then changed."

"I felt like," Andrea starts again, "I hate to use broad words or broad descriptions without giving specifics. But I just felt like towards the latter part of the administration, I felt like there was more turmoil and a divide among the American people."

"During Obama's second term?"

"Yes. And I'll even say that I think it had more to do with the media, than it did actually with Obama. Because the media will take one particular thing. I don't like what the media did in terms of race, and the whole emphasis on law enforcement officers. And, so I think in Obama's wanting to empower African Americans, and we do need to protect the Black people who are getting shot by cops, I just felt like it was too much of an emphasis on that, to where we ended up being more racially divided."

"Okay," I say, taking a deep breath and working hard to listen respectfully. Just thinking of the racial profiling by police and police violence against people of color angers me greatly. I remind myself she didn't say racially motivated police shootings were okay. She said just the opposite.

I take another breath as Andrea continues. "But at the same time, as Trump has taken office, it has flipped to where more African Americans feel like, you know, the whole MAGA is now a racist thing."

"So you thought," I say, "you thought that the country had gotten divisive. And you were thinking that Hillary would be more divisive and Trump would be less, is what you thought at the time?"

"Correct. And then from a military perspective; not that I'm pro-war by any stretch. But I do feel like the prior administration was taking funding away from the military, which I didn't particularly agree with either."

Elizabeth interjects, "and I don't like the fact that there were more people on food stamps during Obama's eight years in office. I think the numbers of poverty, people on food stamps, should decrease. That means the president's doing a good job. And I trusted Trump to make more jobs and to do a better job than Obama did. And I think Hillary would have done the same old thing."

"Okay," I say turning to Larry. "Where are you politically?"

Larry laughs. "For me, I'm a policy person more than a person-person. I wish we'd just abandon these party systems. That would be great, we could just pick a policy. So when I look at individuals, I learn what kind of policies they're going to lean toward. You know, I used to think the left was pretty moderate. But now, I think the left is going ultra-liberal. For me it came down to tax policy. And, trying to develop programs that I felt were going to get the country moving in a certain direction."

I nod and he continues.

"There's this nationalist type approach, I think, that people see with Trump, that it's all about us. But for me, I looked at it when that rhetoric was being put out there. I'm like, yeah, 'cause what do you care about first? You care about your family. You care about your neighbors. You care about your friends, you care about your town and your communities. And to me there's just so much noise, you have to try to read through what's being put out there, and try to get down to, okay, what does this person truly believe, and where are they going to go? What kinds of policies are they going to put in place that I think is good for the country? Like, for instance, some tax policies. I'll come back to that. I think, there's placating on the left. On the right too, but I think the left is placating. I think they placate, sometimes, to certain, you know, minorities. Look, this, they're going to take this away. And the poor are getting poorer, right? They're going to make you poorer. And the left are going to take care of you. There's so much noise and opinions, that you have to try to filter through them." He pauses for a minute to think. "I did not vote for Trump in the primary. I was a Rubio person in the primary. I liked his energy, I liked what I thought that he was going to bring, some of the things he was saying. I thought we were going to get the policies that I like. But, maybe Trump is a person I would not identify with, just because of his background, who he is, but I was very intrigued to see the potential for somebody to come in that wasn't Washington D.C. entrenched."

"He wasn't a politician," Andrea says, nodding.

Larry nods. "Now, I find it hard to believe that a guy of his status wouldn't understand D.C. and how the games are played, but we weren't going to get somebody that was entrenched in politics. I get that he understands how it works."

"His family were New York developers," Jon says.

"Yeah," Larry agrees. "Absolutely, he'd understand how it works. But I felt he was going to be like a free thinker. And, the way his brain goes, I thought, this could be very interesting. I agree with his nationalist approach. I'm not opposed to helping others, but there are so many things we can do in our own country to help lift people up. That's the part I identified with most, compared to with Hillary, because she was going to do the same policies as Obama. I did not agree with the Affordable Care Act; I've seen what it's done to premiums in my own organization, and it's caused mandated penalties. The message of the Affordable Care Act was that 'we want to take care of minorities, but yet, we're going to penalize you if you don't get insurance.' Like, it doesn't seem like it fits the Democrat's philosophy because they're supposed to be all about helping and lifting up and providing."

"Yes," Andrea chimes in.

Larry continues. "And Hillary's scandal. I mean, again, there's noise. And I don't trust her, you know? She's been in the White House, and who knows what she's been a part of? So for me, again, it was more policies than people."

"So," I say, "Andrea and Elizabeth said they were more anti-Hillary more than pro-Trump. It sounds like you were a little bit of both, but it sounds like you were more pro-Trump, and a little bit of anti-Hillary. Is that right?"

Larry laughs. "It's so funny, because I don't wear on my sleeve that I hate you, or I love you. You know, they're saying what they're saying to try to get elected. So they're going to be on their guard or they placate certain people to get where they need to get to. But, I did not hate Hillary. There were just some trust factors with her. I mean, there were also trust factors about Trump before he got elected."

I nod.

"But, you can get that with anybody," Larry continues. "When we're going into closets from college, trying to figure out the things that they did to see that now maybe they're not worthy of office, because of something they did 50 years ago."

"Uh huh," I say.

"You know," Larry says. "I have three older sisters. My mother was a psychologist. My boss is female. I've been around powerful women my entire life. For some people, that might have been an issue seeing a female in the White House. Not for me. Being around women my entire life, I think that would be great to have a woman in the White House."

"That's a good point," says Andrea.

"I would love to have seen Condoleezza Rice," Andrea says.

"Yeah, absolutely," Larry responds.

Andrea laughs. "So, I mean, there you have an African American female."

"Yeah," I say.

"So, to your point," Andrea says to Larry, "for me as well, it had nothing to do with the fact that she was a female. 'Cause I would have been perfectly okay with a female."

Larry nods, "I saw, here's a business person coming in, who has a nationalist approach, who wants to secure our country, bring jobs back into our country, going to get everybody working, going to get people off these programs, whether it's Medicaid or on food stamps, or any kind of assistance, whatsoever, we're going to build this community up, and get everybody working. We're all going to just move this train down the track."

Elizabeth leans forward. "I am very interested in the economy and the stock market doing well, because I'm getting close to retirement, and that's important. And I want my husband to have a job and not be reverse discriminated against, because he's a white male, and I have had some concerns about that, in trying to make things more diverse. I too would be perfectly happy to vote for a woman for president. I just don't believe in government giving away money. I believe every able-bodied person should work, and I think there shouldn't be any fraud in the government systems or programs."

NOTE

1 Pseudonyms used for participant anonymity.

CHRISTINE SALKIN DAVIS AND JONATHAN L. CRANE

INTRODUCTION

Bodily Experiences in a Trumpian World

Early morning January 2017, I joined a dozen of my colleagues at the condo of one of our faculty members for coffee and doughnuts to fortify ourselves for a cold march across uptown Charlotte. One or two thousand women and supporters were expected to march, and we were excited. This was my first protest march. After the disappointing election results, I wanted to lend my body to the cause and make a point. Hillary may not have won, but throughout this election, women – and their allies – had experienced their voices being heard. Now, after the stunning defeat, they still – especially – wanted to be counted. In the end, there were over 10,000 people attending and as a result it was more of a shuffle than a march, but it was exciting. It felt like a movement. I was reminded of Rebecca Traister's (2018) words in her book on women's anger and social justice, "in the fury of women lies the power to change the world" (p. xxviii).

A short three months earlier, the toxic viral clip, a vulgar display of noxious male braggadocio dominated the close of the interminable 2016 Presidential campaign. A cocksure Donald Trump, boasting about sexual assault on a hot mic in the company of D-List celeb Billy Bush, said, "You know I'm automatically attracted to beautiful women, I just start kissing them, it's like a magnet. You know when you're a star they let you do it. You can do anything. Grab them by the pussy. You can do anything" (Transcript: Donald Trump's taped comments about women, 2016, para. 9). There is a long history of candidates and politicians caught on tape uttering words from beyond the pale. As a rule, such statements have led to resignations, public censure, embarrassing mea culpas, and, usually, a chagrined exit from the public stage. No longer.

It was also not just the outlandish candidate whose conduct was alarming. From the onset of the race for President, the news media reported stories of angry Trump champions verbally and physically assaulting protestors and detractors, and Trump's responses to this string of attacks ranged from

DOI:10.1163/9789004436329_003

peevish repudiation, to doubling down, to telling silence. Black Lives Matters and other protesters at Trump rallies were beaten by the crowd and then, as if taking a beating was just not punishment enough, imperiously rebuked by Trump himself (see, for instance, Diamond, 2016; Johnson & Jordan, 2015; Parker, 2016). Of one incident, Trump supported the violence, saying, "Maybe he should have been roughed up" (Johnson & Jordan, 2015, para. 1).

Throughout his campaign, Trump profited by strong support from white supremacists and Nazi sympathizers, who were, in the scandalous and unfortunate phrasing of the Clinton campaign, "a basket of deplorables" (Chozick, 2016, para. 1). As the election neared, white supremacist and racist language ramped up, fueled by support from the presidential candidate himself. The website www.nohomophobes.com counted a 25% increase in homophobic language in Twitter messages the week before the election. *The New York Times* (Kristof, 2016) reported that "The Times made a video of Trump fans at his rallies directing crude slurs not just at Hillary Clinton, but also at blacks, Latinos, Muslims and gay people … [Trump] has unleashed a beast and fed its hunger, and long after this campaign is over we will be struggling to corral it again" (paras. 7–8).

I had many reasons to oppose Trump this election. My sister has cerebral palsy. I am the second generation of immigrants who fled persecution and poverty in Europe. I have a beloved family member of blended ethnicity. I am a woman who has seen far too much of men like Trump, and, like many others, I am a 'metoo.'

So when Trump won the election, after his "grab her by the pussy" remark (Transcript: Donald Trump's taped comments about women, 2016, para. 9); his mocking of a reporter with spasticity (a symptom my sister and others with cerebral palsy sometimes share) (Donald Trump mocks, 2015); his vilifying immigrants; his attacking Hillary Clinton and other women, also blacks, Latinos, Muslims, and gay people; his approving of violence from his followers, and his followers beating Black Lives Matter protestors at his rallies, and then Trump rebuking the *protestors* (see, for instance, Diamond, 2016; Johnson & Jordan, 2015; Parker, 2016); his strong support from white supremacists and Nazi sympathizers; and the increase in homophobic language; there was no way his presidency was acceptable to me.

The morning after the election, I caught an early flight to go to Philadelphia for NCA – our National Communication Association academic convention. I had gone to sleep the night before to ominous exit polling, but still hoped for a political miracle. The miracle did not come and when I awoke at 4 am, I got the news. My husband Jerry was drafted into the Vietnam War when he was 19. He didn't want to go to war, but he considered it his patriotic duty to say yes to his country. "I'm proud I did what my country asked me to do," he told me time and again. We have been together for 36 years and I have always known him to fly an American flag at his house before we married, and at every house in which we've lived together. This morning after the election, after we saw the news, I couldn't find him anywhere. When he reappeared, he told me he had been outside to take our flag down. "This is no longer the America I fought for," he said, "no longer the America this flag represents. The flag will stay down as long as Trump is President." As of this writing, the flag remains stowed in the garage.

When Trump won, it seemed that the entire country was okay with his vilification of experiences that mirrored my own and the experiences of people I hold dear, and I was dismayed, distressed, distrustful, and depressed. I remember boarding the plane to Philadelphia, walking down the aisle of the plane, and looking into the faces of people seated, wondering, "did you vote for Trump? Did you vote for Trump?" I felt betrayed by my fellow citizens. I didn't know who to trust anymore. And all I could think was, "don't you realize, people will die as a result of this election?" As I moved through the week at NCA, that phrase echoed in my head like a horrible mantra: "people will die, people will die."

I wanted to do something, to fix something, but, as a writer and ethnographer, the only thing I knew to do was to provide a forum for people's stories. This seemed like a concrete action, so I sent out feelers for interest in contributing to a book about the stories of people whose bodies were affected by the election. Except for one soon-to-be-former Facebook friend who joyously suggested I invite Hillary to contribute to the book, "since she now had plenty of time on her hands," as if this was a football game and she was a trash talker on the side of the jubilant winning team, there was a great deal of support for the project, especially from Patricia Leavy who generously offered to include the book in her personal/public scholarship series with Brill/Sense Publishing.

One week after Donald Trump was elected President, our 20-year old African-American undergraduate TA rushed into class at the last minute.

"I'm so sorry I'm late," she said breathlessly. "I had to meet with the chief of police!"

"I was assaulted at the library last night," she said, wiping a tear from her cheek.

"I'm okay now. Really."

"I was at the library, studying," she said. "A group of white guys surrounded my table and said awful things to me. About my race. Calling me lazy and ugly. Yelling that I had an illegitimate baby. They told me I didn't belong here. That I didn't belong in college."

"Awful things. I can't repeat it all."

"They wouldn't let me leave. They just kept yelling. They surrounded me. They wouldn't let me leave." The tears returned, harder this time.

"I was so humiliated. But I didn't do anything to ask for it, I promise."

We should note that Alicia, a double major soon to apply to competitive graduate programs, has no baby, and was studying by herself in a quiet corner of the library in an end-of-semester push to graduate with high honors, not that such an explanation is required. We, sadly, also have to point out that there were other people in the library that night, and not one came to her aid.

As Alicia described her attack, in a traumatic flashback, three separate incidents that I have never shaken came back to me. Age 17, sexually assaulted when a bullying date drove me to his apartment against my objections and once inside, tore at my clothes, and took me captive. I still have lucid flashbacks in my sleep, dreaming I am fighting off an attacker. Age 19, car dead, late at night, alone in a shopping center. Two guys in motorcycles encircled my vehicle as I sat trembling, locked in my broken-down beater. Age 21, 2 a.m. in Myrtle Beach with a girlfriend at a pay phone, when a group of guys got out of their cars to surround us. For an interminable hour they ignored our protestations, physically prevented us from leaving, and insisted we come with them. In all those instances, I told few people, convinced I was to blame for allowing myself to be in a vulnerable situation.

As my own experiences of fear, assault, guilt, and blame wrenched me back to an immutable past I thought had been left behind, another of our TAs spoke up. "When I was raped, I was sure it was my fault." She turned to face Alicia. "But it wasn't your fault. It was not your fault."

It took me decades to understand that truth and even now it is clear the past can return with a vengeance. As she told us about her experience, in a group of two instructors, one graduate Teaching Assistant and 2 undergraduate Teaching Assistants, all the women revealed we too had been sexually assaulted or harassed multiple times. Violence against women is not new, but what was evident that day was that the election motivated haters of a myriad of marginalized, gendered, and transgressive bodies, and emboldened them to loose their hate and to use violence and the threat of violence as a weapon of control. What Alicia – and the rest of us in that room – were experiencing was a new wave of efforts to reconstruct white American hegemony and restore white male conservative bodies to a position of leadership and control over clamorous, rebellious bodies, whom they perceive to have forgotten their proper place and trespassed against what they consider to be 'traditional' values and the 'natural order.'

That's when we realized how important this book was going to be.

Trump's victory certainly seems to have authorized a full-bore return of the repressed – as an ominous maelstrom of threats and assaults loose traumatic memories of victimhood, bullying, marginalization, and terror in those who Trump vows to lock up, deport, exile, and stigmatize. Trump's rise reanimated fears consigned to the past – not forgotten, just succeeded by a guarded optimism that things had improved; after all, the Great Recession had not undone us all, and the ACA (Affordable Care Act) did bring healthcare access to millions. We thought we might have some reason to hope that real, positive change was on the horizon as "Forward Together" betokened something more than a neo-liberal tagline that happy times lay ahead. This is not to suggest that Trump destroyed a wholly halcyon present of unalloyed unity; ask any Black Lives protestor or Texan fighting for reproductive rights if this was the best of all possible worlds before Trump decided to run for President. Trump did not ravage Eden, but his popularity ushers in a new era.

Things are different now. Unbound by the rules governing normative civil discourse, Trump's unmoored attacks are the basis of his winning political appeal. Indeed, these snarling attacks may just be expedient political rhetoric for Trump and his bloc, a way to affectively gin up his supporters. And the clamoring cry to "Lock Her Up" may be a bit of genius shorthand for drawing a clear line between the good, the bad, and the ugly, and for making revenge a statement of policy. However, for those who are singled out by Trump's flagrant disregard for the niceties of political intercourse, his words bite. He is a personal threat to many of us who find ourselves on the wrong end of cocked fists, threats, taunts, and acid ridicule. For those of us not-white, not-male, not-heteronormative, not-able, and all others for whom there is no shelter in the Trump coalition, we suddenly find ourselves exiled to the margins with the promise of worse to come. The no trespass signs are up once again. Before Trump's election, many of us had some reason to hope that real, positive change was coming. We were naïve. No one imagined this.

Trump's wholly unanticipated election to the Presidency represented to many a frightening turning point in our nation's history. We believe this pivotal time can be best understood by paying careful heed to the voices of the affected and their mosaic articulation of what the United States means in the wake of a Trump victory.

In some ways, the first two years of his presidency were not as bad as we expected. So far, for instance, at the time of this writing, there's yet been no widespread Muslim ban, no complete repeal of the Affordable Care Act, and, thankfully, Trump has not yet pushed that nuclear button. But in many ways it's been worse than we expected because the daily threats and the political and personal aggressions wear away our optimistic vision of what America stands for, who we are to each other, our national identity, our national self. As Robert P. Sellers (2019) asserted in *Baptist News Global*, "Trump himself is the foundational problem for many of the dangers our nation now faces" (para. 1). He further claimed, "[Trump's] blatant racism is hurting people both directly and indirectly. His claims that our country is being "invaded" by illegal immigrants and refugees from Mexico and Latin America have emboldened irrational people to shout xenophobic, hateful words and to condone or even commit random or premeditated acts of violence" (para.10). Sellers concluded that "these evidences of almost clinical unkindness are startling when they come out of the mouth of America's highest elected leader" (para. 14). Sellers stated that, due to Trump's rhetoric, "… treasures of inestimable value are being lost. Our sense of honor is dying. Our reason to feel proud is dying. Our national soul is dying" (para. 20). Our best, collective dreams are on life support.

Since the election, white supremacist and other far-right extremist attacks and racist, anti-Muslim, anti-Semitic terrorism have more than tripled in the United States. The Southern Poverty Law Center reported a "fourth straight year of hate group growth … [that coincides] with Trump's campaign and presidency" (Hate groups reach record high, 2019, para. 2), and they claim "the number of hate groups operating across America rose to a record high – 1,020 – in 2018 as Trump continued to fan the flames of white resentment over immigration and the country's changing demographics" (Hate groups reach record high, 2019, para. 1). A survey conducted by *The Washington Post* among American Jews reports that almost 9 out of 10 believe that anti-Semitism is a problem in America, and almost that many say it has increased over the past five years. Further, over one-third of study respondents report being a recipient of anti-Semitic remarks or violence (Rubin, 2019). Similarly, the Anti-Defamation League reported that anti-Semitic incidents increased by 99% from 2015 to 2018 (Anti-Defamation League, 2018). David Leonhardt of *The Washington Post* (2019a), argued that "American conservatism has a violence problem" (para. 1) referring to "the pattern of mass shootings by people espousing right-wing views" (para. 3). Leonhardt further said:

> Last year, 39 of the 50 killings committed by political extremists, according to the Anti-Defamation League, were carried out by white supremacists. Another eight were committed by killers with anti-government views. Over the past 10 years, right-wing extremists were responsible for more than 70 percent of extremist-related killings. 'Right-wing extremist violence is our biggest threat,' Jonathan Greenblatt, the head of the Anti-Defamation League, has written. 'The numbers don't lie.' (para. 4)

So, for some people, it's been much much worse than expected. For Muslim women physically threatened for walking down the street; for African Americans shot by emboldened police or threatened with swatting (fraudulently calling emergency services on people of color who are simply going about their lives); for the victims of anti-Latino homicide hate crimes which rose by over 21% in 2018 to a 16-year high (Lopez, 2019); for the over 5,000 refugee children (over 300 under 5 years old) removed from their families at the southern U.S. border (Jordan, 2019; Only now do we understand, 2019; Spagat, 2019), and their frantic parents and families; for the children, babies, and infants at the border who will never be returned to their families because no one cared enough to document their names or their parents' names; for the women and children sexually abused while in immigration detention facilities (López & Park, 2018); for the refugees escaping violence in their home countries who were kept in "dirty, … freezing cells in squalid conditions, … served spoiled food, [and denied] medical care" (Ingram, 2020, paras. 1–2) while in Border Patrol custody; for the factory workers and farmers who have lost their jobs due to this administration's international trade policies; for the 11 people massacred while worshiping in their synagogue in Pittsburgh (the "deadliest attack on Jews in the history of the U.S.," Anti-Defamation League, 2018, para. 3); for citizens of Puerto Rico for whom hurricane relief efforts were deliberately stalled (Acevedo, 2019); for trans people who no longer have health insurance to cover their medical needs, and so on, it has been much, much worse than expected. And we haven't even considered what living this way, being witness to the atrocities, being complicit, from passive indifference to active engagement, is doing to our personal health and collective souls.

For victims of "The Trump Effect," it's been far worse than expected. In terms of creating maximal stress, Trump's racist rhetoric trumps his impeachable offenses, his liaisons with foreign dictators and enemies of the U.S., his government shutdown, his suspension of visas for people of certain Muslim-majority countries, and his continual lies (over 12,000 as of this writing documented by Kessler, Rizzo, & Kelly, 2019). These daily deviations from the norm of decent social behavior cause a continual drain on emotional energy.

Dahlia Lithwick (2019) reports in *Slate*, on the "serious consequences … to transgender soldiers, DACA kids, green card holders, and … families at the border." She further asserts that "meaningless or gibberish or lies or all three, his words still make us anxious, worried, and stressed" (para. 1). She claims:

> The actual psychic toll on our mental health is crippling. The lost sleep, the grinding anxiety, the escalating fears don't just represent squandered time. They start to chip away at your health and at your soul. The healthy response would be to tune it out altogether, but since actual people are actually suffering the brutal consequences, we cannot. And so here we are back in the narcissist's loop, fueling his need to be at the center because, well, there he is at the center. (para. 3)

The Pew Center's (Trump's statements spur, 2019) poll of Americans' reactions to Trump's comments and statements shows feelings of concern (76%), confusion (70%), embarrassment (69%), exhaustion (67%), anger (65%), offense (62%), and fright (56%). William Wan and Lindsey Bever of the *Washington Post* (2019) write that "Donald Trump's presidency may be making some people sick …. Researchers have begun to identify correlations between Trump's election and worsening cardiovascular health, sleep problems, anxiety and stress, especially among Latinos in the United States" (para. 1). They call this the "Trump effect" (para. 7) and quote numerous researchers who have identified the "physical and mental symptoms linked to increased stress" related to the "hateful rhetoric" of the Trump presidency (para. 10). Wan further reports on a pediatrician group's warning that the racism accompanying the Trump administration is having "devastating long-term effects on children's health" (2019, para. 1). Discrimination and racism since the election have resulted in increased stress, heart disease, depression, lower birth-weight babies, and an overall pattern of poorer health. The stress is likely related to the intense pessimism Americans feel about the U.S. The Pew Research Center study reported that 70% of Americans are "dissatisfied with the way things are going in the country right now" (para. 4), 73% think the "gap between the rich and poor" (para. 2) will grow, 77% worry about public education, 60% have a negative view of health care affordability, and 60% are pessimistic about the condition of the planet (Parker, Morin, & Horowitz, 2019).

Even the seemingly good economic news of Trump's presidency (moderate GPD growth and low unemployment) belies the economic reality for most Americans: 44% of all workers, most of whom are adults supporting themselves and their families, are low wage workers – earning, on average, $360-$506 a week with no healthcare or benefits (Kelly, 2019; Ross & Bateman, 2019). In addition, the labor force participation rate is "near its lowest level since 1977" (Uchitelle, 2019, para. 2), reflecting the high number of people who have given up on looking for a job. As David Leonhardt of *The Washington Post* explains, "an outsize share of economic growth flows to the wealthy .... Middle-class income growth has been sluggish for decades. The typical household is still poorer than it was before the financial crisis began in 2007" (Leonhardt, 2019b , paras. 4–5). In addition, despite Trump's claims to the contrary, black unemployment rose in the past year and remains high and, at 7%, is "nearly twice the U.S. jobless rate of 3.8 percent" (Rizzo, 2019, para. 8).

Despite all our intersecting markers of marginality, we editors willingly admit to finding shelter under a protective mantle of white, middle-class, educated privilege. Nevertheless, although we may not be Trump's number one public enemy, we feel, alongside more vulnerable members of the polis, the fierce lash of his tongue. Inciting violence, triggering vulnerabilities and fears, Trump's war on bodies and embodied diversity is a cause for concern. It is also a cause for concern that Trump appeals to so many who do not see themselves as race-baiting haters of those who think, look and act differently. How is it possible that those we count as friends, colleagues, relatives, and neighbors are in accord with Trump, even as they claim to reject his most inflammatory gestures and claims? How can supporters back him while distancing themselves from his rhetoric? How did a substantial and successful coalition of voters learn to read between the lines so as to not countenance a politician's most provocative statements while still supporting his presidency? As communication scholars, we bear the intellectual responsibility for seeking to understand how the vicious populism of Trump has emerged and to limn the scarifying patchwork of embodied experiences that have made difference pay.

There are many people who claim that Trump's hate speech is not to blame for inciting violence. But they are clearly not communication scholars. Communication scholars understand the power of language, the power of discourse to not only reflect reality but to create reality. Leveraging the inferences, judgments, connotations, metaphors, and paranoia in anti-Semitic language inherent in centuries of hate speech to disenfranchise and kill Jews across Europe, Aryan Nationalists of the 19th century constructed a world view and the complex institutions and industrial organization that made the final solution of the Holocaust possible (Dinnerstein, 1991; Evans, 1997; Goldhagen, 1996; Halpern, 1987; Lambroza, 1987). These same discursive elements were revived and recirculated throughout Trump's campaign and have been strengthened and wholeheartedly approved by this administration throughout the first two years of Trump's administration. From the past, atrocities and working models for Othering, haunt us still (Neumann, 2014).

For this book, we solicited contributors who could write either about their personal experiences or who could represent the personal experiences of people whose bodies rendered them especially vulnerable in the aftermath of the 2016 election. We asked them to follow these experiences for the first year of Trump's administration. We wanted to document stories and voices and bodily experiences that allow the reader to better understand what it has been like to live, since the election, in the body of a hijab-wearing Muslim woman, for example, or a person with a chronic illness who relies on the Affordable Care Act for life and death care. We also wanted to include people on both sides of the political divide, so we added interviews – interspersed throughout – with friends who are self-described Trump supporters to understand their experiences and contrast their voices with those of chapter contributors.

As you read these stories, you will encounter four themes: first, a palpable embodied fear and trauma waiting for the other shoe to drop. Dark, in the opening story in the Prologue, offers a raw account of anxieties and sexual assault trauma triggered by the election. Jardine and Simmons, in Chapter 9, open us to the experience of both Black and White Americans who react in fear, and confidence, to Trump's election. Tullis, in Chapter 5, gives expression to the fears of people who rely on the Affordable Care Act for healthcare access. Many other chapters (Mubarak and Bakali, in Chapter 4; Forbes Berthoud in Chapter 2; de la Serna in Chapter 6; and Erdely in Chapter 10) also let us know what it feels like to watch the news as people who look like them and their loved ones are shot, beaten, insulted, and threatened; and what it feels like to wait for the violence to come home. The second theme is one of bodies Othered by this administration. Again, Mubarak and Bakali tell of the Othering of Muslim women in Chapter 4. In Chapter 3, Young Lee and Huff explain what it is like for one's own body to be policed in transit, and in Chapter 2, Forbes Berthoud offers a look into black women's threatened identities in the age of Trump. The third theme of the book details the rending of relationships, a divide rooted in the disbelief that one's family, loved ones, people who have raised us and grown up with us, can't empathize or understand our fears, needs, beliefs, or the deep ways in which the daily onslaught of current event affects the body, mind, and heart. Okamoto and Ivancic, in Chapter 8, and Holman Jones, in Chapter 7, write of the pain of family breaches. The final theme of the book is of border crossings: the internal struggle felt when one's own identity has been torn apart by competing politics. Burt, in Chapter 1, tells of being an Evangelical Christian and woman and liberal; de la Serna, in Chapter 6, brings voices of people who are immigrants and conservative; Erdely, in Chapter 10, witnesses to being a mixed-race couple and a dark-skinned U.S. citizen in a red state. One takeaway from the chapters is that the answers are not always as clear cut as we'd like them to be. Yes, transgressions, fears, and loss are clearly articulated, but nuances and shades of gray abound throughout.

The theoretical bases for this book are many: Foucault's (1979, 1980) concepts of biopower and body politics – the use of bodies as sites of power, or, conversely, of powerlessness, and the similar sounding term, 'the body politic,' the idea that citizens or people residing in a society collectively make up one body. Conflating these two ideas, this book simply asks you to consider, who belongs, or, who is allowed to belong? Which bodies have the power to belong to the collective body, the collective us? Mbembe's (2019) related term, 'necropolitics,' refers to the ways in which death – and threat of death – is used to exert power and control over bodies.

The contributors in this book tell stories of the making-illegitimate, or making-transgressive of certain bodies, and this is the first step in the practice of malign biopower, holding power over another's body. The ultimate form of powerlessness is to be rendered illegitimately-bodied. Illegitimacy is a function of time and place, a consequence of random genes and chromosomes appearing in the "wrong" time and place, or of bodies doing the "wrong" thing, or the right thing in the "wrong" time or place. For instance, bodies can be illegitimized by being blamed or criminalized for performing functions that bodies do normally, but are performed at a socially "wrong" place or time (e.g., being on the "wrong" side of a borderline, or grocery shopping while wearing a hijab). Sometimes, a body is illegitimized by moving to a different place (e.g., refugees). Other times, a body is illegitimized by a transformation of place (e.g., U.S. government displacing Native Americans following successive migrations of Europeans to the Americas, or ethnic cleansing or political violence transforming a country into one from which residents are forced to flee). The label of transgression can be imposed by any authority, be it civil, religious, military, educational, criminal, or juridical, and is reinforced and reified from within the community and populace. In the exercise of pernicious biopower, bodies are dehumanized by language that Donna Haraway (1985) calls 'making monstrous,' and what Eric King Watts (2017) terms the 'zombification' of bodies of color – monsters and zombies, by definition, deserve to die.

As the stories in this volume make plain, this argument is central to the idea of place and belonging. Violence, brutality, and poverty render some bodies 'out of place,' but when these illegitimated bodies try to find 'a new place,' they are 'dis-placed' by violence at the borders (Stierl, 2016), or by policies that cast a blind eye to the needs of arriving migrants (Ryegiel, 2016). Stierl (2016) reminds us that the violence, terror, abuse, and abandonment some immigrants find as they seek refuge are the same baleful fates that drove them from their countries of origin. Of course, as co-inhabitants of our shared biological ecosystem, our attempt to eradicate Others from this system is to metaphorically reject or amputate part of ourselves, suggests Shildrick (2019). In this act of violence, we pluck out our own eye in order not to see the evil we do. Amputation of family ties, community ties, human ties, make us all unhuman and inhumane (Shildrick, 2019). Especially salient to this argument are the voices of radical feminists and critical race scholars who remind us that hegemony, patriarchy, and white supremacy are the discourses of the dead, desiring the deaths of women, people of color, and those who are perceived to be unable to contribute to the economics of the collective (Daly, 1978). If affording "dignity to the body [is] a tribute to that person and representative of our common humanity" (Brazier, 2015, p. 164), then a refusal to treat another person with dignity is an affront and a message of inhumanity, i.e., a method of dehumanizing the other person (Brazier, 2015). This dehumanization leads to social death and then the literal death of certain people – people of color, people from 'unwelcome' ethnic or religious backgrounds, people with the 'wrong' bodies. The Trump administration has declared some people as less than human, unworthy to share in the life of our country, our freedoms, and the bounty of our culture; too many of us have built our own Walls and declared some people not 'us.'

Some examples of treating bodies as transgressive in U.S. history include kidnapping, enslavement, and lynchings of people of color; forced removal of Native Americans and other indigenous people from their ancestral lands; criminalization and punitive punishment of actions specific to certain, marginalized, bodies, such as criminalization of women seeking to end pregnancies (and not the responsible fathers), selling and possession of certain drugs (e.g., crack cocaine, used primarily by poorer African-Americans) and not others (e.g., powdered cocaine, used primarily by wealthier white Americans); loitering laws targeting homeless people; withholding of rights (and, thus, bodily autonomy), from some bodies and not others (e.g., marriage rights and restrictions, bathroom access bills, immigration restrictions for certain countries or origin); inciting war and violence against certain bodies through inflammatory rhetoric; immigration policies that result in border fatalities, either through mistreatment of immigrants at borders (Stierl, 2016) or through indifference or unwillingness to assist arriving refugees (Ryegiel, 2016); unprovoked police brutality against people of color resulting in unjustified deaths; or reproductive oppression (O'Donnell, 2018). Sadly, the plight of Americans of the Muslim or Jewish faith or Latin origin, Americans who are Other-gendered, Americans who are differently bodied or darker skinned, and refugees who are escaping political violence, are only the newest examples of those targeted by weaponized biopower.

Once bodies are rendered transgressive or illegitimate, it is a short step to socially and literally Other, marginalize, dismiss, and discard those bodies through, for example, re-placing them – re-moving them to places deemed more appropriate for enemy bodies, including prison, reservations, concentration camps, and the grave. Transgressive bodies are killed or allowed to die for the purpose of subjugating the body, as an individual act of disempowerment, or as a social act to serve as a warning to other similarly transgressive bodies to remain 'in their place.' In the final step, such bodies are rendered, as Judith Butler (2004, 2009) says, ungrievable in their deaths and the dehumanization is complete. Guilt is purged and order is restored (Burke, 1969). Further, the dead bodies are displaced and disposed of in unnamed graves and mass burials. In addition, the ignominy of silence surrounding the policy of inflicting suffering and death bars the grievability of these displaced bodies (Stierl, 2016).

In this discussion of dehumanization and displacement, it's helpful to remember that many Trump's supporters were once themselves fearful people who didn't feel part of the national conversation, who saw their world fading away, who felt themselves no longer belonging, who feared losing the secure foundation they always thought would be there for them. This age-old fight over power and control has no beginning and no end, only constant struggle in a landslide of horrific headlines and divisive, anger-stoking, fear-inducing news.

This book asks us to think through tough narratives. Our challenge in this book is to represent the unrepresentable, to represent experiences that are alien for many people, which are terrifying, in a way that allows other people to feel and empathize with that terror. This book invites us to step into the perspective of the Other, to remember and honor all our most human stories that, woven together, make up the collective 'us'; the collective 'U.S.' In this book we take a narrative approach to understanding the experiences represented by the contributors. Communication scholars assert that humans are story-tellers, living, representing, and understanding our lives through stories. Stories help us understand each other, and create a way to share our experiences. Scholars understand that we are born into a personal, familial, and cultural story which has already begun, and we live out our lives as stories with plots, characters, motives, and meanings. Sharing narratives is an effective way to enhance understanding between people, and gives voice to underrepresented and marginalized people. Seeing the experience of others through a narrative lens enhances empathy and leads to stronger interpersonal connections (Davis & Warren-Findlow, 2011; Fisher, 1984).

Was my premonition correct? Have people died as a result of this election? Consider the victims of shootings and racial violence, children and adults dead at the U.S.-Mexico border, or remember Heather Heyer, the 'Unite the Right' protestor in Charlottesville, Virginia who died when a neo-Nazi deliberately rammed his car into the crowd. Or read the note left by a husband and wife in Washington State who died by murder-suicide in 2019 and claimed the reason for their death was their inability to afford medical treatment for serious health problems (Iati, 2019). No, America is not yet great.

POETIC RESPONSE

Resistance Marching

Wonder in resistance marching, tens of thousands of feet, bodies demanding justice, compassion, love. Me-too bodies and never again bodies. My turn bodies, black lives bodies, shattered bodies, bodies that matter. One body of diverse bodies, bodies breathing, deep breaths,

from the heart, breathe in,
find the life-affirming air,
energy of love.

Wonder in the energetic giddiness of body after body, voices raised, signs held high, cannot be contained.

You may be in charge,
but hear us here, now, justice
cannot be contained.

Secure in Sunlight

It's hard to focus with all the me-toos and why-nows and didn't-tells and don't-believing going on.

Grabbing and catcalls
weigh you down, not a cat, not
yours, hear and react,

resist,
news obsessed,
bad news breaking,
harvesting
fears paralyze,
raining,
crashing,
shelter within, peace
washing, love counting, safety
now; you are here, calm,

secure in numbers,
sunlight,
strength.

REFERENCES

Acevedo, N. (2019, October 18). HUD officials knowingly failed to 'comply with the law,' stalled Puerto Rico hurricane relief funds. *NBC News.* Retrieved from https://www.nbcnews.com/news/latino/hud-officials-knowingly-failed-comply-law-stalled-puerto-rico-hurricane-n1068761

Anti-Defamation League. (2018). *Audit of anti-Semitic incidents: Year in review 2018.* Retrieved from https://www.adl.org/audit2018#executive-summary

Brazier, M. (2015). The body in time. *Law, Innovation, and Technology, 7*(2), 161–186.

Burke, K. (1969). *A grammar of motives.* Berkeley, CA: University of California Press.

Butler, J. (2004). *Precarious life: The powers of mourning and violence.* New York, NY: Verso.

Butler, J. (2009). *Frames of war: When is life grievable?* London: Verso.

Chozick, A. (2016, September 10). Hillary Clinton calls many Trump backers 'deplorables' and GOP pounces. *The New York Times.* Retrieved from https://www.nytimes.com/2016/09/11/us/politics/hillary-clinton-basket-of-deplorables.html

Daly, M. (1978). *Gyn/ecology: The metaethics of radical feminism.* Boston, MA: Beacon Press.
Davis, C. S., & Warren-Findlow, J. (2011). Coping with trauma through fictional narrative ethnography: A primer. *Journal of Loss and Trauma, 16*(6), 563–572. doi:10.1080/15325024.2011.578022
Diamond, J. (2016, October 14). Protestor attacked at Trump rally. *CNN Politics.* Retrieved from https://www.cnn.com/2016/10/14/politics/donald-trump-rally-protester-attack/index.html
Dinnerstein, L. (1991). Antisemitism in crisis times in the United States: The 1920s and 1930s. In S. L. Gilman & S. T. Katz (Eds.), *Anti-semitism in times of crisis* (pp. 212–226). New York, NY: New York University Press.
Donald Trump mocks reporter with disability (Video). (2015, November 26). *The Guardian.* Retrieved from https://www.theguardian.com/us-news/video/2015/nov/26/donald-trump-appears-to-mock-disabled-reporter-video
Evans, E. N. (1997). *The provincials: A personal history of Jews in the south.* New York, NY: Simon & Schuster.
Fisher, W. R. (1984). Narration as a human communication paradigm: The case of public moral argument, *Communication Monographs, 51*(1), 1–22.
Foucault, M. (1979). *Discipline and punish: The birth of the prison* (A. Sheridan, Trans.). New York, NY: Vintage Books.
Foucault, M. (1980). *Power/knowledge: Selected interviews and other writings, 1972–1977.* (C. Gordon, Ed., C. Gordon, L. Marshall, J. Mepham, & K. Soper, Trans.). New York, NY: Pantheon.
Goldhagen, D. J. (1996). *Hitler's willing executioners.* New York, NY: Alfred A. Knopf.
Halpern, B. (1987). Reactions to antisemitism in modern Jewish history. In J. Reinharz (Ed.), *Living with Antisemitism* (pp. 3–15). Hanover, NH: University Press of New England.
Haraway, D. (1985). A manifesto for cyborgs: Science, technology, and socialist feminism in the 1980s. *Socialist Review, 80*, 65–107.
Hate groups reach record high. (2019, February 19). Southern Poverty Law Center. Retrieved from https://www.splcenter.org/news/2019/02/19/hate-groups-reach-record-high
Iati, M. (2019, August 10). Couple dead in apparent murder-suicide left notes saying they couldn't afford medical care, police say. *The Washington Post.* Retrieved from https://www.washingtonpost.com/nation/2019/08/10/couple-dead-apparent-murder-suicide-left-notes-saying-they-couldnt-afford-medical-care-police-say/
Ingram, P. (2020). Women testify about squalid conditions in Border Patrol detention centers. *Tucson Sentinel.* Retrieved from http://www.tucsonsentinel.com/local/report/011420_detainee_lawsuit/women-testify-squalid-conditions-border-patrol-detention-centers/
Johnson, J., & Jordan, M. (2015, November 22). Trump on rally protestor: "Maybe he should have been roughed up." *The Washington Post.* Retrieved from https://www.washingtonpost.com/news/post-politics/wp/2015/11/22/black-activist-punched-at-donald-trump-rally-in-birmingham/
Jordan, M. (2019, July 30). No more family separations, except these 900. *The New York Times.* Retrieved from https://www.nytimes.com/2019/07/30/us/migrant-family-separations.html?campaign_id=60&instance_id=0&segment_id=15693&user_id=47b1765b4c08ea07ab9e635ec259c3fe&regi_id=72789483ing-news

Kelly, J. (2019, November 25). The frightening rise in low-quality, low-paying jobs: Is this really a strong job market? *Forbes*. Retrieved from https://www.forbes.com/sites/jackkelly/2019/11/25/the-frightening-rise-in-low-quality-low-paying-jobs-is-this-really-a-strong-job-market/#6dff02e54fd1

Kessler, G., Rizzo, S., & Kelly, M. (2019, August 12). President Trump has made 12,019 false or misleading claims over 928 days. *The Washington Post.* Retrieved from https://www.washingtonpost.com/politics/2019/08/12/president-trump-has-made-false-or-misleading-claims-over-days/

King Watts, E. (2017). Postracial fantasies, blackness, and zombies. *Communication and Critical/Cultural Studies, 14*(4), 1–17.

Kristof, N. (2016, August 13). Donald Trump is making America meaner. *The New York Times*. Retrieved from https://www.nytimes.com/2016/08/14/opinion/sunday/donald-trump-is-making-america-meaner.html

Lambroza, S. (1987). Jewish responses to pogroms in late imperial Russia. In J. Reinharz (Ed.), *Living with Antisemitism* (pp. 253–274). Hanover, NH: University Press of New England.

Leohardt, D. (2019a, August 5). Conservatism has a violence problem. *The Washington Post.* Retrieved from https://www.nytimes.com/2019/08/05/opinion/el-paso-shooting-republicans-trump.html?rref=collection%2Fbyline%2Fdavid-leonhardt&action=click&contentCollection=undefined&region=stream&module=stream_unit&version=search&contentPlacement=1&pgtype=collection

Leonhardt, D. (2019b, December 15). Why you shouldn't believe those G.D.P. numbers: The statistics keep on rising, but they don't track the well-being of most Americans. *The Washington Post.* Retrieved from https://www.nytimes.com/2019/12/15/opinion/gdp-america.html

Lithwick, D. (2019, August 21). The demoralizing reality of life under Trump: Every day is the same, but still awful. *Slate*. Retrieved from https://slate.com/news-and-politics/2019/08/demoralizing-reality-of-life-under-trump.html

Lopez, R. (2019, December 2). The shocking rise in anti-Latino hate crimes. *Salud America!* Retrieved from https://salud-america.org/the-shocking-rise-in-anti-latino-hate-crimes/

López, V., & Park, S. (2018, November 6). ICE detention center says it's not responsible for staff's sexual abuse of detainees. *ACLU.* Retrieved from https://www.aclu.org/blog/immigrants-rights/immigrants-rights-and-detention/ice-detention-center-says-its-not-responsible

Mbembe, A. (2019). *Necropolitics*. Durham, NC: Duke University Press.

Neumann, K. (2014). Introductory essay: Historians and the yearning for historical justice. *Rethinking History, 18*(2), 145–164.

O'Donnell, K. (2018). Academics becoming activists: Reflections on some ethical issues of the Justice for Magdalenes Campaign. In P. Villar-Argaiz (Ed.), *Irishness on the margins* (pp. 77–100). London: Palgrave Macmillan.

Only now do we understand the true cruelty of Trump's family separation. (2019, October 29). *The Washington Post.* Retrieved from https://www.washingtonpost.com/opinions/only-now-do-we-understand-the-true-cruelty-of-trumps-family-separation/2019/10/29/8294ef9e-f9cf-11e9-ac8c-8eced29ca6ef_story.html

Parker, A. (2016, March 10). Black protestor is sucker-punched by white Donald Trump supporter at rally. *The New York Times.* Retrieved from https://www.nytimes.com/politics/first-draft/2016/03/10/donald-trump-rally-protester/

Parker, K., Morin, R., & Horowitz, J. M. (2019, March 21). *Looking to a future, public sees an America in decline on many fronts*. Pew Research Center: Social and Demographic *Trends*. Retrieved from https://www.pewsocialtrends.org/2019/03/21/public-sees-an-america-in-decline-on-many-fronts/?wpisrc=nl_daily202&wpmm=1

Rizzo, S. (2019, March 26). Trump's outdated spin on the black unemployment rate. *The Washington Post*. Retrieved from https://www.washingtonpost.com/politics/2019/03/26/trumps-outdated-spin-black-unemployment-rate/

Ross, M., & Bateman, N. (2019, November). *Meet the low-wage workforce*. Metropolitan Policy Program: Brookings Institute. Retrieved from https://www.brookings.edu/wp-content/uploads/2019/11/201911_Brookings-Metro_low-wage-workforce_Ross-Bateman.pdf

Rubin, J. (2019, October 24). What Jews think about anti-Semitism. *The Washington Post*. Retrieved from https://www.washingtonpost.com/opinions/2019/10/24/what-jews-think-about-anti-semitism/?wpisrc=nl_faith&wpmm=1

Ryegiel, K. (2016). Dying to live: Migrant deaths and citizenship politics along European borders: Transgressions, disruptions, and mobilizations. *Citizenship Studies, 20*(5), 545–560.

Sellers, R. P. (2019, August 20). The president is correct: There IS an insanity gripping our nation. *Baptist News Global*. Retrieved from https://baptistnews.com/article/the-president-is-correct-there-is-an-insanity-gripping-our-nation/#.XYWLMedKg0o

Shildrick, M. (2019). (Micro)chimerism, immunity and temporality: Rethinking the ecology of life and death. *Australian Feminist Studies, 34*(99), 10–24.

Spagat, E. (2019, October 25). Tally of children split at border tops 5,400 in new count. *PBS News Hour*. Retrieved from https://www.pbs.org/newshour/nation/tally-of-children-split-at-border-tops-5400-in-new-count

Stierl, M. (2016). Contestations in death – The role of grief in migration struggles. *Citizenship Studies, 20*(2), 173–191.

Traister, R. (2018). *Good and mad: The revolutionary power of women's anger*. New York, NY: Simon & Schuster.

Transcript: Donald Trump's taped comments about women. (2016, October 8). *The New York Times*. Retrieved from https://www.nytimes.com/2016/10/08/us/donald-trump-tape-transcript.html

Trump's statements spur feelings of concern, confusion, embarrassment. (2019, June 18). Pew Research Center: U.S. Politics and Policy. Retrieved from https://www.people-press.org/2019/06/19/public-highly-critical-of-state-of-political-discourse-in-the-u-s/pp_2019-06-19_discourse_0-05/

Uchitelle, L. (2019, July 11). Unemployment is low, but that's only part of the story. *The New York Times*. Retrieved from https://www.nytimes.com/2019/07/11/business/low-unemployment-not-seeking-work.html

Wan, W. (2019, August 2). Racism has devastating effects on children's health, pediatricians warn. *The Washington Post*. Retrieved from https://www.washingtonpost.com/health/racism-has-devastating-effects-on-childrens-health-pediatricians-warn/2019/08/02/ce5fc96a-b313-11e9-8f6c-7828e68cb15f_story.html?wpisrc=nl_tyh&wpmm=1

Wan, W., & Bever, L. (2019, July 19). Trump's presidency may be making Latino's sick. *The Washington Post*. Retrieved from https://www.washingtonpost.com/health/trumps-presidency-may-be-making-latinos-sick/2019/07/19/4e89b9f0-a97f-11e9-9214-246e594de5d5_story.html

CHRISTINE SALKIN DAVIS AND JONATHAN L. CRANE

DIALOGUE 2

"I wasn't wearing MAGA hats anywhere," Larry adds.

Andrea nods, "I'm sensitive to what other people would feel, and I would not want to make someone feel uncomfortable, or feel like I'm against them, or I don't like them, because we have different views. So, for me, I would just rather not flaunt a MAGA hat." Andrea laughs. "I think, I think with Trump you either have, diehard supporters, or people who absolutely hate him. There's not a lot of in-between."

"Yeah," says Elizabeth. "During the time leading up to the election, I wouldn't tell anybody I was in favor of Trump, because people I was around were so negative about Trump. And all the name-calling of Trump supporters, and calling us a basket of deplorables and racists, and all the bad names. And basically calling us uneducated. I didn't want to argue with everybody, but I had my reasons to vote for Trump, as far as immigration. I take a hard line on immigration. And he was a businessman. I thought that would be good for the country, versus what Washington has been doing with things like the deficit and spending."

"The deplorables," Larry says with a grimace. "That's why for the people in the polling business, it totally blew them away."

"I think the media proved that they're very biased," Elizabeth says, "because they had been predicting that Hillary would win. And I think it showed that they had agendas and biases."

"Do you think this election was unusual in that regard, where people would be treated differently because of who they were going to support?" Jon asks.

Elizabeth nods. "I think it definitely was different with this election. I think I felt different about people's reactions because people are negative now about politics. If you share your opinion, people will make a comment. Everybody seems entitled to share things on social media, and it was anything goes, as far as what you can say. Say you're going to move to Canada. And I say, move to Canada if you want to! He's your president too. In my lifetime, I don't remember people, I mean, seriously talking about 'he's not my president.' It was always, 'election's over, you've got your president, move

DOI:10.1163/9789004436329_004

on.' And I think it's been the most negative election. I think people are more willing to speak their minds, speak out, maybe they're not worried about being polite. I think society is less polite, and more willing to just be rude. Call people rude names."

Larry adds, "there were so many people who were Trump supporters and not broadcasting it. They're not out there shouting from the rooftops and wearing red MAGA hats. But they identify with the policies and the nationalistic approach, and things that were going on. It's like, I don't really like to say I am the biggest Trump guy in the world."

"Why? You support his policies? Why would you not want to let people know?" Jon asks.

"I have had to keep my thoughts to myself when we discuss immigration at church," says Elizabeth.

"I feel like he's doing a good job," says Andrea. "In some ways, he needs to work on some things. But, have I benefited so far from some of his presidency, as we've just had our tax returns done today? We have. So, from that perspective I support him. But I think he is perceived by so many in a bad light, I don't know that everyone would be open-minded enough," she laughs, "to understand my support."

"I'm a former military person," says Larry. "Going into this election, the way his brain works, the stuff he said about John McCain, 'I like the people who don't get captured.' I was like, wow, it really wasn't a good thing to say. But again, being a policy person, and knowing which way he was going to lean, he's one part of the three branches of government. So, you know, he can guide it. But, we've just had the midterm elections and now we're going to see what the next two years look like, because now we have a divided Congress. So, what can he truly do?"

"Go back to the primaries," I say, "when Trump was just starting to run in that large field of candidates."

Andrea says, "Initially we were like, there's no way Trump will end up being the Republican candidate. Then the further it went along, and it seemed more people resonated with the fact that he's not a politician, he truly has the best interest of the United States in mind to represent the common person, although he was a billionaire. But he was a common person in terms of, he hadn't been in Washington so long that he was jaded, unable to realize what the majority of the American people deal with. I think people resonated with that. And then it's like his support ended up getting larger and larger, and larger. So I was looking at this, I was like, oh, my God, really? But I was still thinking, okay, I was never a Cruz fan. But, Rubio was the one that I liked;

I just liked his delivery. He was very, convincing; he spoke very confidently and seemed to be very knowledgeable about policies in the debates. So," Andrea continues with a laugh, "so, yeah. When he ended up becoming the nominee, it was like, okay. Well, it is what it is. And then I started getting a little nervous because, well, these are our choices. We've got Trump and Hillary." She laughs again. "And then, I'll never forget, the night of the election,"

"We fell asleep," Larry interrupts. "And I woke up at 2:30, three o'clock in the morning and I went to my phone. And I'm like, he won. And it didn't feel like a win. It was more of a shock. Oh, my God, Trump actually won."

Jon laughs. I, too, am amused at the irony of our having the exact same reaction from different sides of the aisle.

"You were shocked and surprised, and then what, for you?" I ask.

"Well," Larry says. "that's who I voted for, so obviously I felt like, okay, well,"

Andrea laughs. "We'll see. We'll see what happens. And, let's hope that what we put our trust in him to do, let's hope that it actually makes America great again." She laughs. "I was like, okay."

Elizabeth says, "I think Trump's win showed that the voters really wanted a change from Washington controlling, and the media controlling, everything. To regular people having their say, and saying they don't like that Washington's making the laws and doing things without listening to regular people. And Trump is something different. He hadn't spent his whole life in Washington as a political person. He could apply more business-like decisions."

AMY BURT

1. A TRUMP-HAUNTED LANDSCAPE

PROLOGUE: ELECTION DAY, 2016

It started as a social media post in response to other social media posts: let's get a group photo on Election Day! Let's show support for Hillary and for each other! Pics or the zeitgeist didn't happen! And so we met in the middle of town during lunch hour, working women, moms, retired women, straggling in for a shared five minutes. I was thrilled to be in this photo and imagined it would become one of my treasured possessions. Most of us lacked the pantsuit, the appropriate attire for Election Day, and showing that We're With Her definitely had a dress code. The Facebook threads leading up to that Tuesday included ideas for borrowing or procuring items to create the simulacra of pantsuits. After scouring thrift stores, I ended up with a borrowed Brooks Brothers suit from a septuagenarian fashionista who was thrilled at its usage in this context, and she and I marveled at the profundity of this moment, imagining the women who had come before us and those who would come after us. I thought of the women in my own family who had been involved in party politics and nonpartisan democratic practice in a variety of capacities, and thought about the privilege of voting, much less voting for a woman to serve in the highest elected office in this land.

Election morning, I called a family member, wanting to share the excitement. I was unprepared for her silence: I hadn't thought that she wouldn't share my joy in the moment, even if she wouldn't cast her ballot the same way. Politics, like many other topics, was an area in which we agreed to disagree, but we could usually find some common ground. Not that day, and I continued on with my planned activities: to the polls, to the workplace, and on to the photo op.

The photo isn't great: some eyes are closed, some people are obscured by others in front of them, but what's clear is the sense of excitement that shows in that photo. Our faces have that kind of joy you see in pictures of small children: authentic smiles, gleeful, defiant grins, tangible swagger at what we thought of as a moment where history changed. It changed all right, but not in the ways we anticipated.

 | DOI:10.1163/9789004436329_005

The Christ-Haunted South

There are ways in which I exist as both self and Other within my community. As a middle-aged white woman who was raised within two distinct Christian faiths from which I diverged, I "pass" in my small Southern community, and my ideologies are inferred by my embodiment. But I was not raised in the South, and so I am "Other" in ways that I feel deeply when beholding specifically Southern Christianity, especially as it's enacted within churches aligned with the Southern Baptist Convention.

O'Connor noted that "While the South is hardly Christ-centered, it is most certainly Christ-haunted" (1969, p. 44). Churches are such a common fixture of the landscape of middle Georgia that a cursory Google search found no fewer than eighty Christian churches for a town with a population of 25,000. Christ-haunted, indeed. This haunting bleeds into secular experiences: store clerks trill "Have a blessed day!"

A lifetime of performing gospel music (in the car, in the church, later for larger audiences, in venues both sacred and secular) has provided me with intersectional opportunities as a community member who straddles belief categories as both/and, neither/nor. This essay examines lived experience of bodily trauma and memory to move through the time beginning with Trump's candidacy and ending after the inauguration in early 2017.

As someone raised within a Christian tradition, the idioms of my faith are Christ-friendly, and gospel music connects me to this tradition in ways hard to explain considering that my beliefs might be best summed up as "Other," and yet. Gospel music. Like a vegan lured down the street by the smell of barbecue, gospel music calls to me. I number among the "unchurched" largely because churches don't *just* sing and play music. They insist on talking, and in those moments, my doubts about translations of texts, about the real or imagined messages of them predicated upon shared cultural constructs framed for a purpose of this world rather than the next come flooding back, and I argue inherently with what's being said or read. Usually.

Since being old enough to buy lottery tickets, I've attended few churches regularly. I've attended some sporadically, or as a "One and Done" experience. The churches where I linger usually draw me with their praise music. My love for gospel music came from my paternal grandparents. Growing up in an area with spotty radio reception (thanks, granite outcroppings) meant that you could talk, be silent, or sing in the car, and sometimes they picked option C. Because of this, I could sing "Old Rugged Cross" and "In the Garden" along with the congregation that day at the Church of Christ at my

Grandma's funeral, and singing along with my family, with a church full of people who loved Gram, was a beautiful thing.

JANUARY 2017

One day, at the gym, I heard a sliver of a melody – a song I *almost* knew. A few days later, I tracked down Barbara (not her real name), the singer, to ask if she remembered the song. She started singing, "The Sweetest Name I Know," and memories of hearing Gram and Grandpa sing in the car came back to me, and I held onto Barbara's hand and cried a little. Later, I'd remember that that was *almost* the song – the song they'd sung was "Every Day with Jesus is Sweeter than the Day Before," and those songs are so alike as to be cousins, or sisters – the sort that, especially from a distance, you'd swear one was the other.

Barbara launched into another song, and I sang along, still holding her hands, when she asked if I'd come to her church on Sunday. She and her mom, a sharp-dressed nonagenarian, just *love* this church. It was the answer to their prayers.

Barbara and her mama perform femininity in a way I've always admired: they Dress for Life. I doubt that I would ever see Barbara or her mama not fully dressed, made-up, and accessorized, and I would hate to miss it should they ever have a yard sale. Both of them sport elaborate styles that I can only think of as hair-dos: upsweeps, deliberate curls, living testaments to the adage "The higher the hair, the closer to God." Both have long, painted nails, and their eyelash game is always on point. Between the sentiment and the thrill at being talked to by one of the pretty girls, I'm sold on the idea of the church visit, and so I agree, only later to learn that their pastor was one of the evangelical Christians who traveled to Washington for Trump's inauguration. I feel like I've been gut punched.

The Trump-Haunted World

My world became Trump-haunted. A specific type of white male privilege preceded me into a literal sanctuary: a specifically holy space. During the 2016 election season, I didn't really think Trump would win the election, largely because he was so despicable in so many ways, and while news of his antics, his incivilities, his bullying, and his crimes kept stacking up, the moment that took my breath away was learning that Trump had been accused of child rape. As a survivor of childhood sexual abuse, I felt unsafe in ways that were at odds with the current details of my life, but trauma affects the brain and memory. The brain has systems in place for allowing us to determine who we can trust and who we can't. Lachmann writes that Trump's "unapologetically authoritarian manner … is similar to abusers, predators, sexual harassers, and seething misanthropes that so many people, females especially, have been forced to endure" (2017, para. 2).

The idea that the minister of Baldwin Baptist Church (not its real name) had attended Trump's inauguration felt to me as an overt approval of the man I've come to think of as the Predator in Chief. As a child, I was told not to tell, and I didn't; the people who could have protected me didn't have all of the information. Having a secret, I felt simultaneously outside of their love, and outside of the love of a God who (it seemed to me) could have and certainly should have protected me. The adult me has (through a lot of work, a lot of therapy) rewritten that script, but my ideas about the God of my grandparents reverted after the election to my childhood idea of a scary, disinterested deity. All at once, I again felt unheard, unseen, and unprotected, because Trump was elected by an overwhelming majority of white evangelical Christians who overlooked a myriad of evidence and allegations of assault, misogyny, and bad behavior to support, promote, and join forces with a man who brandishes a Bible as a weapon.

What *Time* referred to as "a public celebration of Jesus" (Dias, 2017, para. 6), the inauguration had six religious leaders, five Christians and a rabbi, a record, according to an inauguration scholar (Stack, 2017, para. 2). *Forbes* noted that Trump's inaugural address was singular in a few ways: it was shorter than any speech since Jimmy Carter's and its tone was bellicose (Morgan, 2017, paras. 3, 5).

Reading Trump's address, one sees that women are significant by their absence. *Vox* commentator Crockett noted that "Trump only used the word 'women' twice," both in reference to "men and women," once when he mentions "the forgotten men and women of our country, and again "in reference to the men and women of military. He does mention "Mothers and children trapped in poverty in our inner cities," but *Vox* reporter Emily Crockett (Trump's inauguration speech, 2017, para. 13) notes, it's "interesting that (Trump) never specifically talks about women's issues after a campaign that was so strongly defined by gender on both sides."

Scholars of U.S. Presidential rhetoric Campbell and Jamieson note that two features that separate the inaugural address from other epideictic speeches, are that it functions to "(unify) the audience by reconstituting its members as 'the people' who can witness and ratify this ceremony" and it "rehearses communal values drawn from the past" (1985, p. 396). The absence of the category of women would suggest that Trump and his administration consider women of so little value that they are not worthy of mention. The past that the "communal values" seem to be drawn from harkens to a time when women had no legal rights and could neither witness nor ratify anything of note.

While women were absent in the body of the inaugural address, they were protesting in droves. Estimates for the women's marches in the U.S. hover around four million, and over a quarter of a million additional worldwide. To put the numbers in perspective, there were twice as many marchers in the U.S. as there are active members in all branches of the military, and the four million mark is roughly 1.6% of the entire U.S. population (Chenoweth & Pressman, 2017, paras. 5, 6).

On my way to Baldwin Baptist Church on the Sunday after the Trump inauguration, I'm seized with my familiar childhood fear: Something Bad is going to happen. I call a friend, crying, on the way to church, and she and I go through a worst-case scenario, and discuss how I can leave if things get weird. "But I'll be sitting by the pretty girls!" I think to myself, realizing that my warring pathological desires to act like my shit is together while simultaneously not condoning Trumpism by my mere presence may have to work through their differences for the next hour.

At the church, I'm struck by the few cars in the parking lot for a church of this size, but I arrive early, wanting clear access to the exits. I greet Barbara, at the front with the praise team, and go and sit by her mama. Both of them look fabulous, and it occurs to me that perhaps by the time I'm in my nineties I'll have mastered double-lined lower lids.

On this last Sunday in January, the pastor begins by talking about his time at the inauguration, and how thrilling it was to be there. His sermon that day is built around a passage from the New Testament that "prayers, petitions and thanksgiving be given by all men, for kings and all who are in authority, so that we may lead a quiet life in all godliness and dignity" (1 Timothy 2:1–2). I'm thrown out of the text by the use of "all men," spending some time wondering if women are included, and, as always, decide that if I have to ask, the answer is no.

Reading along in one of the Bibles that the church has provided, I move into the next part of the passage where it's suggested we pray for the leaders so that we may "lead a quiet life," and think about what I'm hearing about Trump's administration, and agree that I'd like to live a quiet life, and I can agree to pray that they make good decisions, so that ALL people can have a quiet life.

The cognitive dissonance of agreeing with part of a message while disagreeing with another part strikes me. As with most things Biblical, I'm taking my agreement out of context. The next couple of lines in 1 Timothy go on to discuss the ways in which women shouldn't adorn themselves as to be showy: don't wear pearls or gold (1 Timothy 2:9) and, oh by the way, women don't get to be leaders in the church because Adam was born first, and he wasn't the one who did the deceiving, that was Eve (1 Timothy 2: 12–14). I begin thinking about how the situatedness, the physical embodiment, the historical and geographical contexts of an author impact the writing, and recall the "Prologue to the Wife of Bath's Tale," and her claims that men wrote the Bible which is why women are treated poorly within the stories (Chaucer, 2014, p. 179). Famously, she cites Paul's poor opinion of women when he says that it's better to marry than to burn, meaning, I've always imagined, that if passion is so great that sexual congress is inevitable, marriage is preferable to eternal damnation.[1]

The pastor goes on to talk about how he's been on a personal mission to pray the Lord's Prayer with people at least once a day, and how he's spent every day of the last year asking strangers to join with him in prayer. He recounts how he went up to a guy at the gym (the biggest and baddest guy there!) and prayed with him. I think about how approaching strangers when you're in a body (white, straight, male) that many associate with power may be easier than in any other embodiment. This is privilege.

Trump's evangelical connections smack of this sort of privilege, and many of the clergy who publicly supported him preach a specific message that many find controversial. Prosperity theology, as it's known, says it's God's will for the faithful to be wealthy, and that "sickness and poverty … can be broken by faith" (Livni, 2017, para. 6). Many Christians feel that this gospel in no way lines up with Christ's teachings, as it steers clear of his warnings about the dangers of wealth and power.

Trump's affiliation with televangelists has been life-long. He and his parents were members of Norman Vincent Peale's church, Marble Collegiate in Manhattan, where his first marriage took place, and, in fact, Trump hosted Peele's 90th birthday party in 1988 at the Waldorf Astoria. Peale's message of positive thinking and self-realization reached millions through television and radio (Dias, 2016, "God is Green," para. 2). Trump's coterie of famous preacher friends includes Joel Osteen, Franklin Graham, and Liberty Baptist University's own president Jerry Falwell Jr., who says that Trump reminds him of his daddy (Dias, 2016, para. 6).

Inaugurations function, in part, as a celebration of the electoral victory, and the shout outs to Jesus may have been by way of thanks to Trump's voters: 81% of white evangelical Christians voted for him (Dias, 2017, para. 6). What separates evangelical Christians from others? Graham's son, Franklin, famously stumped for Trump, and "rallied evangelicals to polls in every state" (Dias, 2017, para. 8).

I left the church dispirited and exhausted, bone-weary. My relentless judgment of others in no way made me happy. Perhaps I lost track of the reason I went to the church in the first place. I went because a friend had asked me: it was important to her, and she wanted me there. And it had meant a lot to Barbara that I was there, that much was apparent when she'd introduced me to her friends and family. Perhaps my comfort was, in many ways, beside the point.

Your Easter Heart

A few weeks later, as I'm leaving the gym, Barbara runs up and hands me a pink piece of paper, a flyer for her church's Easter service. "I'm singing three songs!" she tells me. She's holding my hand. I put the flyer in my purse and hold her other, hand, too, and we stand there in the hall and sing together two verses of "Were You There When They Crucified My Lord?" in imperfect but heart-felt harmony. It occurs to me, looking into her eyes, that me judging other people is antithetical to the purpose of Easter, and that if Christ's ideas had been easy, they might not have killed him.

The flyer, a pink heart, has my name printed on it, in large, careful lettering. Inside it says "Come and join us for a Resurrection Celebration! Baldwin Baptist Church," along with the date and time, and a reminder: "Bring your Easter Heart with you!" My Easter Heart and I head out to Baldwin Baptist Church, this time taking a friend along for moral support. The friend, Diane (not her real name), had jumped at the chance to attend the Easter service, and, it turned out, had once been a regular at that church. The minister and several members greet her warmly. During the service, she squeezes my hand, tears in her eyes.

The Easter Service is filled with music, as Barbara promised, and she and the praise team sound great. The music is interspersed with the usual readings from the New Testament, detailing how Jesus's tomb was found to be empty on Easter morning. Near the end of the service, we're handed hearts and asked to write our names on them, and in so doing, give our hearts to Jesus. Lining up, we go to the front of the church and tack our hearts onto a large panel of sheetrock. The praise team sings "He's Alive!"

I later think about this participatory part of the service, and how it allowed the congregation a way to connect to each other and to a community of faith in a tangible way. Reflecting back on the minister's personal prayer mission, which, too, was about connection, and about transforming the present. Years of rote recitation of the Lord's Prayer can render it into a string of nonsensical phonemes, and yet the act of reciting the prayer with a stranger within a different, an unexpected, context may have the power of reinscribing the text with sacred meaning. The more I think about this personal prayer mission, the more I reflect on the idea of connection. It is a desire to connect with others that drives my love of gospel music, combined with a desire to reconnect with my past within an environment that I recognize.

EPILOGUE: INTO ACTION

I wanted to write this essay to grapple with a few fundamental questions that have plagued me. Can a shared vernacular lead to the opportunity for real discourse about issues that keep us divided? Or the question behind it: if we can't find ways to talk with people we look like, how can we hope to talk with people who are unlike us? The problem is this: I don't have an answer. I remain both Christ-Haunted and Trump-Haunted. The ubiquity of Fox news blaring from TVs in restaurants, salons, gyms, and coffee shops means that I don't have to be looking for Trump to find him: he is everywhere and nowhere. Hauntings become synecdochal (Wenno & Holmgren Troy, 2008), a part for the whole relationship, wherein Trump's image, his name, the doings of his administration all become the sign of the perpetrator, the Predator in Chief. Conversely, everywhere I see images and words of Christ, on billboards and bumper stickers. "Ghosts," O'Connor noted, "can be very fierce and instructive. They cast strange shadows" (p. 45). They can show us who we are as well as who we don't want to be.

I haven't been back to Baldwin Baptist Church, but have started attending Our Town Baptist Church (not its real name), where, not coincidentally, some of the women in the Election Day photo worship. That Election Day photo has become a token of a transformational moment. The women in that photograph were galvanized by Hilary's loss and moved to act, in ways large and small. Some of the women knitted pink hats with cat ears and wore them as symbols of resistance. Some of the women marched in Washington, Atlanta, and elsewhere. Some registered voters in the area, while others became poll watchers, and many worked to reenergize the local Democratic Party, canvasing for candidates, working to bring debates and information about issues to the people. Some of them had been doing these forms of civic engagement all along. All of them practiced kindness with each other and with the people in their families and communities.

I had coffee with the pastor of Our Town Baptist Church one day, and we were talking about things large and small, when I made my big confession: I'm scared of Christians who voted for Trump, and I don't even know how to talk to them about the things that matter: issues of equality, social justice, love of people. My questions are accusations masquerading as questions, pointed barbs covered in venom. I want to ask my family member why the hell she voted for Trump, but I'm too scared of what she'll say, so I remain quiet. The pastor was silent for a minute, and then he said that he knows God's love is so big that it can heal all the brokenness. And in that moment, I believed him.

When Trump was elected, many other Republicans also gained office, and through an odd series of events, I met one of those elected in November of 2016, our local representative at the state capital. Needing to ask him about funding for an organization, I used a mutual friend as entry into the discussion. During our conversation, the talk turned to the news of the day, which included accusations and allegations of abuses of power. I heard him say what I'd heard from other white Southern Republicans of a certain age: "It's hard to say anything anymore without somebody taking offense." This has historically been the point at which I jump in with vitriol, but I heard pain in his voice, and I was able to respond with what I thought was true. I told him that I'm sure it seems that way, and that there are groups of people who haven't been heard who have a lot to say, and it's a great opportunity for the rest of us to learn from them. I didn't have to agree with him, I didn't have to argue with him. I was able to listen and to offer up my own truths about that topic. I felt heard. We were quiet for a minute, and then took our leave of each other. Later, I told our mutual friend that I truly enjoyed meeting him, and was told that the politician thought that I was good people. Maybe reaching out to one person at a time is the only way we can change the world and ourselves.

NOTE

1 The Wife of Bath, it should be noted, is justifying her five marriages. I would remember, too, later, that the story she tells is about a knight who is found guilty of rape, and the women who intercede on his behalf.

REFERENCES

Campbell, K., & Jamieson, K. (1985). Inaugurating the presidency. *Presidential Studies Quarterly, 15*(2), 394–411.

Chaucer, G. (2014). *The Canterbury tales*. New York, NY: Penguin. (Original work published 1387 and 1400)

Chenoweth, E., & Pressman, J. (2017, February 7). This is what we learned by counting the women's marches. *The Washington Post*. Retrieved from http://www.washingtonpost.com/news/monkey-cage/wp/2017/02/07/this-is-what-we-learned-by-counting-the-womens-marches/?noredirect=on&utm_term=.61b6619d28b9

Dias, E. (2016, April 14). How Donald Trump gained support from evangelical outsiders. *Time*. Retrieved from http://time.com/donald-trump-prosperity-preachers/

Dias, E. (2017, January 20). Trump inauguration: Donald Trump wooed evangelicals. *Time*. Retrieved from http://time.com/4641780/trump-inauguration-faith-religion-evangelical/

Lachmann, S. (2017, February 6). You are not alone in being retraumatized by Trump. *Psychology Today*. Retrieved from http://www.psychologytoday.com/us/blog/mewe/201702/you-are-not-alone-in-being-retraumatized-trump

Livni, E. (2017, January 20). The clergy at Trump's inauguration belong to a church that believes poverty is a punishment for lack of faith. *Quartz*. Retrieved from https://qz.com/890765/trump-inauguration-gospel-of-success/

Morgan, N. (2017, January 23). The astonishing rhetoric of President Trump's inaugural. *Forbes*. Retrieved from http://www.forbes.com/sites/nickmorgan/2017/01/20/the-astonishing-rhetoric-of-president-trumps-inaugural-address/#12e3f02a4190

O'Connor, F., Fitzgerald, S., & Fitzgerald, R. (Eds.). (1969). *Mystery and manners*. New York, NY: Farrar, Straus, and Giroux.

President Trump's inauguration speech, annotated. (2017, January 20). *Vox*. Retrieved from http://www.vox.com/a/president-trump-inauguration-speech-transcript-annotations

Stack, L. (2017, January 18). The religious speakers taking part in Trump's inaugural ceremony. *New York Times*. Retrieved from https://www.nytimes.com/2017/01/18/us/politics/inauguration-speakers.html

Wennö, E., & Holmgren Troy, M. (2008). *Space, haunting, discourse*. Newcastle: Cambridge Scholars Publishing.

CHRISTINE SALKIN DAVIS AND JONATHAN L. CRANE

DIALOGUE 3

"It's like the State of the Union the other night," Larry says. "I mean, you go, okay, protect the country. Check. We've got, you know, the lowest level of unemployment among African Americans and females. So, check. GDP now is running record highs, the GDP we've seen in the last year went up 4%. Check. The number of women that are working. Women's rights when it comes to having their children, and expanding that. I'm like, okay. Trying to reduce costs on medications, working on the opioid issues. It's like, okay, even if you didn't like the things he said that were taped and recorded about females, his multiple marriages." Larry continues. "And it's funny, really, the economy was moving in a very positive direction under President Obama. We were in a horrible mortgage situation when Obama came into office; it killed the economy as Bush was coming out, because we believed everybody needed their own home. So I think there were a lot of good things that Obama put in. Economies are cyclical, regardless of who's in office. It's going to go up and down. So is Trump now getting to inherit a very climbing economy? And now the numbers are great. So you could say, if Hillary was in office, would these numbers be what they are today? It's a very valid question. So, you know, how much has Trump impacted the economy, shaming companies, and not moving certain things to Mexico?"

"So how do you feel about your vote now?" I ask.

"I'm happy about the low unemployment rate, says Elizabeth. "North Korea, we are beginning progress."

Larry says, "You know, now we're attacking media, and, now we have media which is more opinionated. So, that's why I come back to the noise and everything else, and it's fine, because I'm more about local government and state government. I care about what my city council and my county commissioners are doing. I look at state policies and how we're helping education work around the state. And how we are working our taxes to fund roads. And local things like that. But I just wish people would not live in that federal bubble between Republicans and Democrats. You're concerned about what was said on the State of the Union, but here locally we're going

DOI:10.1163/9789004436329_006

through a revaluation now with properties. And, are our local city councils and the commissioners going to stay revenue neutral? That's something that really affects people that nobody seems to think about, but we care about, you know, fake news."

Elizabeth says, "there is no comparison between now and before the election. The economy is excellent. I did not like the fact that Obama wasn't tough on immigration, and he had an aunt living in Boston for 20 years, I think, on government subsidies when she overstayed her visa, and he did nothing. She lived there illegally at the time he was president."

"After the election," Andrea says, "I was cautiously optimistic perhaps."

"What were your thoughts on the day after the election?" I ask. "If I had asked you the day after the election, what are five things that you think are going to happen in the next year with this country? What would you have said?"

"Oh, gosh. Oh, wow," Andrea says. "It was a long time ago. Military. I know that military funding was one of his campaign promises. There had been cuts in the military, we were going to pull out of some countries where we had been and didn't need to continue to be. I know he never served in the military, but he has made appearances when a deceased soldier comes back home, and pays condolences to the family. Again, that could be a media thing. I just see it more through media I think now than I did from Obama. So I do feel like there's been more of an emphasis on the military."

Larry says, "Trade agreements. When you talk about pulling out of NAFTA, if he can get it passed, it does make sense if you're trading with somebody and somebody's abusing you, and it's not a fair exchange, wouldn't you want to try to make things fair? So we're going to renegotiate and redo this. Now, his methods might not be what everybody would want. And how he puts things out there, might not be the typical speech that you've heard from people that have sat in that office before. But, hey, we've been losing in this deal. If it's winning or losing with another country, I'm all about winning. So, how can we make things better for us?"

I nod.

Larry continues, "And, you know, I looked at some of the trade agreements that he talked about trying to redo. If it's regulations to allow corporations to move more quickly and more efficiently. The government had gotten big, you know, so the question was, how do we cut through some of the red tape? And, reduce the size of government so it functions better."

"There's trade-offs with it," interjects Andrea. "What was the report that I saw last week about China?"

Larry says, "You're talking about the trade deficit with China?"

"Yes, just last week," Andrea says.

"It might have been the trade deficit with China."

"Had a decrease."

"You know, Larry says, "we did our taxes recently. I expected that to be a complaint in the left leaning publications, and you should read some of the comments, 'I just did my taxes and guess what I'm paying, I've never paid in ever. And so how's this supposed to be helping me. The rich are getting richer. I'm paying more.' We paid for the first time ever too, but we went back and compared our tax amount with our income, and now we're by far, way better off. We're in a better position. And I would say we're not rich people. So, it helped the middle class. It's going to get the middle class going."

"I can see the value to be concerned for those less fortunate," says Elizabeth, "those who can only make minimum wage, and have trouble supporting themselves and their family on minimum wage, and the homeless, health coverage, making it affordable. I just don't think that taking jobs from people is the best solution. I don't think that there's a lot of problems being solved, because government programs could spend billions of dollars to help support people in poverty, and there's a lot of private groups, charities, non-profit religious groups, that do things to feed the homeless, get them places to live. What I've seen is that the problem seems to get bigger and worse, not better, the more government programs we have. I just believe we need a different approach. We need to get ahead of the problem to prevent the problem. I'd start with the idea of adults being held responsible, or accountable. By age 18, you need to support yourself."

DIANE FORBES BERTHOUD

2. BLACK WOMEN'S EMBODIED IDENTITIES AT THE NEXUS OF POLITICAL MOVEMENTS

Intersectionality, Resistance, and Power in the Post-Obama Era

What do we stand for?
Love and not fear.
The storm is brewing,
More change is near.

What seeds are we planting?
What can we learn?
How do we connect?
How do we know when it is our turn?

Can we smash the paradigm?
Open the door wide to inclusion?
The lines are no longer blurry,
There is no delusion.

We can't sit back and do nothing
We have to decide who we want to be
We are stronger together
Solidarity is the key

Can we listen to learn?
Hear a story
Make a friend?
There is a call to action
Get ready to prepare
We can't win this fight alone
And it's scary out there

There are warning signs ahead
Open your eyes to the truth and you will see
The power to change is here!

DOI:10.1163/9789004436329_007

It is you!
and
It is me!
(Clara, study participant)

The Obama effect has been extensively researched, pointing to the 44th president's historic rise in politics, his inspirational rhetoric and leadership, and his influence on grassroots organizing, political activism, and community leadership (Harris, Moffitt, & Squires, 2010; Jeffries, 2013; Marx, Ko, & Friedman, 2009; Welch, & Sigelman, 2011). After eight years of an unprecedented two-term presidency of Barack Obama, and the relative comfort and confidence of his supporters that a Democratic successor would prevail in the 2016 election, many were stunned and shaken upon the election of the Republican candidate, Donald J. Trump. Among the populations that have been adversely affected by this political and cultural shift are Black women, who have been caught for years in a symbolic and narrative struggle of their embodied identities. Black women who live at the nexus of "Black Lives Matter" and "Not my president"/"My pussy is not up for grabs" positionalities encounter complicated embodied experiences of the political and cultural landscape. This chapter gives voice to these positionalities through the documentation and analysis of women's narratives to contribute to a robust understanding of the body politic.

This essay offers a set of narratives that constitute an interlocking and dynamic mosaic of perspectives, feelings, and orientations that capture complex and nuanced experiences of Black women in response to the Trump presidency. Black women's written narratives in this chapter speak to the intersectional bodily experiences that are constituted through and by their psychological and political positionalities in the first twelve months of this presidency.

The 2017 Women's March serves as a starting point to capture Black women's narratives of resistance and urgency. Mirza (2009, p. 2) notes that Black women's resistance has been more than a "mere response to invisibility and erasure from the dominant discourse of race, class, and gender"; their activism has sought to achieve political empowerment and social justice.

Drawing on intersectionality as a conceptual framework, I document the ways in which Black women are affected by this presidency and discuss critical incidents that have defined and shaped their activism. This intersectional analysis addresses multiple axes of location and elucidates the simultaneous and interlocking oppressions that Black women experience that are sometimes not represented in feminist studies, although feminists of color and anti-racist feminists have emphasized this intersectional approach to understanding women's lives and experiences. It is challenging to respond to and incorporate multiple oppressions because they are simultaneous, inseparable, interlocking, and constantly shifting, and must be approached as such (Carastathis, 2013; Mann & Huffman, 2005), but the concept of intersectionality leads us to reject the viewpoint that women's identities are fragmented and solitary units. Women's experiences and identities are internally heterogeneous, complex, and constituted by dissonances and internal differences, as well as internal and external relations of power (Carastathis, 2013; Heywood & Drake, 1997). Mirza (2009) posits that racism, patriarchy, social class, and multiple systems of simultaneous and intersecting systems of oppression structure Black women's positionality at any given moment, thus creating specific and varied patterns of inequality and discrimination.

Forbes' (2009) conceptualization of the body dialectic also guides this chapter, as it addresses the (in)visibility of Black women and the tensions that arise from the workings of hegemonic social and political discourse, in which Black women's bodies become sites of political, historical, and cultural struggle. The chapter captures this struggle and the ways in which Black women choose to resist colonization and oppression. Bodies, in this essay, will refer to the physical, intellectual, political, and psychological elements that constitute our identities. The narratives in this chapter, therefore, constitute a holistic and nuanced representation of the complex corpus of Black women's tenuous positionality in U.S. society, particularly in the face of a Trump presidency. Narratives from women of middle to low-income and rural areas, and from immigrant women and Black and women of color can strengthen feminist scholarship and research as it enriches the perspectives and life narratives of women as a whole. To fully understand Black women's experiences in this political era, I explore power through narratives in a mosaic of voices of struggle and resistance to this presidency.

BLACK WOMEN'S EMBODIED EXPERIENCES

The social, organizational, and political experiences of women of color include disproportionate patterns of sexual harassment. In addition, Black women are more likely than any other group to experience racial discrimination, and intimate partner violence. While murder is a leading cause of death for women, Black women face a significantly higher murder rate than other groups of women. Furthermore, Black and indigenous women experience stalking, rape, and/or physical violence at a rate of 30–50% greater than Hispanic, White, Asian, or Pacific Islander women (Baker, 2005; Harris-Perry, 2011; Petrosky et al., 2017). Black women and other women of color, therefore, occupy precarious positions in U.S. society and organizations. As a result, Black women may experience greater anxiety and anger in response to state-sponsored or state-sanctioned oppression (Ashley, 2014; Cozier, Wise, Palmer, & Rosenberg, 2009; Harris-Perry, 2011).

The (Re)Emergence of Political Movements in the Millennial Era

In this section, I offer a review and brief history of the intersecting social and political movements that are integral to Black women's lives: The Women's March and Movement of January 2017 and the Black Lives Matter movement, founded in 2013. Black women find themselves uniquely positioned at the intersection of these movements because of their simultaneous and interlocking identities as woman *and* Black. The tensions between these movements, especially in their causes and foci, come into sharp contrast during the Trump election and presidency, and threaten their political viability.

The Women's March

In the fall of 2016, a month before the presidential elections, a recording of Republican nominee Trump emerged. In an *Access Hollywood* conversation with the show's host, Billy Bush, Trump discussed his experience seducing women: "I moved on her, and I failed. I'll admit it .... I did try. I've got to use some Tic Tacs, just in case I start kissing her," Trump said. "You know I'm automatically attracted to beautiful – I just start kissing them. It's like a magnet. Just kiss. I don't even wait. And when you're a star, they let you do it. You can do anything. Bush interjected: "Whatever you want," Trump responded: "Grab them by the pussy. You can do anything" (Fahrenthold, 2016, p. 1).

In the final presidential debate shortly after the lewd recordings surfaced, Trump appeared to stalk Democratic nominee Clinton on stage and assumed an argumentative and aggressive stance throughout the event. He later, in an exchange of remarks with her, referred to her as "such a nasty woman." This term set off a firestorm on social media. "Nasty woman/en" emerged as a battle cry, an empowering anthem among women and other supporters who responded with robust proclamations asserting their rights, freedoms, and power. Trump's use of "nasty" to describe the first woman Democratic nominee of a major political party was highly gendered. His discursive choices and approach throughout the debate were focused on using Mrs. Clinton's gender against her. "Nasty woman," intended as a moral, physical, and political form of abuse, worked to re-energize the women's movement and the March that directly followed the day after the president's inauguration.

The stated mission of the Women's March was to:

> harness the political power of diverse women and their communities to create transformative social change. Women's March is a women-led movement providing intersectional education on a diverse range of issues and creating entry points for new grassroots activists & organizers to engage in their local communities through trainings, outreach programs, and events. Women's March is committed to dismantling systems of oppression through nonviolent resistance and building inclusive structures guided by self-determination, dignity and respect. (Women's March, 2017, para. 1)

The Women's March represented an expansive local and global movement of resistance and solidarity that sought to protect women's rights and freedoms. Rooted in the values of justice and equality, the March also raised awareness and took a stand on immigrant rights, the environment, gun violence, and the degradation of women. Sister Marches were organized in many other cities around the globe, including Nairobi, Paris, Sydney, Barcelona, Brussels, and Tel Aviv, in more than 75 countries. The March's primary focus was to challenge the Trump administration. Groups that partnered with the movement against the new administration included Black Girls Rock, Girls Who Code, and the Muslim Women's Alliance (Rogers, 2017). Participants held signs that read "Get your Little Hands off my Uterus"; "This Pussy Grabs Back"; "My Pussy is Not up for Grabs"; "Protect our Future"; "Love Trumps Hate"; and "We the People: Women's March." With a diverse representation of women and girls of different races, religions, and ethnicities, and allies all over the world, people stood together to resist the oppressive ideologies of the presidency. A keen representation of the movement was captured in one of the signs, an adaptation from a prayer, which scholar and activist Angela Davis popularized: "I am no longer accepting the things I cannot change. I am changing the things I cannot accept."

Black women contributed to the March's creation and growth as they joined forces to meet the president's degrading and oppressive discourse with staunch resistance and outrage. With threats to health care, women's freedoms, and continued empowerment, Black women spoke up and were critical in shaping the political and cultural backlash. They mobilized around racial justice, while Hispanic women mostly organized around immigration. In an effort to ensure a democratic and inclusive movement, Black women demanded meaningful representation and involvement of racially and ethnically diverse women in the leadership of the March (Fisher, Dow, & Ray, 2017; Taylor, 2019). Black women's intersectional identities are implicated in attacks against dark-skinned immigrants, Black children and youth, educational excellence, and economic justice. On both the frontlines of the Black Matter movement and in other forms of community-based activism and protest, Black women's lives depend on protecting their communities.

The Black Lives Matter Movement

Some Black women identified closely with, and were very involved in advocacy and activism of, the Women's March, and others were more closely engaged with the Black Lives Matter movement. The murder of Trayvon Martin, an unarmed teenage African American, and the acquittal of his killer enraged many and gave birth to the Black Lives Matter movement in 2013. The movement strengthened over the next four years, as African American men and women continued to be subject to police brutality and unjust outcomes in the courts. The all too frequent acquittal of the perpetrators and their many acts of violence and murder left deep hurts and strong feelings of betrayal, anger, and frustration in communities of color. With little justice and relief from repressive policing found in the courts, and targeted efforts to address community concerns meeting with little or no sympathy from the powers that be, the movement expanded.

Chatelain (Chatelain & Asoka, 2015) notes that as a Black woman, she viewed the movement as fundamentally about her life and the lives of those she loves. She found the "Black Lives Matter is feminist in its interrogation of state power and its critique of structural inequity. It is also forcing a conversation about gender and racial politics that we need to have" (p. 57). The Black Lives Matter movement highlighted gendered police violence and critical issues such as economic inequality and discrimination against LGBT people of color. The movement adopted an intersectional approach to activism, seeking multiple and diverse perspectives that draw on community strengths and resist reliance on a single issue or a singular voice. Important issues addressed in this intersectional approach include mass incarceration, unemployment, the regrettable state of our K-12 educational system, and unrestricted access to public spaces (Carney, 2016; Chatelain & Asoka, 2015).

Next, I will use narratives and commentary to personalize and elucidate the intersectional experiences of Black women in the aftermath of Trump's election.

BLACK WOMEN'S NARRATIVES

The narratives presented in this chapter offer critical insights into the impact of the Trump presidency on selected Black women, based on repeated interviews with Black women throughout the year after Trump's election, about their experiences of President Trump and his presidency, and their thoughts and perspectives on the Women's March. The narratives elucidate the intersectional experiences constituted through and by their psychological and political positionalities over the first twelve months of the 45th presidency. These women's voices reveal complex and nuanced sensemaking processes about events and decisions related to this administration and the politics of resistance.

The Women's March

First, the narratives bring to light diverse reactions to the Women's March, varying from strong support to rejection of the March's leadership and organization. They capture the tensions between the active, outward resistance and internal, invisible turmoil Black women experience in political, organizational, and social contexts.

For instance, Lynn, an African American woman who is a 50-year old mother of two, explained why she attended: "I had to! There are moments in life where this is the only option. I had to be present, and bear witness to this." She viewed the Women's March as even more important than the inauguration of Barack Obama, of whom she was a staunch supporter. "Attending the March was like the equivalent of being on a plane that was crashing. Are you going on stay on it or jump?," she asked. The crashing plane was her analogy for Trump's election and presidency in the U.S., and her attendance at the march with a multigenerational group, including her mother and her daughter, represented three generations united in protest. "Taking my daughter was one of the best forms of parenting," she explained, "modeling the way. I wanted to show her the power of choosing to be part of something versus choosing not to do something in the face of feeling helpless. January 21 … was the first day to do something." As Lynn described it, the election of Trump signaled an urgency, a greater call to resist, particularly in light of his recorded statements about women and his attitude about them/their bodies. Her actions were focused on empowering her daughter to respond to misogynist and oppressive ideologies, particularly when they come from our leaders.

Lynn's physical reaction to the March was particularly memorable. "I almost vomited – it was so shocking at the March," she said. Lynn detailed being "packed in like sardines" at the March and seeing a White family in front of her family with a two-year-old holding a sign that read: 'Yeah, I wanted to fuck her …. I wanted to grab her pussy.' "I gasped," Lynn said. "A 2-year old, a block from the White House and the president that resides here said this about women. The only thing this 2-year old has to say about him was this? I was gutted! … The family had the courage to let the 2-year old have the poster. That was powerful."

In addition to the large numbers of women and supporters and being "packed like sardines," which elevated the power and community of resistance, the experience of seeing the two-year-old protestor's placard made Lynn sick to her stomach. Encountering a toddler displaying a poster with shockingly vulgar language emphasized the grotesque discourse about women coming from our president. Lynn's view was not that the family-approved placard was obscene or the family misguided; rather, she lauded the family's move as "powerful," calling attention to the ways in which misogynistic discourses from the top down can shape the next generation and degrade women in our society as a destructive normative practice.

Sasha, an African American professor in the Northeast, who chose not to attend the March, lamented:

> The March did not represent me; it represented White, liberal feminist women, who were upper class and highly educated. They had no interest. When the talk of the March was in the works before Trump was inaugurated, all leaders were White women. All White women. It was not until there was a backlash about the women's exclusivity that a change was made. There were White women who created a table, picked out the materials for table, location, tools, how high the table was going to be, then they went and invited others. Is the table too high? Can we fit comfortably? Is the material what we need? You created and

> set the foundation that may not have worked with other women affected by this man in unique ways THEN you invited us to talk .... Incredibly problematic.

Kylie's narrative illustrated the complex and contradictory responses of the Black women participants to the March and our newly elected president. As Kylie said,

> I never would have attended the March because I'm still pissed that White women largely supported Trump. So that March was their issue and [their] need to absolve themselves of guilt. But I did support those who attended because the leadership and organizing was quite diverse and it obviously resonated with their big vision for what CAN BE if all women come together to resist patriarchy.

On the one hand, while Kylie herself would not attend, she supported others who chose to do so, acknowledging the value of a collective and unified resistance to the patriarchal ideologies of the 45th presidency.

Natasha demonstrated her support of the Women's movement through her purchase of multiple pink "pussy" hats, which also dovetailed with her hobby of collecting artifacts from historic periods. She stated that she likes having conversations about what artifacts mean and she looks forward to talking about the hats. Her narrative highlighted women's unity around resistance in a way that departed from the other informants. She said, "that hat symbolized that women were coming together around these political issues." Her narrative also revealed how some Black women do not rely entirely on the Women's March as a locus of political resistance. She noted that Black women were always planning, always coming together. As a member of a Black sorority, she mentioned that the Divine 9 (nine historically Black Greek letter organizations – BGLOs) always have a platform for service and leadership in our communities.

> Did they have a voice? [Pertaining to Black women's leadership in the March's organization]. Black women have their own voice. We have been having our own voice ... if the media wants to pick it up. Black women just feel more empowered. We have had to take certain positions of empowerment when it comes to our voice, and we have done that.

Natasha's discussion demonstrated a resoluteness and sense of intrinsic empowerment that characterize Black women's historical and organizational experiences. Black women's socialization typically necessitates speaking up and speaking out. Since Black women collectively are less likely to be protected by White patriarchy, a privilege which some White women enjoy, Black women have developed internal and external coping and resistance strategies to preserve their identities and dignity. A common resistance strategy that Natasha's account highlighted is the search for ongoing social and community support that is central to Black women's sustenance and success (Bell & Nkomo, 2001; Shorter-Gooden, 2004; Thomas & Hollenshead, 2001).

Similarly, Catherine's narrative revealed a nuanced response of resistance. She chose not to attend the March in protest. She did not want to "experience anything that had his [the President's] name on it." From her perspective, she did not want to add numbers to the media frenzy that she saw in the March's representation. Further, she explained, because of her disgust about the Florida electoral results, "I did my darndest to spend no money in the state" when she visited a few weeks after the election. Instead, "I ordered something online for a relative and had it shipped to an address outside of the state. I was resentful." In her account, she emphasized that she wanted to be sure that people who contributed to the President's ascendancy did not benefit in any way from her.

The March, sparked by outrage about the election of the 45th president, further disenfranchised women of color – Black women in particular – who may have felt aligned and connected to the outrage against the president, but structurally and systemically were excluded through lack of representation at the leadership levels of the Women's March. The presidency further exacerbated Black women's marginal status in political and organizational systems of resistance. Black women's positionalities in the Trump era have shifted in light of the administration's policies and statements related to education, police-community relations, and healthcare (ACA, Muslim ban, DACA, and response to Charlottesville). The participants' accounts of their experiences elucidated the centrality of Black women's histories and socialization related to agentic strategies at both the community and individual levels.

Black Women's Experiences of Patriarchy and Privilege

Sasha's narrative reflected the anger and divide that Black women sometimes experience in feminist activism, which has too often excluded women of color, poor women, immigrant women, and other marginalized populations of women. The cultural and historical experience of inequality highlights the importance of developing a more holistic intersectional approach to mainstream feminist analysis of women's social disadvantage. Not surprisingly, in the effort to remediate previous forms of marginalization and color-blind theory, feminists of color and anti-racist feminists have emphasized this intersectional approach to understanding women's lives and experiences, which, as we stated earlier, are heterogeneous and complex (Carastathis, 2013; Mirza, 2009). In so doing, we can better grasp the specific reasons Trump's election felt so devastating to so many different communities. Sasha described her experience:

> The bottom dropped out of me – I had a feeling in my stomach. The bottom of my stomach dropped out when he was up [in the polls]. It was the wee hours of morning. I remember a moment after midnight. 'I really think he might win this.' I had a nightmare of people revolting, a friend saying, 'Get up! Put your tennis shoes on. We're going to the street.' Black people dropped everything and went to the streets with torches in the street.

In Sasha's account of her dream, she described: "Smoke was coming from torches that filled up the air. It was like a wilderness background." Sasha's account illustrated her confusion and consternation. "I woke up and I was in a daze. It felt kind of like when you are really, really sick, … high off medicine and you feel debilitated. There is nothing you can do. You can't move, you can't. … All I could do was lay on my couch with no hope of getting comfortable." As a Black woman, the threats were many and the depression that followed those days were palpable for her. Sasha's bodily experience reflected her emotional state: weak, frightened, powerless.

> NCA was the day after. That day my colleague picked me up and we were driving. I forced myself to take a shower. My body was incredibly anxious. I had to go to NCA. I was anxious about potential encounters with colleagues. What colleagues am I going to have to encounter and see their body language and know they voted for him? I was also anxious about encountering White women. There was something about the White women who were so ride or die for her [Clinton].

Sasha's reaction to White women's support for Clinton was based on her belief they were blind to unjust and corrupt policies Clinton influenced or instituted as a senator that disenfranchised Blacks in America. Neither choice of candidate seemed optimal for Black women. "She's [Hillary Clinton] got blood on her hands, and they were blind," she said. Sasha's anguished account illustrated the complication of intersectional positionalities as Black and as woman, with divided yet integrated perspectives on the 45th president and the first woman nominee of a major political party. Sasha's gender and racial identities collide and clash, and her reaction to going to a meeting of one of the largest professional conventions and having to face her mistrust of White women captured the (dis)connection between Black and White women. Despite commonalities across gender, status, and profession, she and her colleagues were still split along racial and some political lines.

Sasha's narrative illustrated the complexity of her positionality. On the one hand, she was distressed about the 45th presidential election because of the dire political and social consequences for her as a Black woman, and on the other hand, she explained that she aligns with the first woman candidate. She was clear about her reservations about Clinton because of what she viewed as unjust and corrupt policies that disenfranchised Blacks in America, but neither political candidate seemed optimal for Black women.

Natasha drew strength from being able to survive tough times and framed her experience following the election as "an experience of empowerment. All that we went through and we're still here." The Trump era for Natasha has been one, in part, of empowerment, as she noted that this period was not particularly alarming and represented nothing at all that was new in the life of the American polis. She saw the same misogynistic enactments and oppressive discourses at play throughout her lifetime. "This era reminded us of a time they want us to forget."

Born and raised in the South and now a higher education administrator in a large Southern institution, Natasha referenced the history in the U.S. – "a time" that led to the Civil Rights era, when Blacks could not vote, lynchings were commonplace, and there were bloody struggles for freedom and human rights. She also addressed the murder of a woman near her city, in which Black men questioned why the young woman "put herself in that situation. It wasn't about the situation; it was the outcome." This assault and subsequent murder referred to in Natasha's narrative implicated Black men as unsupportive of the woman and apparently blaming the victim. She also discussed Black men's response to the Bill Cosby case. They were skeptical of some Black women's claims against the actor. Natasha stated, mimicking Black men's voices: "He didn't penetrate her. He didn't penetrate her. Why is she saying anything? Rape is only if it's a violation of a body." In her account she noted her experiences on social media and in her community: Black men from HBCUs (Historically Black Colleges and Universities) were silent. Her narrative implied ways in which Black men have supported White patriarchy in condemning Black women and ineffectively using their voices to support them in sports and work discussions, but not to seek justice and compassion in Black women's experiences. "I feel less supported. Black women are not as supported by Black men in the way that they want to be. In everything Black women do, it's associated with Black sons, men. Children dying on the street, I think Black women have been very vocal about, 'It could be my son,'" she said. She lamented in her narrative that this dynamic is not reciprocated, that of men advocating and supporting women in Black communities.

Natasha's experiences and reflections are even more poignant and critical to her in this era, particularly as they relate to the ways in which Black people and women – where she is at the intersection – have been discursively and physically threatened and assailed (Charlottesville, disrespect to Black policy makers and journalists, and shootings of unarmed Blacks). The empowerment and agency from her perspective is evidenced in Black women's resilience and resolution to continue to organize, resist, and lead in multiple contexts, despite the political, social, and systemic challenges and the oppressive sociopolitical and economic conditions.

Lynn also spoke of ways Black women support each other in reference to a contentious exchange when veteran journalist April Ryan asked Trump about his policies and campaign promises to urban communities. In response, the president at first lauded his accomplishments with Black communities. When Ryan pressed and inquired further about whether he had met with the Congressional Black Caucus (CBC), the political body specifically focused on increased access, empowerment and advancement of African Americans, Trump responded in a casual and dismissive manner by asking Ryan to set up a meeting. "I'll tell you what, do you want to set up the meeting? Do you want to set up the meeting? Are they friends of yours? Set up the meeting! Let's go, set up a meeting" (Yu, 2017, p. 1), Trump commanded Ms. Ryan, who both in the moment and online asserted that she was reporter, not a convener. Lynn, discussing this exchange and its impact on her, spoke of Ryan with pride, as both she and Ryan are alums of an HBCU, and she admired Ryan's strength and resilience in the face of the current administration's hostile stance toward the media.

> She's [Ryan] in her heyday [having previously referenced a university award of excellence that Ryan recently received]. She's embodying Black womanhood – the way that her Black female body tells this narrative to express her disapproval of Trump. On the one hand, "Are

> they friends of yours?" [citing Trump], and through that [the public display of his disrespect towards her], she maintained her role space.

Ryan's resilience and professionalism resonated with Lynn and she reflected with pride that Ms. Ryan persevered in her questioning and asserted her professional role as a reporter. I saw the interview as well and discussed my reactions with Lynn. I too felt disappointment and outrage watching a professional Black woman, an expert in her field, being so publicly denigrated and cavalierly dismissed. To complicate matters, the president commanded Ryan to perform administrative duties unrelated to her position. April Ryan reflects me, to some degree, with similarities in gender, race, class, education, occupational status, and age. As well, her work is concerned with the economic, political and overall well-being of urban communities of color. As I watched her, I thought there are so few of "us" (Blacks and Black women) in any context in the current White House, and there are few whose work focuses on the concerns of people of color. When such an incident occurs, I experience it as a great loss and disappointment. From the President's exchange with Ryan and subsequent ones with journalists who have brought similar concerns, it seemed as if my values and concerns have been discounted. The president, through his actions, communicated his priorities and values, which did not include me or my communities.

In respect to Trump's actions, Sasha's sentiments captured the complex intersectionality of her class as highly educated, middle-class, with a terminal degree (Ph.D.), yet feeling insecure in her status as a Black woman. She also communicated the recklessness of his decisions and approach to policy making, one that jeopardizes vulnerable populations, such as immigrant children and the LGBT community.

> I carry a lot of privilege. Having certain degrees; SES (socioeconomic status), but at the same time it appears that there is a person in this presidential position, and formal rules and social norms of politeness are out the window. He just doesn't play by the rules. [My] privilege has afforded me some security and that security is dwindling quickly. You never know the next group that will be under attack. The rug will be pulled from under your feet – DACA and dreamers and the LGBT [community] – fighting for these rights for many years. These groups might be first to be under attack. I don't trust him, what he's capable of doing. We see that with Charlottesville. There could have been so much more said and done. How this president feels about me. Again, I feel insecure.

Sasha bemoaned the way in which Trump's comment about "very fine people on both sides" condoned the acts of hate in Charlottesville and she emphasized how little he did to make a strong statement rejecting bigotry and violence.

Similarly, Catherine complained about Trump's glib statements concerning African Americans, such as "The Blacks love me" and "What have they got to lose?"

> I didn't take him seriously. That was done from a disrespectful place. "What have they got to lose?" ... He was looking for political one-upmanship. His maleness – was all of what he embodied. All of what he embodied was around [being] a man, a privileged person, from a privileged perspective. His manhood was more important to him and he said it because he knew he could, and because he knew that in this still very patriarchal system, he reigned supreme from his penis. That's where his power came from .... He knew better than we did that America was not ready for a woman in office. He knew that anybody who showed [up] with a penis would have won!

Catherine offered her assessment of the central component of Trump's presidency: patriarchy, male privilege, and social and political collusion that sustains such a system. She also referenced his Charlottesville comments and failure to issue a staunch rebuke against White supremacists:

> His response was not unexpected. I wasn't shocked. After he said "Grab them by the pussy!" I wasn't shocked about anything after that. I was not offended. I wasn't hurt. I just wanted to hear from people like President Obama. I kept looking to see what he would say .... I was looking to him for that moral leadership. I was looking to him after the first repeal of Obamacare. When he [Obama] spoke that's where my faith in human behavior came from for that bit of nourishment. Who is going to speak on behalf of the people? No matter what, the ACA [Obamacare] was still helpful. Why is nobody saying that? ... I don't take Mr. Trump seriously as a president. I am not one of those people .... I don't respect him as a president. I am still looking and waiting for the president to show up. I have come to a place of some relief that he is not my president. I am waiting for the president to show up and, in the meantime, I can be doing other things while I wait.

Catherine communicated a mental and positional displacement of Trump. She also spoke about her resolve to make more of a contribution to her community as a response to the president's lack of leadership and to empower herself and others to work for change.

The Body Dialectic

The idea of the body dialectic captures the complicated tensions of visibility and invisibility and Black women's bodies as sites of political, cultural, and social struggle. Forbes' (2009) theory about the body dialectic in relation to Black women's experiences centers on the ways in which organizational and political discourse (con)scripts Black women as both visible (physically and sexually) and invisible (organizationally, intellectually, and professionally). This conceptual framework represents the tensions of the invisibility and organizational positionality of (Black) women as denigrated Other. From political, economic and social perspectives, Black women in the U.S. seem invisible and are ranked below White men, White women, and Black men. In contrast, they are hypervisible in terms of sexuality, physicality, and denigration of their bodies – intellectually, physically, and professionally. For instance, former First Lady Obama, despite her Ivy League education, professional achievements, and philanthropy, was depicted in multiple media outlets as a large Black woman with too much attention paid to her physicality – her arms, body shape and type, and her clothing (Brown, 2012; Dowd, 2009; McAllister, 2009). "If I were not a celebrity, I'd be invisible," actress Viola Davis remarked recently, pointing to the ways in which Black women's beauty, accomplishments, and contributions have been overlooked in multiple contexts (León, 2018; Noble, 2013).

The Trump presidency seemed to have provoked Black women's increased resolution and agency in the form of diverse offerings in poetry, writing, and spoken narrative that expressed women's resistance and staunch challenge to erasure, misogyny, and denigration. Black women's discursive choices to deepen engagement with social support groups, more conscious parenting, increased scholarship, art, and political organizing constitute a clear resonance of "Not on my watch" and "Not my pussy" as these Black women re-position and make visible their lives and values.

Responding to Trump's infamous comment, "I wanted to grab her pussy," in tears, Lynn bewailed: "I'm so deeply disappointed in this country that that didn't shut it down. Nobody said NO! Everybody just played along. What does that say about this country's progress, equal rights, and how we think about women?" Lynn felt angry and worried about his election and its implications for her as a parent, for her two African American children, and the direction our country was going. Lynn's feelings of disappointment and fear were rooted in the positionalities of Black women in U.S. society who face greater rates of assault, harassment, and interwoven systems of oppression that impact Lynn's experiences as a mother and professional (Baker, 2005; Harris-Perry, 2011; Petrosky et al., 2017).

Sasha reflected on the President's tepid response to Charlottesville as well as her general uneasiness and insecurity during this political season:

> There could have been so much more said and done. How this president feels about me .... Again, I feel insecure. I feel uncertain about what is to come, also, uncertain about the financial/economic future. I have felt – personally – I'm just between a rock and a hard place. I see it all around me – political unrest .... Sometimes I shut myself away from the news, engaging in conversations. It's so taxing – psychologically taxing .... I feel I can be doing something, but I can't. Physically I just can't. I feel like the cost is too great. As Black women, we have been treated as *mules*. In the long run, you're just so great at it, but it's a guise. In fact, it kills us. People are using us for their own good and for their own gain. At the same time, I recognize that and I don't want to do that .... I have to put in the cost for someone else to reap the benefit.

I found Sasha's discourse here impactful and jarring, as she spoke of a familiar dynamic of Black women's emotional and psychological labor in society, particularly as it relates to contending with the simultaneous complexities of racism and sexism (Bell & Nkomo, 2001; Shorter-Gooden, 2004). Her particular reference to Black women being treated as "mules" speaks to what Black women's identities have embodied in multiple contexts – burden bearers, caretakers, and bridges. Her narrative addressed the difficult work in which Black women often engage to bring about change, which she experienced as "taxing" and at times debilitating. Forbes' work (2009) on the body dialectic elucidates this experience, as it communicates the embodied paradox of Black women's positionality at center and margin, visible and invisible, in positions of elevation and denigration, as well as the social and psychological expectations for Black women. Research has also highlighted the value of intersectional frameworks to understand Black women's lived experiences, their physical and psychological well-being, and the relationship of their experiences of discrimination and denigration in society to Black women's health outcomes (Brown, 2012; Cozier et al., 2009; Dowd, 2009; Noble, 2013; Settles, 2006).

Sasha recalled her experiences as the Charlottesville events were unfolding and described re-thinking how she saw young White men. She recounted her feelings of insecurity (physical and psychological), and, as she discussed earlier, her disappointment in the president who failed to establish a moral position to protect the vulnerable in Charlottesville, which by extension, meant failure to protect or speak up for Blacks.

> I was moving from downtown to a smaller suburb and I remember learning about it through a CNN alert on my phone. I was initially confused. What's happening? ... I was just floored. I had to watch on my phone .... I remember that the people who were moving me were young White males and I remember just the fear. I actually called up a girlfriend to come: "I need you to be with me. I need to have someone else there." There was a fear. You should also make sure you have other people there [she thought to herself]. Something about their demeanor, their physical appearance. The event [Charlottesville] made me hypervigilant. What is it going to trigger in them?

Lynn also shared that since the Trump election she experienced her son's Boy Scout troop differently.

> [They are] working class White people. I go to the first meeting and the Assistant Scoutmaster, he's militaristic to boys. I witnessed him saying: 'Boy Scouts is about hierarchy. There are ranks for a reason.' My guts are tying themselves in knots. It gets worse. In his rhetoric, he says even though there are ranks, there is room for democracy – 'just like our country and the recent elections, boys, and it was Trump and that other individual running for office.' The White man said: 'Trump and that other individual who ran for president' and then he chuckled and looked at another White man knowingly. It took everything in me not to say: 'You know you *do* have some Sanders and Clinton supporters here!' I came home and I was pissed! I think that that is all about the White patriarchy overall. But now! I am really tight-lipped if it will lead to violence. And this guy is talking about that at a Boy Scout meeting. I am worried that those men who run the troop don't have eyes for who my son is and an interest in who he may be in that space of intersectionality.

Lynn not only spoke of her invisibility, but her son's as well, in a mostly White working-class space with a troop leader who is a strong supporter of the President and who does not appear to explore the implications of his leadership of this diverse troop of young men. Lynn also described the physical reaction of her guts "tying themselves in knots" as her body contained the stressful experience of erasure and disbelief. I asked her what her approach would be if her son remained a part of the troop, and she responded, "My approach to the troop? – I'm going to help plan a fundraiser, involve myself with something positive and I will get a better feel." I shared with her my experiences in similar spaces with other parents, and how I have disengaged from regular interactions with those groups where I have felt that my perspectives were unwelcome or where I felt invisible. I shared that I drop off and pick up, and keep the close interaction with my child after the meeting:

> My response to the energy ... all my windows rolled down and [I] pulled my dress up and put my painted toenails, feet dangling in the window [while waiting for my son]. What am I up to? You're not going to run me out. Not only am I there, I recline and pose .... Nobody spoke to me; approached me. What would they have said? 'Hello!' [but] I'm the invisible woman. My experience [is], you don't miss me. I'm a loud laugher. I'm gregarious. You don't miss me. In this space, I'm invisible or I need to be blocked and I'm refusing to accept [that]. It's not empowering; it's certainly isn't.

CONCLUSION

This chapter centered on Black women's narratives that illustrated the complexity of Black women positioned between two resistance movements: Black Lives Matter and the rejuvenated Women's movement. Intersectionality as a conceptual framework captures the complexities of women's identities along multiple axes of location. Within this framework, gender and racial identities are interconnected and interlocked (Carastathis, 2013).

The practice of highlighting these women's stories develops inclusive discourse that details Black women's experiences in the production of knowledge about our political and organizational systems. Their experiences highlight the intersectional and complex experiences of resistance and the fight for social justice. Black women's resistance has been more than a "mere response to invisibility and erasure from the dominant discourse of race, class, and gender"; their activism has sought to achieve political empowerment and social justice (Mirza, 2009, p. 2).

In this chapter, I focused on the complexity of identity – fashioned from individual and collective experiences of subjection – by focusing on Black women's narratives, which disrupt hegemonic and essentialized identities that are (re)produced through complex, interwoven networks of social and organizational positions and practices (Holvino, 2010). The narratives revealed diverse perspectives about Black women's alliances with the Women's March, the Women's Movement, and related initiatives, as well as complex and nuanced standpoints about their relationship with White women as colleagues and political and organizational leaders and figureheads.

The study also contributes to Black feminist and intersectional scholarship. Deeper analyses need to be developed to understand the fluidity and depth of Black women's experiences in this historic season of the dawning Trump era. The small sample size of respondents limits the study's generalizability across all Black women; rather, the narratives capture individual experiences and offer provisional insight into the depth and complexity of selected Black women in the Trump era. Future research needs to extend this initial work by seeking out a larger sample of Black women from diverse backgrounds to deepen our understanding of women's experiences and learn why Black women are so alarmed and deeply troubled by Donald Trump's Presidency.

By highlighting Black women's narratives, this chapter illustrated the impact and intersection of identity-based political and social movements, which emerge out of struggle and stand in resistance to oppression. Their forms of resistance contribute to knowledge production and subjectivities that reveal varied responses to the March, organizing strategies for Black women that involve seeking social and professional support and affirmation. Through their accounts, the study revealed the ways in which Black women's embodied identities and resistance challenge and disrupt oppressive ideologies and practices that characterize the Trump presidency.

REFERENCES

Ashley, W. (2014). The angry Black woman: The impact of pejorative stereotypes on psychotherapy with Black women. *Social Work in Public Health, 29*(1), 27–34.

Baker, C. N. (2005). Blue-collar feminism: The link between male domination and sexual harassment. In J. E. Gruber & P. Morgan (Eds.), *The company of men: Male dominance and sexual harassment* (pp. 242–270). Boston, MA: Northeastern University Press.

Bell, E., & Nkomo, S. M. (2001). *Our separate ways: Black and White women and the struggle for professional identity.* Boston, MA: Harvard Business School Press.

Brown, C. (2012). Marketing Michelle: Mommy politics and post-feminism in the age of Obama. *Comparative American Studies: An International Journal, 10*(2–3), 239–254.

Carastathis, A. (2013). Identity categories as potential coalitions. *Signs, 38*(4), 941–965.

Carney, N. (2016). All lives matter, but so does race: Black lives matter and the evolving role of social media. *Humanity & Society, 40*(2), 180–199.

Chatelain, M., & Asoka, K. (2015). Women and Black lives matter. *Dissent, 62*(3), 54–61.

Cozier, Y. C., Wise, L. A., Palmer, J. R., & Rosenberg, L. (2009). Perceived racism in relation to weight change in the Black women's health study. *Annals of Epidemiology, 19*(6), 379–387.

Dowd, M. (2009, March 8). Should Michelle cover up? *The New York Times*. Retrieved from http://www.nytimes.com/2009/03/08/opinion/08dowd.hyml?_r=1

Fahrenthold, D. (2016, October 8). Trump recorded having extremely lewd conversation about women in 2005. *The Washington Post*. Retrieved from https://www.washingtonpost.com/politics/trump-recorded-having-extremely-lewd-conversation-about-women-in-2005/2016/10/07/3b9ce776-8cb4-11e6-bf8a-3d26847eeed4_story.html?utm_term=.69f63604251a

Fisher, D. R., Dow, D. M., & Ray, R. (2017). Intersectionality takes it to the streets: Mobilizing across diverse interests for the Women's March. *Science Advances, 3*(9), eaao1390.

Forbes, D. A. (2009). Commodification and co-modification: Explicating Black female sexuality in organizations. *Management Communication Quarterly, 22*(4), 577–613.

Harris, H., Moffitt, K., & Squires, C. (2010). *Obama effect: The multidisciplinary renderings of the 2008 campaign*. Albany, NY: SUNY Press.

Harris-Perry, M. V. (2011). *Sister citizen: Shame, stereotypes, and black women in America*. New Haven, CT: Yale University Press.

Heywood, L., & Drake, J. (Eds.). (1997). *Third wave agenda: Being feminist, doing feminism*. Minneapolis, MN: University of Minnesota Press.

Holvino, E. (2010). Intersections: The Simultaneity of race, gender and class in organization studies. *Gender, Work and Organization, 17*(3), 248–277.

Jeffries, M. P. (2013). *Paint the White house Black: Barack Obama and the meaning of race in America*. Stanford, CA: Stanford University Press.

León, F. (2018, November 18). Viola Davis: "If I were not a celebrity, I'd be invisible." *The Root*. Retrieved from https://www.theroot.com/viola-davis-if-i-were-not-a-celebrity-i-d-be-invisibl-1830503920

Mann, S. A., & Huffman, D. (2005). The decentering of second wave feminism and the rise of the third wave. *Science & Society, 69*(1), 56–91.

Marx, D. M., Ko, S. J., & Friedman, R. A. (2009). The "Obama effect": How a salient role model reduces race-based performance differences. *Journal of Experimental Social Psychology, 45*(4), 953–956.

McAlister, J. F. (2009). Trash in the White House: Michelle Obama, post-racism, and the pre-class politics of domestic style. *Communication and Critical/Cultural Studies, 6*(3), 311–315.

Mirza, H. S. (2009). Plotting a history: Black and postcolonial feminisms in 'new times.' *Race Ethnicity and Education, 12*(1), 1–10.

Noble, S. U. (2013). Google search: Hyper-visibility as a means of rendering Black women and girls invisible. *InVisible Culture*, (19).

Petrosky E., Blair J., Betz C., Fowler K., Jack S., Lyons, B. (2017, July 21). Racial and ethnic differences in homicides of adult women and the role of intimate partner violence – United States, 2003–2014. *Morbidity and Mortality Weekly Report, 66*, 741–746.

Rogers, K. (2017, January 10). Women's March on Washington: What you need to know. *The New York Times*. Retrieved from https://www.nytimes.com/interactive/2017/01/10/us/politics/womens-march-guide.html

Settles, I. H. (2006). Use of an intersectional framework to understand Black women's racial and gender identities. *Sex Roles, 54*(9–10), 589–601.

Shorter-Gooden, K. (2004). Multiple resistance strategies: How African American women cope with racism and sexism. *Journal of Black Psychology, 30*(3), 406–425.

Taylor, K. (2019, January 18). Turning the women's march into a mass movement was never going to be simple: The reason goes to the heart of inclusive, democratic movement building. *The Nation.* Retrieved from https://www.thenation.com/article/turning-the-womens-march-into-a-mass-movement-was-never-going-to-be-simple/

Thomas, G. D., & Hollenshead, C. (2001). Resisting from the margins: The coping strategies of Black women and other women of color faculty members at a research university. *Journal of Negro Education, 70*(3), 166–175.

Welch, S., & Sigelman, L. (2011). The "Obama effect" and White racial attitudes. *The Annals of the American Academy of Political and Social Science, 634*(1), 207–220.

Women's March. (2017). Women's March Mission. Retrieved from https://www.womensmarch.com/mission/

Yu, R. (2017, February 16). Trump asks Black reporter to set up meeting with Black lawmakers. *USA Today.* Retrieved from https://www.usatoday.com/story/money/2017/02/16/trump-asks-black-reporter-set-up-meeting-black-lawmakers/98017336/

CHRISTINE SALKIN DAVIS AND JONATHAN L. CRANE

DIALOGUE 4

"How has the reality of the past two years compared with your initial expectations?" I ask.

"I would say, pretty much equal, because my expectations weren't high to begin with," Andrea says with a laugh. "I know you're thinking, how could you vote for somebody and not have high expectations, but I voted for him with some reservation because he was the first of his kind – for lack of a better term – to be president. I guess most of the time they have come in with military background or political experience, and he didn't."

"Mm-hmm," I nod.

"So in terms of my reservations," Andrea says, "even during the campaign, he wasn't very polished. I liked him for being candid but those were also some of the same reasons that I didn't like him, because he was so candid." She laughs.

"Yeah," Larry agrees.

"I think the reality is still true today to where a lot of the expectations I had, I feel he's delivered but at the same time, I still think that he is not very polished and says things that he shouldn't say – or could say them differently," says Andrea.

"I think Trump has ideas that are very unconventional, they sometimes seem bizarre," Elizabeth says. "Some have worked, and some … have not, but he has said a lot of things that he's gotten away with, that really were improper, and a lot of his past behavior and things he's said against women, I don't agree with. I would say his negatives are his attitude toward women and his bias toward minorities."

"Leading into the elections," Larry says, "some of my co-workers and I talked about, let's look at his kids. Okay, here's a billionaire, who's had several kids. To listen to all them talk about …"

"… how he was as a father," Andrea interrupts,

"… how he was as a father," Larry continues, "how he was as a businessman, I heard Don Junior talk about him and he told a story of one Saturday morning, Don Junior was at home and his dad goes, 'why are you

DOI:10.1163/9789004436329_008

not at the office?' And I was like, I can relate to that as a hard-working person, and coming from hard-working people. That really struck a chord with me. And during the Republican National Convention, his kids were up each night speaking and that was pretty impressive. His kids, yeah, are from different marriages, but yet all of them just have this affinity to him and how he is. And to me that said a lot."

"Yeah," Andrea says, "He can't be all bad, look at his kids."

Larry continues, "so once he was elected, I expected him to run it like a business. I expected he was going to see things from a bottom line standpoint. And I hoped that some of the rhetoric and things that he said leading up to the election, if you look at the debates and how he was in debates and how he would say things. I was thinking, okay, well, maybe that was to get elected, to stir up his base, because people do just about anything to get elected. But once he was elected, I would expect him to run the country like a business and to tamp down on how he was putting things out there. I expected he would run this ship, and do these things, and reunify this country, and here we go."

"And?" I ask.

Larry says, "Well, I think there was a learning curve for him that he did not expect, even having control of both houses he had people in his own party still not on his side with certain issues. I don't know if he expected that. I learned that he seems to be someone that really wants loyalty. Which makes you think back to his kids, you know, they're just so loyal to him, but it's, like wow, there's just seems like there's this loyalty factor and if you sway a little bit it's like, you know, *Survivor*, or you've been voted off the island. And, that part was a little bit surprising to me. Because I thought he would be so focused on the day to day running of the country. I thought some of these things would go away and we wouldn't be living on Twitter and saying the things we were. So, you know, he tweets yesterday about North Korea and now things are great and we have a great relationship and he expects their economy to do these great things and all these great things about North Korea and you're like, okay. So yeah, there's just things that come out, things that he's said that I thought would have been put away once he got in."

"When he was elected," Elizabeth says, "I expected the economy to grow and get better. I expected the stock market to be well, and I expected tax breaks. And I expected a stricter immigration enforcement. In my personal opinion, there should be zero illegal immigrants in the country, we should just secure our country and its borders, and only have people who are legally here. We should have everyone identified, and there's been some progress on immigration, but I don't think it's been enough."

I clarify, "since Trump was elected, there has not been enough?"

Elizabeth nods. "Since he's been elected, there's been more talk than, I think, action. I think if it requires us to use our military to secure our borders, we should. If it's to stop criminals from coming in, drugs from coming in, we should do it. And to just be able to identify what comes across our borders, people, drugs. I'd rather have the military do that than be in foreign countries, fighting wars."

EUN YOUNG LEE AND BILLY HUFF

3. AIRPORT (IN)SECURITY

INTRODUCTION

We are sitting at RSW, the Fort Myers, Florida International Airport, and we are on our way to the National Communication Association's annual conference in Philadelphia. The exhaustion on our faces is the result of the late-night news that the Republican presidential candidate, Donald Trump, has just been elected the 45th president of the United States of America. We are trying to fathom what the results will mean to us, while being thankful that we don't have to be in classrooms this week facing questions from students.

We move through the tiny small-town airport today with ease. We don't yet know that our own bodies will soon realize this place is a site of political contestation, oppression, and privilege thanks to the Trump presidency. We talk to each other about how relieved we are that we are on our way to an academic conference where we anticipate a welcome opportunity to process what the next four years will bring.

This chapter recounts our own bodily experiences in airports, including the arrivals and departures that brought us there, in the first two years of the Trump presidency. Our stories concern the bodies of two individuals. One of us is a South Korean, female, able-bodied, middle-class, cisgender, heterosexual, non-US citizen, who is 'temporarily' allowed to be in the U.S. with a work visa and is in the process of getting a green card (officially known as a permanent resident card). The other is a white, U.S. citizen, able-bodied, middle-class, queer, transgender man, who is 'legally' male but is subject to and dependent upon being correctly read by TSA personnel for safe passage through security. Logging our experiences while moving through airports, we aim to shed light on how our different *positionalities* affect our body politics, both in the space of airports specifically and the public sphere more generally. While un-layering the complexity of the relationships between our intersectional identities and our bodies, we illuminate the structure of hegemonic power undergirding body and spatial politics in the age of Trump, and we hope to unveil the physicality of body politics that fluctuates contingently with the political environment.

 | DOI:10.1163/9789004436329_009

The airport is a place where surveillance is not only omnipresent, it is also a space in which authoritative and repressive acts become routine. Salter (2008) writes of airports, “There is a pedagogical function of airports …. Passage through airports condition and normalize particular identities, certain authorities, and normalize ways of managing the mobility of populations” (p. xii). When processed through the stages of an airport, one’s physical body is politicized. This politicization of the body in airport space opens one up to a space of vulnerability. Shome (2003) points to “the centrality of space in the production, organization, and distribution of cultural power” (p. 39) while raising the question “how might thinking of power spatially both disrupt and add to our understanding of how power works?” (p. 41) Taking her question seriously, we strive to tackle the discourse of power manifested through space.

The airport in particular has become one of the most contentious spaces in U.S. political discourse due in part to one of Trump’s first executive orders, a “travel ban,” that has provoked heated and contested reactions, which include claims of potential violations of the U.S. constitution. According to Parks (2007), “in the context of the U.S.-led war on global terror [the airport] has possibly become ‘the place,’ a charged and volatile domain punctuated by the shifting regimes of bio-power” (p. 185). Foucault also identifies how power is discursively formed through the use of space and institutional practices (Foucault, 1980). In the machines of surveillance, our (foreign) bodies, moving through airports, raise questions about which bodies count as American (this term is hegemonic in itself), and which bodies are automatically read as potential threats. Who counts as a citizen in this new order? Who is allowed to travel undisturbed?

People from all over the world arrive at the airport with the shared purpose of travel. They depart, however, to different places, and they travel for a multitude of reasons. Movement through the airport is inseparable from the experiences of travel it makes possible. The airport is a locus that allows us to make sense of our own experiences of sameness and difference – our own arrivals and departures – as we move through a seemingly new world in which Donald Trump is now President of the United States.

NOVEMBER 9, 2016

Billy

The National Communication Association’s annual conference immediately follows the election of President-elect Donald Trump. I feel so fortunate to have a week to process the meaning of this election with like-minded people and to also put a week between the election and my return to classrooms jam-packed with Trump supporters and students who are not "following politics." I am relieved to be in a large "blue" city, and there is a constant supply of queer panels. There are active protests in Philly every night, and the election is a notable topic of concern in every panel I attend.

One thing that strikes me in the queer panels I attend is a general lack of conversation about sex. We know that Trump's administration will take aim at our queer bodies. We know that many of his supporters crave the complete eradication of our queerness. I don't know what form the hate directed our way will take or how bad it will become, but I cannot stop thinking about how important it will be to refocus our attention on sex in what will soon come to be known as the "Trump era." We know from our history, in the words of Gayle Rubin (2014), that "disputes over sexual behavior often become the vehicles for displacing social anxieties, and discharging their attendant emotional intensity" (p. 143). Rubin instructs us that "sexuality should be treated with special respect in times of great social stress" (p. 143). I fear that this is just such an era. I don't yet consider that my valorization of present pleasures and my impatience with those at the conference positing queer futures not focused solely on sex is firmly rooted in my own privileged blindness, but I will soon learn this lesson as I travel during the onset of the Trump era.

Eun Young

It is weirdly reassuring that I am not the only one on earth who is going through an extreme mixture of feelings about the election. As a person who doesn't have a right to vote in the U.S., it is strange to think how much this election will affect my life, the life that I seem to have little control over. The decision was not made by me, but I have to figure out how to deal with the consequences. Meeting up with colleagues and friends with whom I share similar backgrounds, puts me at ease; all of us have passports from countries outside the U.S. Attending panels in which many panelists forthrightly admit that they cannot read the paper they wrote a year ago validates my insecurity. It is oddly comforting.

Many critical intercultural scholars like myself express concerns about how the newly elected president's bigotry will impact our lives. I share their concerns, but I don't really know how they will play out.

FLASHBACK – JUNE 12, 2016

Billy

I arrive at the Philly airport after the annual Philadelphia Trans Health Conference, five months before the election. I have just begun regularly injecting Testosterone, and it is my first trans conference. Little do I know that President Donald Trump will soon advise the Center for Disease Control to discontinue use of the word "transgender." I do not know that the Trump administration will plan to roll back a rule issued by President Barack Obama that "prevents doctors, hospitals and health insurance companies from discriminating against transgender people" (Pear, 2018, para. 1). I cannot foresee that I will soon sue the state of Florida for excluding gender confirmation surgeries from all of their available insurance plans, and I do not know I will worry that a Republican-leaning Supreme Court could decide my case.

I am fraught with anxiety about returning to Florida, a place where the landscape is dotted with "Trump for President" signs, and where I am still the only trans faculty member at my university. I make my way through security with ease. I am not yet visibly "male." My physical appearance and identity documents appear to align. I sit down in the terminal and focus my attention on the television reports of a mass shooting at a gay nightclub in Orlando, Florida on Latin night. In response to the shooting, then presidential candidate Donald Trump (@realDonaldTrump, 2016) tweets, "Appreciate the congrats for being right on radical Islamic terrorism, I don't want congrats, I want toughness & vigilance. We must be smart!" I am furious that Trump would use a massacre as an opportunity for self-promotion, and I am even more worried that my fellow queers will adopt the anti-Islamic bait that Trump dangles before us. I do, however, take solace in a misplaced optimism that Trump will never be elected president.

As I sit sobbing in that airport in Philly, I cannot imagine the ways that Trump's anti-Islamic insults will come to weigh on my own white trans body in airports, and the multiplied fears and material affects these insults will wreak on the non-white bodies of countless others. I have done my homework about traveling while trans, and I learn from others that as long as I carry letters from my therapist and doctor explaining my transness, I will not have much trouble. I have not yet thought to pay attention to the ways that "Islamophobia [is] … a specific form of racism, one that draws its logic in part from the figure of the Muslim terrorist as an especial threat to

LGBTQ communities" (Puar, 2017, p. 224). I am unaware of my complicity and the fact that while I have documents to signal myself a "safe" citizen, my access will come at the cost of people of color. I will come to pay attention to the ways that the Trump administration will use the anti-LGBTQ sentiments of some primarily Middle Eastern governments to justify anti-Muslim sentiment. I sit in the Philadelphia airport on the morning of the Pulse Nightclub shooting consumed by present injustices and in complete ignorance of the shadow that Trump's figure will cast on my queer and trans community in the very near future.

NOVEMBER 13, 2016

Eun Young

Since I moved to the U.S. from South Korea, my passport has become one of my most precious possessions. It is my worst nightmare to imagine losing my passport in a foreign land. For that reason, I rarely travel within the U.S. carrying my passport. I do carry my U.S. driver's license. Until today, I never had a problem using my driver's license as a form of identification at any U.S. airport.

I am at the Philadelphia airport after the conclusion of the National Communication Association's annual conference and a few days after the election, and I don't think much of the fact that I don't have my passport when I walk up to the security desk to show my identification. I didn't have any problem getting here from Florida, so I am expecting to go through security with no trouble. After days of comforting conversations and academic dialogues, I am more optimistic about the future. I show my driver's license to the person behind the desk. I'm confident from previous experience how to travel within the U.S. as a non-citizen. I have learned the protocol for how foreigners do airports in the U.S. In light of my conspicuous non-white body, I adopt the blandest look possible and do not make small talk. I don't need attention. I don't want attention.

This time, however, the situation is very different. For the first time in a decade, I am asked to present another form of identification, which is not 'temporary.' They want to see a passport. Looking down at my drivers' license they hand back to me, it says 'temporary' on the bottom right corner. I scream in my head "but, this is a domestic trip!" I quickly realize, however, "Shit, I am not in my home country. I can't make a fuss." I don't have my South Korea issued passport. It is safe at my Florida apartment. There is little

I can do now. To the Philadelphia TSA, my Florida issued driver's license isn't enough. At this very moment, I am reminded that I do not belong. As much as I wish to argue my case, I remember the protocol for how foreigners make it through airports. I curb myself.

The security agent speaks into his walky-talky, "We have a secondary here …" Secondary means secondary search, which is an extra search that involves patting-down my body and looking through my luggage. Standing at the secondary search station, I am a second-class citizen. Before November 2016 and the election of Trump, nothing like this ever happened to me. The fear toward bodies of color is at an all-time high with Trump's anti-Islamic agenda. So is my fear.

Once they finally decide that I am not an alien threat, they let me in. I search for Billy. I can't locate him, although we parted from the same spot. I am sure Billy will be waiting on me here since I was so delayed. After an anxious several minutes, I see Billy. We are both exhausted and frightened. This is going to be a long f(l)ight.

Billy

I feel fortunate to have had a free evening at the end of the conference to meet a casual hook-up from Scruff (a gay/queer hook-up site). He was a hot, black, trans top who directs a women's center at a small Philadelphia college. He had a full black beard, and a sexy gap between his front teeth when he smiled. Given my experience at the conference, I decided it was more important to fuck than to participate in another election protest. Where I live, my sexual options seem limited to straight, married guys who are attracted to masculinity, but are terrified of being gay. I need it. I am haunted by the election. I am also haunted by what I missed, libidinally, from the conference, and having sex is my way of insisting on the pleasures of the present moment. It is also a pleasure that might soon be illegal.

The surveillance process in airports is always anxiety-provoking for trans people (and people of color, particularly Muslim people). According to Spalding (2016), "The TSA checkpoint incorporates two of the foundational assumptions that undergird post-9/11 security: namely, the elevation of willful practices of transparency before state actors as a key element of citizenship and the reduction of identity to a bodily phenomenon that can be determined absolutely given the appropriate use of requisite technology" (p. 466). This time the woman at the scanner guesses "woman" which lately results for me in an invasive secondary search (sometimes a strip search).

Although the development of masculine secondary sex characteristics has been slow, I have an enlarged clitoris that registers as an anomaly on body scanners that compare my body to that of a normative "female." I plead for her to rescan me as male, but she refuses and calls her supervisor. The supervisor looks directly at me and says, "We have to make a call when it comes to you people."

I'm not a confrontational person, and as the supervisor puts on her latex gloves and signals for me to follow, I know that I would usually have just followed. Something stops me this time. It isn't my politics or the sense of injustice that stops me in my tracks. It isn't Trump's looming presidency, and it isn't euphoria from the protests I attended. It is because my body is marked with bruises from the hot, BDSM sex I had hours before. This is the first time I have ever stood up for myself during security screening. I can only describe the decision as a complicated mix of shame that she will know what kind of sex I had the night before and indignation that the "female" TSA agent thinks it is appropriate to search me. TSA regulations require same-sex searches, and she regards me as female. "This is why conversations about sex are so important right now," I think to myself with righteous conviction. For me, this experience highlights the ways that my gender identity and expression, my queer sexuality, and my body's confrontations with regimes of power are inseparable.

These instances in which it becomes clear that my "maleness' depends upon recognition from others are always frustrating for me. I insist that a male TSA agent search me. He is obviously horrified by the prospect. Meanwhile, someone in the line shouts, "Stop holding up the line, Tranny!" He is ironically wearing a safety pin to represent himself as an ally to marginalized people. The supervisor gives in and rescans me as a male (as indicated by the state issued identification I am obliged to show them). No search is necessary this time. I look for Eun Young, unaware that she is enduring a secondary search. I am lucky this time, but my friend and colleague is not.

DECEMBER 2016

Eun Young

I am traveling to Ohio for winter break. I remember the Philadelphia airport incident from last month and contemplate whether or not to bring my passport to the airport. I end up not bringing it. This is my small act of resistance. This time, no one has a problem with my driver's license.

JANUARY 2017

Billy

It is two weeks after the inauguration of Trump. I am flying to Bloemfontein, South Africa where I am a research associate with the Institute for Reconciliation and Social Justice at the University of the Free State (UFS). I am going to consult on the development of UFS's first center for gender and sexuality. Even though Trump has just become president, he has already reinstated the "Mexico City Policy" which bars international non-governmental organizations that perform or promote abortions from receiving U.S. government funding (Koran & Masters 2017). I do not know how this decision will affect the center at UFS or how I will be received there as a citizen of an imperialist power.

This is also the day that Trump signs an executive order halting all refugee admissions and temporarily barring people from seven Muslim-majority countries from traveling to the United States. My Muslim colleague planned to accompany me on the trip, but because he is in the U.S. on a temporary work visa from Canada, he is afraid he will not be allowed back in the U.S. My fears about passing through airport security are this time "trumped" by an overwhelming feeling of privilege. It might not be easy, but I will be let back in.

One of the things that interests me most about the comparative study I am beginning regarding treatment of queer and trans subjects in the two countries, is the fact that while queer and trans people receive full legal equality in South Africa, social acceptance seems lacking. I am especially nervous about my movement through the airport. My travel to South Africa is unremarkable, and I hope for the same for my return home. When I arrive at the tiny airport in Bloemfontein, a rural town in the middle of the country, I brace for the worst. I make it quickly through security. I am not even asked to remove my shoes. Everything is going to be fine.

I decide to buy a coffee, and as I approach the counter, I immediately fear I am in trouble. The woman working behind the counter squints her eyes and her face hardens. "What are you trying to be?" she asks me. "I'm trans," I answer. "That's amazing!" she exclaims. "My mom is transitioning too. May I ask you some questions?" I talk to the woman behind the coffee counter for an hour. Her questions are direct and genuine. We talk about sexual politics, gender, and globalization. We talk about Trump. We talk about how progress feels like the natural state of things when it's happening, but how we have both learned in entirely different contexts that social progress is not a given. It is and always has been a result of struggle. I realize I have learned the most about this struggle in airports during the early days of the Trump era.

Eun Young

Without any specific plans for air travel, I hear the news about Trump's travel ban, which bars people from seven Islamic countries including Iraq, Iran, Syria, Yemen, Libya, Sudan, and Somalia from entering the U.S. for 90 days. This brings me relief and fear simultaneously. South Korea is not on the list, so it won't be necessary to worry about my international trips too much. What scares me is the capricious and unpredictable nature of the administration's decision-making. South Korea's political climate can be so quickly and easily shaken up in relation to what North Korea happens to be doing at the moment, and North Korea was once marked as part of the "axis of evil" by the Bush administration.

A month ago, I was finally able to file my petition to get permanent residency in the U.S. Watching the news about the travel ban on TV, I decide not to make a trip back home this summer. For the last couple of years, going home has been an annual treat. When filing the petition for a green card, my attorney advised me not to make any international trips. I was told that international travel is legal, but it is strongly recommended not to move in and out of the country while the petition is in process. Who knows what could happen? The news about the travel ban, however, seals the deal. I am not going home. I am not making any international trips until my petition goes through. I can't afford to take any risks. My colleague asks me if I am going home this summer. I say no. He understands. He tells me he didn't either when he was going through the same process years ago. He adds that as an Iranian, he isn't sure now what he and his family are going to do about international trips. Holding permanent resident status doesn't seem to guarantee their security. The fact that South Korea isn't one of the countries on the list does not comfort me. Everything seems too fragile and uncertain. I feel a bond with all those people who won't be able to see their families due to the ban.

FEBRUARY 2017

Billy

I arrive at the Gainesville, Florida local airport for the first time since I started working at University of Florida. I'm heading to an international conference on "Diversity in Higher Education" in Amsterdam. Despite having grown a fairly substantial beard, I am still regularly misgendered, and I know airport security at this small airport will likely not know how to read me. I am heartened when I walk up to the screening area and realize they are only using a metal detector. As long as I don't make the machine "beep," my sex/gender is irrelevant.

I wish I could say the same for my carry-on bag. In addition to the books I planned to read on the plane, my bag also contains a couple of large dildos, condoms, and lubricant. I am going to Amsterdam after all. I guess the sexual paraphernalia looks to the agent like a weapon, because he pulls my bag aside and forces me to wait there as he removes everything from my bag in front of all of the other travelers (including my boss). I would normally have been horrified, but after everything I have been through, I can't help but find the situation slightly amusing. The trip to Amsterdam is amazing. I am read as a man (called sir) by a stranger in Amsterdam for the very first time.

NOVEMBER 2017

Eun Young

I am at the RSW airport, and I am on my way to Dallas, Texas, again for the annual NCA conference. I am thinking about last year; the day Billy and I were on our way to Philadelphia and the day we returned to the Philadelphia airport exactly a year ago. Since then my legal status has changed. I am now a permanent U.S. resident. The debate over the travel ban executive order is still before the Supreme Court. Changes are rapid, DACA (Deferred Action for Childhood Arrivals), sanctuary cities, refugee quotas, H1B (working) visas, the diversity green card lottery system are all in play as Trump works to reshape immigration policy. Who knows what else I am missing? I am grateful that my petition for permanent residency went through, and I have my green card in hand. I no longer have to think about whether or not to bring my passport whenever I travel in the U.S. I have to admit, this is nice. It is just simply nice. Of course, it is about more than having one less thing to carry. It is about a whole different level of ease my new status provides me. Sure, I am an immigrant, which means, especially now, I am still vulnerable when I cross a border. But, this is the most secure status I have had as a migrant body in this alien country.

I am making my first domestic trip since I got my green card. I have the urge to use it. I am disappointed; I am not asked to present any identification other than my driver's license. But, having that little card in my pocket, I can't avoid thinking about privilege. I personally feel more privileged than I did a year ago. My status is invisible, but that doesn't change that I now have the privilege to feel 'just fine' while traveling. I think to myself the green card is worth a well spent eight-grand. It is a shiny validation securing my presence in this land. But then, this question pops in my head: how many people can afford that much money for a green card?

MAY-JUNE 2018

Eun Young

Again, sitting at the RSW airport in Florida, I am full of excitement about going home. Yes, my home, South Korea. It has been two years since the last time I made a trip to Korea. The moment my plane lands, I am completely at ease. I feel free; free from constantly checking up on myself, free from justifying my presence, and free from any agony of instability. Being home was great before, but this time, it is more than great. It is an extremely interesting time to be in South Korea. The U.S., North Korea, and South Korea are going through the final stages of negotiations to hold the 'historic' summit between the U.S. and North Korea. At home, I am eagerly watching the news: one day the summit is on, and the next day the summit is off. It is eventually held on June 12, 2018 in Singapore, but, once again, unpredictability and uncertainty create fear. With my U.S.-bound flight booked for June 17, my fear isn't necessarily about not being allowed back in the States. There are just so many what ifs. When I think I finally have something secure, the green card, I come to realize that even then, I can't escape from geopolitics as I move across the globe.

When I was packing for this trip, it felt easier to travel without all those papers and documents to prove that I deserve to re-enter the States upon my return. But now, as I am about to come back to the U.S., the anxiety kicks in. I feel vulnerable because I don't have any of the 'papers' that I used to carry with me as an international student and then as a worker with an H1B visa. Along with my South Korea passport, the only thing I have this time is my green card. It is still shiny because it hasn't been much used. Knowing that I don't need anything other than my green card and passport to enter the U.S. does little to stop my body from reacting anxiously as I go through customs. With my new status, I don't yet have a new protocol. Walking up to the self-customs machine at the Detroit airport, I experience self-doubt. I imagine a range of unpleasant scenarios in which my card doesn't go through or there is no record of me. I find it bitterly funny that my life depends on a little plastic card.

Boarding my connecting flight to Fort Myers from Detroit, I go over my encounter with customs. It was quite pleasant. If it was not the most pleasant experience, it was surely better than other times. Reasons? I will never really know. I put my green card back in my passport pouch. Leaving the Fort Myers airport and heading to my other home in Florida, I am finally at ease. Yes, finally.

Billy

I am once more at the Gainesville, Florida airport. This time I am on my way to Los Angeles for an on-campus interview at UCLA for the position of Director of the LGBT Campus Resource Center. I don't have words to describe how desperate I am to get this job and leave Florida. My desperation is compounded by my Uber ride to the airport. The driver remarks that there must be an exodus of academics leaving the University of Florida. He has noticed an upswing in demand for rides to the airport from academics lately. He offers that, as a Trump supporter, he is glad to see us go. He announces his position, but it is not always so easy to tell someone's politics. I am becoming accustomed to moving through a sea of strangers in Florida who might very well want me gone. I am not offered the position.

JUNE 26, 2018

Eun Young

Driving to campus, I hear the news on the radio that the Supreme Court upholds the travel ban. Is this really it?

NOVEMBER 7, 2018

Billy

It's been two years since Trump was elected president, and I am sitting with Eun Young again at RSW on our way to the National Communication Association's annual conference. Yesterday was the 2018 national midterm election. There is some good news nationally. More women were elected to national and state office than ever before. A number of people of color were elected, and many of our elected representatives are now people who identify as LGBTQ+. Several attempts to curtail the rights of transgender citizens were thwarted, and Florida passed an amendment that will restore voting rights to over a million citizens of the state who have felony convictions. The state of Florida, however, elected their Republican candidate, Ron DeSantis, to the position of governor, and their current Republican governor, Rick Scott, was elected to the U.S. Senate. My desire to leave Florida is stronger than ever.

I am also preoccupied with a recent report from *The New York Times* regarding a secret memo from the Trump Administration's Health and Human Services department that narrowly defines "gender as a biological, immutable condition determined by genitalia at birth, the most drastic move yet in a government wide effort to roll back recognition and protections of transgender people under federal civil rights law" (Green, Benner, & Pear, 2018, para. 1). I think about what this change will mean for me as I move through the world (including the airport), but I have learned a lot about my own privilege in the last couple years. According to trans advocate, lawyer, and scholar, Dean Spade (2018):

> The Health and Human Services memo leak is aligned with a broader patriarchal and authoritarian ideology about enforcing a gendered worldview that constrains everyone, especially those most touched by state systems that target and control the lives of poor people and people of color. This new move dovetails with the administration's work to embolden and expand resources to the military, police and immigration enforcement. All of this strengthens the violent enforcement of race, gender and class hierarchies in our lives. All of them will directly result in increased sexual and gender violence in the lives of the poorest people. (para. 14)

As I sit in the airport preparing to present this very chapter on a panel in a couple days, I ponder the transformations I've made in my thinking alongside the transformations of my body over the past two years. In this time of increased vulnerability, I've learned the most about my own privilege. I travel through the world, and I am terrified, but at the end of the day, I know that if someone is detained, I am white, and it will likely not be me.

At the conference, I attend panels that engage heterosexism, genderism, and racism. I am no longer frustrated by the lack of conversations exclusively about sex. I am grateful for the emotional labor spent by my queer colleagues of color who graciously give their time at the conference to explain to mainly white academic audiences the ramifications of their privileged blindness. I now understand the immense privilege of thinking of sex apart from considerations of race, class, ability, and gender, etc. and apart from regimes of power that manifest in unjust policies informing immigration, law enforcement, colonization, and yes, even airport (in)security.

Eun Young

Sitting at the Fort Myers airport with Billy while glancing at TV screens that are still broadcasting midterm election results, I am glad that our flight to NCA in Salt Lake City isn't in the early morning because I was up late last night watching the news. Due to the close races, it is several days before we find out that Florida's a red state again. Our hope for the election of Florida's first Black governor is unfulfilled. Waiting in line to get on our plane, Billy and I spot some people wearing "Rick Scott, Make Washington Work" t-shirts. Billy and I look at each other. I flashback to 2016, and the t-shirts overlap with the infamous MAGA red hats.

At NCA, I recover the hopes and aspirations that left me in the wake of Trump' victory. Inspiring panels on racism, Whiteness, critical pedagogy, intersectionality, and more, really help me rechannel my thoughts toward what I can do rather than feel sorry for myself. These dialogues push me again and again to take a good look at my own prejudice and privileges. These dialogues give me tools for navigating critically through a myriad of junctures at which my positionality crosses with someone else's.

On the last day of the conference, Billy and I finally have some free time until our night flight. We decide to go to a restaurant. I regret our choice immediately upon walking in. There is a sign up front that reads, "We have the right to refuse to serve anyone." I have heard about such policies, but I have never noticed such a sign before. Traveling with Billy for the last four years, I have come to realize it is indeed a privilege not having to think twice about being welcome whenever I walk into a public establishment. Now I feel extremely uncomfortable, not only with being in an exclusive restaurant, but also with the fact that it was me who suggested it.

At the airport on our way home, I am still processing what happened today. I am savoring the luxury of sailing through security with a driver's license that does not say 'temporary.' I feel torn. On one hand, I appreciate the ease with which I can now travel. On the other hand, I feel overwhelmed to know how much more work still needs to be done. Not everyone is as privileged as Billy and I feel right now.

ON BOARD

Logging our itineraries throughout the last two years, including our trips together to the NCA conference, has been a tremendously teachable experience. Our bodies moving through various airports inside and outside of this country, together and separately, sharpen our attentiveness not just to our respective positionalities, but to moments and spaces through which our positionalities intersect and then diverge. Airports indeed are spaces where we experience difference and similarity, privilege and marginalization. In a quite literal sense, we travel to and leave from each other's worlds (Ghabra & Calafell, 2018; Lugones, 2003). Our travels help us grasp that "recognizing and sitting with our privileged and marginalized positionalities opens a plethora of possibilities for alliance building" (Ghabra & Calafell, 2018, p. 51). We aren't naive to think these momentarily shared feelings can save us, but we are glad to know we are on board to have each other's backs through the Trump presidency and beyond.

REFERENCES

Foucault, M. (1980). *Power/knowledge* (C. Goron Edition). New York, NY: Vintage Books.

Ghabra, H., & Calafell, B. M. (2018). From failure and allyship to feminist solidarities: Negotiating our privileges and oppressions across borders. *Text and Performance Quarterly, 38*(1–2), 38–54.

Green, E. L., Benner, K., & Pear, R. (2018, October 21). 'Transgender' could be defined out of existence by the Trump administration. *The New York Times*. Retrieved from https://www.nytimes.com/2018/10/21/us/politics/transgender-trump-administration-sex-definition.html

Koran, L., & Masters, J. (2017, January 24). Trump reverses abortion policy for aid to NGOs. *CNN*. Retrieved from https://www.cnn.com/2017/01/23/politics/trump-mexico-city-policy/index.html

Lugones, M. (2003). *Pilgrimages/peregrinajes: Theorizing coalition against multiple oppressions*. Boulder, CO: Rowman & Littlefield.

Parks, L. (2007). Points of departure: The culture of U.S. airport screening. *Journal of Visual Culture, 6*(2), 183–200.

Pear, R. (2018, April 21). Trump plan would cut back health care protections for transgender people. *The New York Times*. Retrieved from https://www.nytimes.com/2018/04/21/us/politics/trump-transgender-health-care.html

Puar, J. K. (2017). *Terrorist assemblages: Homonationalism in queer times, tenth anniversary expanded edition*. Durham, NC: Duke University Press.

@realDonaldTrump. (2016, June 12). Appreciate the congrats [Tweet]. https://twitter.com/realdonaldtrump/status/742034549232766976?lang=en

Rubin, G. (2014). Thinking sex: Notes for a radical theory of the politics of sexuality. In R. Parker & P. Aggleton (Eds.), *Culture, society and sexuality: A reader* (pp. 143–178). New York, NY: Routledge.

Salter, M. B. (2008). Introduction: Airport assemblage. In M. B. Salter (Ed.), *Politics at the airport* (pp. ix–xix). Minneapolis, MN: University of Minnesota Press.

Shome, R. (2003). Space matters: The power and practice of space. *Communication Theory, 13*(1), 39–56.

Spade, D. (2018, October 22). Right-wing fantasies about gender are killing trans people. *Truthout*. Retrieved from https://truthout.org/articles/right-wing-fantasies-about-gender-are-killing-trans-people/

Spalding, S. J. (2016). Airport outings: The coalitional possibilities of affective rupture. *Women's Studies in Communication, 39*(4), 460–480.

CHRISTINE SALKIN DAVIS AND JONATHAN L. CRANE

DIALOGUE 5

"I think one thing that's gotten missed, he's put women in a position of power. Look at Ivanka. And she is pushing women's issues, mothers being able to be home and take care of their children after birth. So, I think she could bring in a softer side from her perspective in life and that he listens to. I think he wants everybody to do well."

"Yes," Andrea agrees, "And he wants America to be safe."

"He wants everybody to do great," Larry says. "He wants everybody to be self-sufficient."

"And not wanting to take the salary," Andrea says. "Or maybe he took it but then gave it away. In other words, he didn't want to be paid. I mean, obviously, I know that you get other benefits by being president."

Larry says, "I want you to walk out of here understanding me as a policy person more than supporting the person, but also know that I think he was the right person to pick at the time, and he could still be the right person for the time, however, some of his rhetoric, he doesn't help himself. I mean, if you know the media already is going to lean left anyway, why give them more myths? So yeah."

Andrea says, "I still think his intention truly is what he's said, to make America great again."

"How is he making America great again?" I ask.

"I'm not sure how to elaborate," Andrea says. "Well, let's talk about the border. He's protecting us. I'm not against people coming here, but I think we need to vet people a little better to make sure that we are still protecting ourselves as well. I mean the terrorist thing is real. So, like the refugees from Syria. If I was in Syria, I would want to come here as well. And there's people we truly need to help. But at the same time, in them coming here, where is the balance in them coming here, being provided housing, being provided money until they can get on their feet again, being given an education. I mean, I even read an article on one particular family, the housing they were provided, the vehicle that they were provided, the jobs that they were given. That's great, but I also think there should be a balance between other people

DOI:10.1163/9789004436329_010

who are already here that we need to help in that same way. So for me, I felt Trump felt the way I did about that. I don't mind people coming here. But we also need to take care of ones who are already here, our veterans. This isn't something new, this is something even prior administrations needed to address. But I do think that his intention is to help make America great by making it safer."

"I think the government has run better under Trump," says Elizabeth.

"Better in what way?" I ask.

"I just think he has shaken up Washington. I don't think it's just business as usual. The politicians, both Democrats and Republicans, making deals to pass laws, and working behind closed doors. They seem to trade favors. I think he's more open. I think he says what's on his mind, and I don't think he tries to hide it. So he's gotten in trouble for it, but he really hasn't tried to pull the wool over anybody's eyes, to hide anything. And that's kind of refreshing."

HADIA MUBARAK AND NAVED BAKALI

4. VIOLENT, OPPRESSED, AND UN-AMERICAN

Muslim Women in the American Imagination

INTRODUCTION

The first Muslims to come to America were Africans, chained, forced into bondage and stripped of their heritage, religions, and families, alongside 388,000 others who were forcibly sent to the Americas between 1619 and 1866 (Curtis, 2019; Gates, n.d.). Despite the presence of Muslims in the United States since its early history, when Republican candidate Donald J. Trump ran for U.S. president in 2016, he frequently repeated widespread rumors about President Barack Obama "being a Muslim" to cast doubt on Obama's identity as a U.S.-born citizen. While Trump did not fabricate the rumor, he exploited the fact that 43% of his own base believed Obama to be a Muslim (Bailey, 2015). It made no difference to Trump that Obama was in fact a Christian, nor that Muslims had been a part of this country much longer than Trump's own family, who arrived to America's shores in the late nineteenth century (Blair, 2000). Rather, Trump's campaign chose to capitalize on the rising level of anti-Muslim sentiments among the general populace. According to polling agencies, Americans' views of Islam in the 2016 presidential election season were significantly more negative than they were within weeks after 9/11, the worst terrorist attack against the U.S. (Telhami, 2015).

Donald Trump's animosity towards Muslims signaled a critical turning point in the history of America's public discourse on Islam. For the first time, what could only be said in private was deemed acceptable for public consumption. In place of the careful and reasoned analysis of America's long line of 43 presidents[1] who recognized Muslims as part of the social fabric of America, Trump is the first U.S. president to openly target America's Muslim minority and cast it as an "Other." Whereas President Thomas Jefferson affirmed that "neither Pagan nor Mahometan [Muslim] nor Jew ought to be excluded from the civil rights of the commonwealth because of his religion" (Spellberg, 2017, para. 8), Trump instead said he would "strongly consider"

 | DOI:10.1163/9789004436329_011

closings mosques for America's 3.3 million Muslim population (Johnson, 2015). In place of George W. Bush's factual distinction between law-abiding, peace-loving Muslim citizens and the terrorists who attacked America on 9/11, Trump has deliberately collapsed the terms Islam and terrorism, Muslims and foreigners, fueling a radical, binary view of the world, as either 'free, democratic and western' or 'violent, authoritarian and Muslim.'

While anti-Muslim sentiments predate President Trump, he was the first U.S. president to introduce central tenets of Islamophobic rhetoric to the White House. The central themes of Islamophobia, amplified by President Trump, are (1) the pervasive identification of Islam as foreign to the history and culture of America; (2) the characterization of Muslims as threatening and dangerous to America's security, thereby morally legitimating policies and actions against this religious minority; (3) the 'essentialization' of Islam –the depiction of a 1440-year-old religious tradition as a monolithic, static, unchanging entity – a view that is completely divorced from history, sociology, and the contemporary politics of the Muslim world; and (4) the insistence that contemporary political, ethical, and human rights problems in the Muslim world stem from Islam, thereby bolstering claims of an imminent clash of civilizations. The Othering of Muslims is endemic to Islamophobia, which is premised on the 'clash of civilizations' theory' (Kumar, 2012; Sheehi, 2011).

The portrayal of Muslim Americans as a dangerous menace to American society, as a religious community who do not fully belong to the rich tapestry of American life, is most acutely felt by women who wear the *hijab*. The modest covering of a woman's hair and body, *hijab* is a visible marker of religious identity. The narratives of women in this chapter illustrate that Muslim women – as subjects whose "Otherness" is most visible by their outward appearance – bear the brunt of Donald Trump's rhetoric on Muslims as an unpatriotic fifth column who pose a security threat to their own country. The women interviewed[2] in this chapter – mothers, bankers, educators, students, pharmacists, civil rights advocates, and homemakers – all tell the story of chronic abuse at the hands of a segment of the American citizenry mobilized by their new president's rhetoric against Islam.

'GENDERED ISLAMOPHOBIA': PRIMARY VICTIMS

The disproportionate impact of Trump's rhetoric on Muslim women speaks to the reality of "gendered Islamophobia," a term first coined by Jasmine Zine, a sociology professor at Wilfrid Laurier University (Zine, 2006).

Similarly, Barbara Perry notes (2014) that Muslim women's experiences with Islamophobia are atypical of hate crimes. While the majority of victims of hate crimes tend to be men outside of the Muslim community, patterns in the Muslim community run counter to this trend. Rather, as Perry notes, Muslim women in particular have borne the brunt of a rising level of Islamophobia since 9/11 (Perry, 2014). This finding is confirmed by the 2018 polling results published by the Institute for Social Policy and Understanding (ISPU), which found that 75% of Muslim women experienced racial discrimination in public, in comparison to 40% of women from other faith communities (Mogahed & Chouhoud, 2018).

It is not a coincidence that most of the victims of hate crimes against Muslims are women. Muslim women's multiple subject positions as female and members of a minority religion (and minority ethnicity, in many cases) amplifies their vulnerability as targets of hate. As social theorists have discovered, there is a strong correlation between racism and sexism (Henley & Pincus, 1978). One of the earliest studies to examine the relationship between the two isms, published in 1978, found that sexism and racism were positively correlated with political conservatism (Sidanius, 1993).

The strong correlation between racism and sexism is critical for understanding Muslim women's lived experiences with Islamophobia, both traditionally and in the post-Trump era. In Edward Said's (1979) foundational work *Orientalism*, he describes how the Orientalist gaze has eroticized the Muslim female subject as overtly sensual. In the present discourse, the vulgar sexualization of Muslim women persists but is intertwined with discourses that frame Muslim women as passive and oppressed victims of their cultures and faith through visual signifiers of their Muslimness, like the *hijab* (Bakali, 2016). Hence, Islamophobia experienced by many Muslim women in the present context manifests as a type of reconfigured Orientalism (Bilge, 2012). Through these visual signifiers, the Muslim female subject undergoes a process of racialization, such that her ethnicity, culture, and selfhood dissipate and she is only identifiable as "Other" or foreign. As such, white Caucasian participants in our study, despite being members of the majority culture, also experienced racism and discrimination intended to cast them out from the mainstream public.

The intersections among religion, race and gender in relation to Muslim women's experiences has received minimal attention in media coverage or public discourse. The story of every woman in this chapter offers a sketch of the experiences of Muslim women in the U.S. during Trump's presidency, their narratives interweaving to paint a bleak image of their lives: one in which their identity as Americans is questioned, their loyalty to America undermined, and their very safety jeopardized.

Our interview selection process solicited stories from *any* Muslim woman who experienced hatred, discrimination or assault during Trump's electoral season and presidency, irrespective of choice of dress. Yet every woman who shared her story with us said she was wearing the *hijab* at the time of the incident. Some of the women we interviewed have modified their *hijab* or no longer cover their hair out of fear for their safety; others continue to wear it, despite challenges. Likewise, a study by Pew Research Center found that nearly two-thirds (64%) of Muslims "whose appearance is identifiably Muslim" say they have experienced discrimination in 2017, whereas only 39% of Muslims who do not have a distinctively Muslim appearance reported experiencing discrimination (Pew Research Center, 2017).

The perception of Muslims as 'other than American' is exacerbated for women who don the *hijab*. The *hijab* – a distinct covering of the hair and body – is mistakenly perceived by many as an attempt to hold on to a foreign cultural tradition and as a reluctance to assimilate. Yet, as Katherine Bullock (2002) illustrates in her extensive survey of Muslim women in Canada, *Rethinking the Veil,* women's choices to dress modestly often stem from a spiritual commitment, not a cultural one. In fact, her study confirms what the authors of this chapter have observed in their respective communities in the U.S. and Canada: immigrant women who were reluctant to wear *hijab* in their native countries due to the stigma it carried, a byproduct of colonial perceptions of the headscarf, felt freer to don the *hijab* in countries like America and Canada, where freedom of religion is celebrated and protected (Bullock, 2002).

The women with whom we spoke reflect a diversity of races, professions, levels of religious commitment, and demographics. Some are recent college graduates; others are in their fifties; some are born in the U.S.; others are immigrants to the U.S.; some converted to Islam; others were born Muslim. The experiences of these women range from having a gun pointed at them and being chased down by a truck driver screaming obscenities at them, to being threatened with death, bullied, denied service, or verbally harassed. Despite the diversity of their backgrounds and incidents, four common themes emerge in their encounter with Islamophobia during Trump's run and election for presidency.

First, all interviewees expressed the view that the political climate worsened during the 2016 electoral cycle and Trump's first year in office. Our older interviewees, those old enough to distinctly remember the post-9/11 climate in America, noted that the hostility they encountered during and after Trump's election was far worse than anything they experienced after 9/11. Our findings are consistent with the Pew Research Center's 2017 polling results, which found that 75% of U.S. Muslims believe "there is a lot of discrimination against Muslims in the U.S." (Pew Research Center, 2017). Fifty percent said that "being Muslim in the United States has gotten more difficult" in recent years (Pew Research Center, 2017).

Second, many of the victims reported unsympathetic bystanders, who saw an incident occur, yet did nothing to intervene. Worse, some encountered law enforcement officials or school administrators who defended the actions of the perpetrators as "freedom of speech," undermined the seriousness of the incident, or betrayed their obligation to protect women who felt vulnerable and unsafe. At the same time, interviewees observed that the haters have ironically mobilized a sympathetic segment of the population, whom – upon witnessing suffering – have stood up against it.

A third common theme among the interviewees is the conflation of terrorism, violence, oppression and hyper-sexualization with Muslim women. Ironically, many of the incidents that Muslim women shared with us reveal the entanglement of a few stereotypes in the minds of their perpetrators: the perception of Islam as inherently violent, Muslim women as oppressed, and Muslims as not "real" Americans. While attacking their victims, perpetrators shouted phrases like "terrorist bit*h," or "you fu*king terrorist, go back to your country; we don't want your oppressed a*s here." The irony of referring to Muslim women as simultaneously oppressed and terrorists appears to elude those who assault them. Even when verbally harassing Muslim women, perpetrators made sexually explicit comments or referred to the women as "oppressed," conjuring Orientalist views of Muslim women as both hyper-sexualized and victims.

Related to this trend, Muslim women also experienced a form of "out casting." The common perception that Muslims are not American, but foreigners, underlies Muslim women's experiences with racism, hostility and assault in the United States. While facing physical or verbal harassment, many of the victims with whom we spoke were told to "go back home." For example, while attempting to run over Maryam – a mother in her mid-20's, who was crossing a shopping parking lot with her toddler – a truck driver yelled at her, "You fu*king Muslim, get out of this country" (M. Najeeb, personal communication, May 16, 2018). Not only did the perpetrators clearly perceive their victims as foreigners who do not belong in their community, but they used this perception to justify their physical or verbal assault.

The number and nature of the verbal assaults Muslim women received during Trump's first year in office are not only alarming, but repugnantly vulgar.

TRUMP USHERS IN A CLIMATE OF FEAR

It was the night of the second primary presidential debate between Hilary Clinton, the Democratic nominee for president, and Trump, the GOP's presidential nominee. The town hall format of the debate gave selected, uncommitted voters a chance to directly ask the candidates a set of questions. That night, Gorbah Hameed, an American Muslim, was one of the few voters chosen by the Gallup organization to solicit responses from America's next president. The young Muslim woman, with sleek black hair and wearing a black leather jacket, expressed her concern about heightened Islamophobia in this country:

> Hi. There are 3.3 million Muslims in the United States and I'm one of them. You've mentioned working with Muslim nations. But with Islamophobia on the rise, how will you help people like me deal with the consequences of being labelled as a threat to the country after the election is over? (Full transcript, 2016, para. 83)

Rather than alleviate her concerns, Trump's response instead entrenched the idea that Americans should be afraid of Muslims. He claimed that Muslims in San Bernardino had seen "bombs all over the apartment" belonging to the terrorist couple, yet had failed to report it – a statement that the FBI and media outlets have proven false (Krieg, 2017). Ignoring the complex psychological, economic, socio-political, and ideological factors that underlie terrorism and violence, Trump lumped together the terrorist attacks in NY, Paris and the Orlando shooting as evidence of "radical Islam." In response to Hameed, Trump declared:

> Muslims have to report the problems when they see them. And, you know, there is always a reason for everything. If they don't do that, it's a very difficult situation for our country. Because you look at Orlando and you look at San Bernardino and you look at the World Trade Center. Go outside and you look at Paris, look at that horrible thing. These are radical Islamic terrorists and she [Hillary Clinton] won't even mention the word and nor will President Obama. (Full transcript, 2016, para. 85)

The careless association between everything Islam and terrorism is a prominent feature of Trump's rhetoric. After the horrific shooting at an

Orlando gay club, which took the lives of 49 people, Trump capitalized on the shooting by Omar Mateen, a U.S.-born Muslim, as an example of "radical Islamic terror." Rather than frame the shooting within America's recent wave of mass shootings, Trump's speech on the very next day connected the Orlando shooting with 9/11. Employing the common trope that terrorists attack America because "they hate our freedoms," Trump said:

> This is a very dark moment in America's history. A radical Islamic terrorist targeted the nightclub, not only because he wanted to kill Americans, but in order to execute gay and lesbian citizens, because of their sexual orientation. It's a strike at the heart and soul of who we are as a nation. It's an assault on the ability of free people to live their lives, love who they want, and express their identity. It's an attack on the right of every single American to live in peace and safety in their own country. (Beckwith, 2016, para. 8)

Yet the complicated patterns of Omar Mateen's life, as a young boy who never fit in, experimented with drugs, drank heavily, and was abusive and violent to the women in his life (Sullivan & Wan, 2016), tells us the story of a troubled, American teenager whose turn to violence stemmed from unresolved social and psychological issues, not religious ones. Yet Trump – and others who subscribe to a clash of civilizations theory – work hard not to allow us to make those comparisons. Mateen's own family members and friends reported that he was not a devout Muslim and that his family's observation of Islam was primarily cultural. His manager told *The Washington Post* that Mateen's behavior offended the sensibilities of his Muslim co-workers (Sullivan & Wan, 2016). These details did not matter to Trump; what mattered to Trump and his campaign was that Mateen was a Muslim, as if his religious background encoded in his DNA an inclination for violence, a ticking bomb waiting to explode.

The empirical reality of Muslim Americans, based on data polling, paints an entirely different narrative. According to a Pew Forum study, a higher percentage of U.S. Muslims reject violence against civilians than does the general public. Seventy-six percent of U.S. Muslims believe that violence against civilians is "never justified," compared with 59% of the general public (Pew Research Center, 2017). The same study found that Muslims are just as concerned about terrorism as the general public. Whereas 82% of U.S. Muslims "say they are either 'very' (66%) or 'somewhat' (16%) concerned about extremism in the name of Islam around the world," 83% of the general public also express this concern (Pew Research Center, 2017). Despite the discrimination that Muslims

(48%) said they experienced between 2016 and 2017, 92% said they were proud to be an American (Pew Research Center, 2017).

Every single woman with whom we spoke said she noted a significant shift in her day-to-day experiences after President Trump became the Republican nominee for president. While most said they had no proof or evidence, they believed that their personal encounters with Islamophobia were directly related to the president's moral legitimation of the masked animosity and hatred that had lay dormant within a segment of America's population. As one interviewee noted,

> I definitely think his presidency heightened a lot of things. Now that the president is very direct about it, they feel like they can be the same way. He exposed people who are like him. You know it [racism] has always been there, but we're seeing more of it because people are not afraid to expose themselves anymore. They just do what they want and say what they want .... They feel like they can say whatever they want without getting in trouble. (L. Salam, personal communication, May 8, 2008)

Dalia Mogahed, the director of research at ISPU, a think tank that conducts research and education on social and political issues related to Muslim Americans, argues that Trump's rhetoric emboldened white supremacy. In an interview she stated,

> The climate created the situation where wearing visible markers of religion invites these kinds of attacks. When you're under so much scrutiny, it impacts how you function in life. You go from being a private individual to being a sort of mascot [of Islam]. (D. Mogahed, personal communication, May 14, 2018)

Fatima Ahmed, who has lived in south Florida since 1993, said she never experienced as much intense hatred from fellow Floridians as she did during Trump's presidential campaign and first year in office. She explained,

> We began suffering since Trump ran for president. I was here during Sept. 11 and I never had to face what I have had to face since Trump ran for office. This happened right after the elections. His hatred was spreading everywhere in the city .... I was here during the Gulf War, Sept. 11 and I haven't experienced such a thing like this before. I even had a more public presence at that time, wearing a big scarf and *jilbab* [long traditional dress]. I haven't seen anything like what we're seeing and feeling now. (F. Hasan, personal correspondence, August 5, 2018)

STRUCTURAL RACISM: ISLAMOPHOBIA, CRITICAL RACE THEORY AND THE LAW

It is not a coincidence that Trump's era came at the heels of America's first black president. The eight years during which Barack Obama served as president witnessed some of the most racism-laden dissent ever directed at a U.S. president. Many Republicans, albeit not all, had capitalized on their base's endemic hatred of Obama. As seasoned politicians and journalists were quick to observe, Trump's election was the "racist backlash" to Obama's presidency (Milbank, 2018). It is important to recognize the connections between rising Islamophobia and deep-seated anti-black racism that has plagued America's history. Within this context, Islamophobia is not a recent phenomenon, but is one of many iterations of an enduring legacy of racism in America. One essential theoretical framework that can be employed to better understand this phenomenon is through a critical race perspective.

Critical Race Theory (CRT) (Taylor, 2009) is a theoretical frame that understands racism as existing through relationships of power, which aim to preserve the regime of white supremacy, while subordinating peoples of color. Within this paradigm, race is understood to be socially constructed. In other words, terms such as 'white' and 'black' do not refer to individuals or group identity. Rather, they indicate "a particular political and legal structure rooted in the ideology of White European supremacy and the global impact of colonialism" (Taylor, 2009, p. 4). One of the primary concerns of CRT is to understand the relationship between law and racial power. The law, as argued by critical race theorists, is a tool that is wielded to maintain racial hierarchies. Consequently, racial categories that are at the supposed 'lower rungs' of the social order are targeted, subverted, and punished through the legal system.

One of the clearest manifestations of structural Islamophobia during Trump's presidency was Executive Order 13769, commonly referred to as the "Muslim Ban." The order institutionalized the notion that Muslims constitute a terror threat, as it primarily targeted Muslim-majority countries. Titled "Protecting the Nation from Foreign Terrorist Entry into The United States," the bill was enacted on January 27, 2017. Although President Trump's administration claimed that the bill did not target Muslims, his previous attacks on Muslims as presidential candidate resonated clearly in the American public. As the GOP frontrunner, Trump first issued a press release and then read his statement on December 7, 2015 at a rally in South Carolina. "As president, … [he stated], he would consider shutting down some mosques" (Johnson, 2015, para. 1).

Trump's language reflects an unmistakable motive for Executive Order 13769: the elimination of Muslim immigration to the United States. Lacking accuracy and nuance, his language conflates terrorism and Muslims, playing on existing stereotypes of Muslims as terrorists. As U.S. Supreme Court Justice, Elena Kagan, argued, Trump's signed executive order should be understood against the backdrop of his anti-Muslim rhetoric. Offering an analogy, she asked, what one would make of a scenario in which a presidential candidate, who is "a vehement anti-Semite and says all kinds of denigrating comments about Jews," decides to ban visitors from Israel after taking office? (Donald Trump, President of the United States et al. vs. Hawaii et al., 2018, p. 16).

In his presidential campaign, Donald Trump promised radical changes in the political landscape. This entailed doing away with political correctness, while pandering to the racist attitudes held by his base of supporters. Trump's executive order signaled an intent to fulfill his reactionary campaign promises, one of which included a complete shutdown of Muslims entering the United States (Johnson, 2015). Executive Order 13769 was challenged by the courts, which led to an amended version of the ban, Executive Order 13780. This version of the ban was also challenged by the courts. Eventually, the ban, in its third formulation, was upheld by the Supreme Court in a 5-4 decision. Through this ban, Trump's presidency amplified the existing fear of Muslims as potential threats to American security.

It was in this political climate that Farah Mustafa encountered an assault that left her traumatized and afraid for her life. A mother of four, Farah had just left the pediatrician's office, where her fourth child, a one-month-old baby, received his first physical check-up. On her way home, Farah stopped at an Indian grocery store in Charlotte, NC to pick up some yogurt for her three older children, who were waiting at home. As she described,

> It was a Tuesday afternoon. It was very hot. It was the first hot day this year, the temperature in the upper 80s. My baby started to cry so I decided to stop [in a parking spot] under the shade to breastfeed in privacy. I stopped my Sedan and went to the back [of the car] and got him. I took him to the front seat to breastfeed him. Within the three to four minutes that I started breastfeeding, a red pick-up truck pulls up next to me in reverse. At that point, I had no reason to be suspicious. I looked over and saw this Caucasian male who was in [his] upper 40s or 50s. He was sitting in his driver seat and just staring at me, without even blinking. I figured maybe he just had a break from work. I look

> over and he's still looking at me...He had opened his driver door and was walking to the back of his truck. I was just looking at [what] he was doing. He moved the front seat forward and grabbed something. At first, I thought he was grabbing a metal pipe, but then when he turned and pointed it at me, I realized it was a rifle. There was just a yard between us. I could see the end of the barrel. (F. Mustafa, personal communication, June 11, 2017)

With a rifle pointing at her, Farah recalled thinking "I'm not going to get shot in this car. I don't want to die here in this car" (F. Mustafa, personal communication, June 11, 2017). She clutched her son and ran zig-zag to the store. She asked the store manager to call 911. When the police came, they affirmed her inclination that the incident may have been triggered by the driver's religious bias and her physical appearance, as a tan-skinned Pakistani-American woman who wears *hijab*. Yet the police officers were never able to find the driver who threatened to take away Farah's life that day. Having parked in reverse, the man's license plate was not captured by Farah or security cameras. A month later, Farah noted that she had not been able to sleep well since the incident:

> I've gotten sleep deprived from this. I'm not sleeping well. I'm not eating well. My immune system is so weak that I get sick right away .... If something had happened to me, what would I do as a mother? What would my kids do? I feel like even the counseling hasn't helped me much. (F. Mustafa, personal communication, June 11, 2017)

An Egyptian-American woman experienced a similar incident that she described as a 17-minute "horror movie" unfolding before her eyes in Tampa, Florida. Fatima Ahmed, a part-time teacher at a local Muslim school, was heading to the mosque where she tutors children after school. All of a sudden, a white Nissan veered in front of her and stopped when the traffic light turned yellow. The driver proceeded to throw rocks at Fatima's car windshield. Confused, Fatima said she initially thought he was throwing out peanuts or garbage. "But when I heard the [sound of] small rocks hitting my door, I figured out it was rocks," she said (F. Ahmed, personal communication, August 5, 2018). This ordeal continued until the traffic light turned green.

They were both within a few yards from the entrance to the mosque. When the Nissan driver noticed that Fatima was turning left into the mosque entrance, he sharply turned left into the entrance before her and proceeded to block her entry into the driveway. Still confused, Fatima explained,

> I kept waiting for him to shift right or left. I honked the horn so he could move. I thought at first it was a mistake.... I thought maybe he got lost or needed help. I drove to his side and rolled down my window [and asked], "Sir do you need anything? How may I help you?" Then he opened his mouth and all this garbage came out. He was cussing so much. He was so angry. He said "I'm going to kill you. I'm gonna get you tonight. I don't care what fu*king language you're speaking. I'm going to get you tonight." So I went as fast as I could go towards the main mosque at a very high speed and he started chasing me. Every curse word came out of his mouth. (F. Ahmed, personal communication, August 5, 2018)

Feeling threatened, Fatima had no safe place to go. Her students would be arriving any minute and this driver was blocking her entry into the mosque. She frantically called the local imam (mosque leader), whom Fatima knew was inside the mosque. He came out to confront the driver. At this point, the driver threw rocks at her car again and said "I'm gonna send someone to get you tonight. You're going to be killed" (F. Ahmed, personal communication, August 5, 2018). When the parents began to arrive to the mosque parking lot with their children, Fatima managed to scream from inside her car, "Stay in the car and keep your kids in the car!" By the time a police officer showed up on the scene, the driver had fled the mosque parking lot. The officer's apathetic reaction to what Fatima experienced as life-threatening nightmare incensed her. Fatima described,

> The police officer told me, 'He just threatened you. He didn't do anything that you can report.' I asked her, 'Are you waiting for me to be killed to report it?'. (F. Ahmed, personal communication, August 5, 2018)

APATHETIC BYSTANDERS AND LAW ENFORCEMENT OFFICIALS

The apathy of bystanders and officials, such as store managers, law enforcement officials, and school administrators, was a consistent theme in our interviews. Maryam Najeeb, a full-time mother in her late 20s, encountered this apathy first-hand when a man attempted to run her over in a shopping parking lot while she was walking with her son. The incident occurred days after Trump took office. At the time, Maryam used to wear *niqab,* a face veil, in addition to the conventional covering of her hair and body. Maryam had just parked her car in front of Target in a huge strip mall in a small Pennsylvanian town. She was crossing the parking lot to enter the store with her two-year-old son when a car driver saw her and began to speed toward her without stopping at any stop signs. Attempting to run her over, he yelled, "You fu*king Muslim, get out of this country" (M. Najeeb, personal communication, May 16, 2018).

When Maryam ran into Target and reported the incident to their staff, they told her she must file a police report. Frightened and feeling alone, Maryam waited inside her car for 10 minutes until a police officer arrived. She described, "The cop comes and is like 'what's the problem?' I explain, 'There is a guy outside, he was trying to run me over'" (M. Najeeb, personal communication, May 16, 2018).

To Maryam's surprise, the police officer began to interrogate her. He asked her, "Who do you work for?" and "Where do you live?" She responded, "I'm filing this police report and you're asking questions about me." The cop asked, "What do you want me to do? You don't have a license plate number [of the truck]." Maryam suggested to the officer that he may want to check the security camera footage. She said, "This a huge shopping strip; there are cameras everywhere" (M. Najeeb, personal communication, May 16, 2018). When the officer left to look at the footage, Maryam requested to look at the footage with him, but he declined and said, "we don't do that" (M. Najeeb, personal communication, May 16, 2018).

By the time the police officer returned, Maryam had been waiting in her car for over 20 minutes with her toddler since she first arrived at Target. The officer returned and told her, "You were too far away to be run over by the car. People do crazy things sometimes, but you weren't in any danger" (M. Najeeb, personal communication, May 16, 2018). Maryam described her disappointment at the police officer's dismissal of her experience and feeling of legitimate fear.

> I felt there was nothing for him to offer to me. He didn't tell me to file a police report; he didn't look into getting the license plate number reported. I said, 'I'm gonna need your name and your card' and he said, 'I don't have a card, but here's my name.' I said, 'I feel very hurt that I'm calling the police for help and I'm not really getting any help. My child and I were in danger and we could have been run over by this guy.' His response to me was 'If you want to dress the way you want to dress and live in this country, then you have to be open to how people are going to respond and what they're going to say. That's their freedom of speech too. (M. Najeeb, personal communication, May 16, 2018)

Feeling betrayed by the very people who were responsible for her protection, Maryam decided to be proactive and filed a complaint to the state trooper office. It turned out that the trooper with whom she spoke was the head of his department. Ironically, her local Muslim community had raised $10,000 for their city's local police station that year. By the end of Trump's first year in office, Maryam decided to stop wearing the *niqab,* face covering, which she had previously worn for several years. She described,

> I stopped wearing *niqab* in December 2017 …. Trump had been in office for a year. I was still receiving a lot of hate. I really felt like I was putting myself in dangerous situations by doing my day-to-day stuff like grocery shopping and just being outdoors. And I have a child with me. I had to make a decision, I had to ask myself, 'is it worth doing something like this that could put myself and my child at risk?' So I removed it [the *niqab*]. Since then, it has not been as bad. (M. Najeeb, personal communication, May 16, 2018)

THE OPPRESSION/SENSUALIZATION DICHOTOMY OF MUSLIM FEMALE REPRESENTATION

There is a long tradition of representing Muslim women in the West. Scholars give it a name: gendered Orientalism. Pictorial as well as literary, what is constant is that Muslim women are portrayed as culturally distinct, the mirror opposite of Western women (Ahmad, 2009). "In the nineteenth century, the depictions took two forms: women of the Orient were either portrayed as downtrodden victims who were imprisoned, secluded, shrouded, and treated as beasts of burden or they appeared in a sensual world of excessive sexuality – as slaves in harems and the subjects of the gaze of lascivious and violent men, not to mention those looking in …. Artists and writers, and even the colonial postcard photographers of the early twentieth century, preferred the sensual and sexual" (Abu-Lughod, 2013, p. 88).

Despite drawing upon imagery from two centuries past, this description above by Lila Abu-Lughod (2013), a Columbia University anthropologist who specializes in women and gender in the Middle East, captures the convergence of sexism and racism encountered by Muslim women today. Sana Khan, a 14-year-old student in Charlotte, NC, had just started high school the year that Trump ran for presidential office. A bright young woman born to Pakistani immigrants, Sana began wearing *hijab* in the seventh grade. She described how her excitement about starting high school quickly turned to despair, as she became the target of chronic bullying. Sana described how she became the target of a group of boys who hurled insults at her every single day during power period, "one hour during which we would eat and meet with clubs" (S. Khan, personal communication, June 17, 2017).

While walking down the hall on the first day of school, a boy yelled, "She has a bomb!" (S. Khan, personal communication, June 17, 2017). When Sana turned back, she did not see anyone. Rather than an isolated incident, to Sana's shock, it reflected a general trend that gradually peaked during the school year. As Sana described,

> During election season, things progressively got worse. I would walk down the hallway for clubs and these kids would start shouting words of abuse about being a Muslim, Islam and being a woman. I first shook it off. I expected the teacher, who was standing directly in front of the boys, to intervene. (S. Khan, personal communication, June 17, 2017)

One day, a boy walked over to her in school and asked, 'Can I ask you a question?' 'Sure,' Sana naively responded.

> At that point, he asked me to do something I'd rather not repeat. It was a sexual act. It was sexually explicit. He said it right in front of a teacher and the teacher did nothing at all. (S. Khan, personal communication, June 17, 2017)

Sana's story tragically reflects the overlapping junctures between Islamophobia and the sexualization of Muslim women. An intelligent young woman, Sana became acutely aware of being targeted for both her religion and gender. In her words,

> Muslim women are very sexualized to the rest of the world. Because of media outlets, there is this perception of Muslim women being oppressed with no one to help them. At the same time there is this overly sexualized perception of women. The boys who were harassing me really relied on these two stereotypes. They hurled a lot of verbal abuse at me, phrases like bit*h, whore; she's got a bomb; she's a terrorist. One day, while I was walking down the hallway … the boys spread their legs across the hallway. I normally wear skirts and dresses with jeans underneath; one of the boys laid across the hallway and tried to look up my skirt. (S. Khan, personal communication, June 17, 2017)

The apathy of teachers and administrators at Sana's high school exacerbated her feelings of despair. When she first complained to her school's administrators, they told her to come back when things got worse. She began to keep a detailed record of the bullying she experienced, documenting each incident. She reported these incidents to her guidance office. Although she followed the school's guidelines for reporting bullying, she still received no feedback from the guidance office. Worse, teachers who were present in the hallways while boys shouted abusive insults failed to intervene. She notes,

> There was a teacher every day when this was going on and the boys would sit right in front of the teacher and they would call out names. And the teacher never did anything. I heard from a lot of the administrators that it was noisy [and] perhaps they [the teachers] didn't hear. I would like to believe that they really didn't hear it, but when someone is shouting abuse literally right in front of you, it's really hard to believe [they didn't hear]. Maybe they were just afraid to intervene. I really don't know why no one said anything. It is really difficult to be a freshman in high school and feel like there is no one who will stand up for you. It became really tough for me as a student to even study or pursue my activities because I was scared …. I felt like no one cared. This was the scariest part for me. When you are a little kid, you really want to believe that you live in a country and a place where these kinds of comments would not be tolerated. To feel like no one really cared to do anything, that was the worst feeling. (S. Khan, personal communication, June 17, 2017)

Sana's ordeal came to an end when a few of her classmates decided to take action to end the daily bullying she experienced. They took initiative by mobilizing students and started an anti-bullying campaign for Sana. They began walking with Sana down the hallway during power period. They contacted the principal about Sana's situation and asked their classmates to do the same. Sana felt grateful for her high school friends who intervened:

> I had no idea that they were putting together this campaign. A lot of my friends, who were walking with me for safety and heard these things directly, started telling others. One girl and boy [whom] I carpooled with started contacting everyone they knew and asked them to email the principal. I even heard that my middle school friends, who attended different high schools, had also contacted the school principal. (S. Khan, personal communication, June 17, 2017)

Sana also related that a teacher from her former middle school, where Sana continued to volunteer, directly intervened in the anti-bullying email campaign. She described, "I told her about it and she was also involved in the process of getting it stopped. I wasn't shy about what was going on" (S. Khan, personal communication, June 17, 2017).

Jennifer Smith, a mother of two and a white Caucasian convert to Islam, also encountered an incident of hatred and sexualization at an elite charter school in Charlotte, NC. Unlike Sana, Jennifer was not a student, but an active parent who frequently volunteers at her children's school.

> I was at the kids' school for Grandparents Day. That is when we invite all the grandparents of the kids from the school to come and experience a day in their grandchildren's school. The kids put on performances and shows. I was in the music room and we were having a book fair. All the grandparents were waiting in line with their grandchildren to buy them books from the book fair. There was a lot of people, about 100 people in a long line out the door. One of the male grandparents was with his wife and approaches me and says, 'Do you have hair under that thing?' I smiled and said, 'Yes I do.' So, he reaches behind me and grabs my scarf and my ponytail and yanks it. And he says, 'Oh yeah, I can feel the ponytail back there.' Then he turns to his wife and says, 'Oh yeah she has hair under there.' He says to me, 'Why don't you just take it off,' and motions with his hands, pointing up and down my body, 'Why don't you take it all off?' (J. Smith, personal communication, May 7, 2018)

Jennifer's experience points to how donning a visual signifier of her Muslimness has subjected her to a form of racialization. Despite being a member of the majority race, she is verbally and physically harassed for her perceived "Otherness," manifested through the *hijab.* Furthermore, she is treated as a sexual object because of perceptions surrounding the Muslim female subject.

"GO BACK HOME": MUSLIMS PERCEIVED AS FOREIGNERS

Islamophobia is fueled by perpetuating the myth that Islam is antithetical to American values and, by correlation, that Muslims in America are not *fully* American or do not belong in this country. A fourth dominant theme experienced by most of the Muslim female interviewees was being told that they were not American or needed to "go back home." Even when born and raised in this country, Muslim American women told us of one encounter after another in which their peers – fellow American citizens – questioned their identity or undermined their Americanness.

One of the most poignant examples comes from Maryam, a 26-year-old Muslim female activist. During the 2016 presidential election, the young activist decided to work at the polls as an act of civic service to her community in a small town in Pennsylvania. Yet her presence at the polling station while wearing both the *hijab* and *niqab* provoked much animosity. A number of people who came up to her polling station to receive their ballots asked if someone else could help them instead of her. One man wearing a red baseball cap with the "Make America Great Again" logo, approached her and said, "Do you know why I am coming out to vote? To make sure people like you don't exist in my world" (M. Najeeb, personal communication, May 16, 2018).

Ironically, while performing a civic duty by volunteering at the polling station, Maryam's American identity was repeatedly questioned. One of the most surprising instances came from a local elected official, who interrogated her "origins," as Maryam elaborated:

> At some point, I even had a local elected official come and say 'where are you from? I haven't seen you before.' I replied, 'I've been (living) here for a few years.' She asked, 'Where did you come from before that?' I told her, 'I moved here from Florida.' She said, 'Well, where are you *really* from?' I said, 'I'm from Virginia.' I guess I was trying to be obnoxious. She was like, 'OK, where is your family from?' Then I said, 'My family is originally from Palestine.' When she asked, 'What are you?' and I said, 'I'm American,' she couldn't take that as an answer. She was like, 'Well where are you *really* from?' I don't know why 'I'm from here' isn't enough. (M. Najeeb, personal communication, May 16, 2018)

Muslim Americans do not have to imagine what it would be like to be treated as foreigners in their own county, to never really belong, to be pushed to the periphery of American culture. They live that reality. Americans' collective perception of the Muslim in America is not that of the cardiologist in Panama City, Florida, working tirelessly to aid the lives of thousands of patients that have visited him in the past 33 years. The public perception of the American Muslim is not that of the Olympian fencer, Ibtihaj Muhammad, winning a bronze medal for the U.S. fencing team in the 2016 Summer Olympics. Nor is it of the world heavyweight boxing champion, Muhammad Ali, or dozens of NFL and NBA Muslim athletes who've shaped their respective sports. Rather, common impressions of the American Muslim have been shaped by Hollywood movies showing Arab fanatics hijacking planes, documentaries about female honor killings, and ideological, hate-laden books that portray Muslim Americans as *American Jihad: The Terrorists Living Among Us* (Emerson, 2002).

The perception of Muslim Americans as foreigners *and* a dangerous menace, a theme perpetuated by our current President, has emboldened assailants and provided justification for their attacks on Muslim women. Maryam experienced the frightening manifestation of this mindset when a man pulled out a gun and threatened to shoot her and her two-year-old son. Walking out of a Marshalls in Allentown, Pennsylvania, Maryam was carrying her toddler when a black truck decorated with confederate flags stopped in front of her.

> The man pulls out a gun and he tells me, 'I have a gun and I'm not afraid to use it.' I'm just like, 'I have a baby that I'm trying to put safely in a car seat.' He just started yelling 'Go back to your country. You are a bunch of terrorists!' I tried to remain calm and just put my child in the car seat so I could get out of there. I then called 911 and told them I have a car blocking me from the back and I have a car parked in front of me. I showed him that I was on the phone with the cops. This was before Trump was president, when he was still running for presidency. (M. Najeeb, personal communication, May 16, 2018)

The verbal assaults hurled by the truck driver who carried a gun reflects the dangerous outcome of conflating Muslims with terrorism and perceiving them as 'immigrants' who do not belong. Similar to Fatima's story above, Maryam's experience reflects how the Othering of Muslim women has contributed to a rise in assaults against them, specifically when they can be identified as Muslim due to their choice of dress.

CONCLUSION

Previous American presidents, both Republicans and Democrats, made clear distinctions between Islam as a faith of 1.8 billion people and the violent minority who waged war against the U.S. In contrast, President Trump and his aides have capitalized on oft-repeated themes that perpetuate a sense of Otherness in the public discourse on Muslim Americans. Most significantly, Trump has carefully played on existing fears of an imminent terror threat against America by portraying law-abiding Muslim Americans as a fifth column, an unpatriotic minority whose presence poses an imminent threat to the security of their own country. By encouraging Americans to view fellow Muslim citizens through the lens of violent and extremist events that do not speak to the reality of Muslim Americans, the administration's rhetoric perpetuates the heightened sense of Otherness that has been cast on the Muslim American community.

Dalia Mogahed, who served on President Obama's Faith-Based Council, argued that the new presidency signals a critical shift in political rhetoric and policy on Islam and Muslims. As she described,

> You had this seismic shift in the way that we imagined our country, from being a place that has always had Islam as a part of its story … to one that had a very different definition of what it means to be American, a definition based on creed and culture, rather than a set of principles that we all agree on. It is a very interesting change and I think the root of it is really the definition of what it means to be an American. It is not a coincidence that Trump started the birther conspiracy theory against Obama …. It underpins his [Trump's] whole narrative: … To be a real American is to be a white Protestant. And everyone else is here as guests, as tolerated guests, some more tolerated than others. But the real stakeholders, the ones who really own this country is this one group. It's a very dangerous ethnic nationalism that some would just call white supremacy. (D. Mogahed, personal communication, May 14, 2018)

The impact of American policymakers' political rhetoric on Islam and Muslims has fallen primarily on women who 'appear Muslim' due to their choice of dress. Participants in this study consistently described a process of racialization through Muslim female visual signifiers. As such, the intersectionality of their race, or perceived race, and gender is fundamental in understanding their lived experiences. The stories they shared paint a disturbing image of American citizens being harassed, threatened and verbally assaulted by other citizens who do not identify them as belonging to the American collective. The narratives they shared point to four dominant themes: (1) the vulgar sexualization of Muslim women; (2), the correlation between their experiences and the political climate of fear ushered in by Trump's electoral campaign and presidency; (3) the presence of apathetic bystanders, law enforcement officials or school administrators, who failed to intervene to stop bullying or abuse; (4) the common perception that Muslims are not American, a theme amplified by our current president, who has repeatedly mentioned falsities that enforce this view, such as the myth that Muslims in New Jersey celebrated on the day of 9/11, when America was attacked on its own soil (Medium.com, 2018).

The perception of Muslims as violent, dangerous and foreign clearly motivates much of the harassment and assault that Muslim women encounter as American citizens and residents. Through personal narratives of Muslim American women, this chapter demonstrates that the notion of Muslims as foreigners perpetuates xenophobic tendencies and offers a false sense of justification for hostility towards Muslim women, who are often uniquely targeted due to their visibility. While facing physical or verbal assault, many of the victims with whom we spoke were called "terrorist" or told to "go back home." The historical and empirical reality of Muslims in America, however, defies perceptions of Muslims as un-American.

The history of Islam in America dates to the first enslaved Africans brought to American shores, slaves who built this country through their hard labor, sweat and tears. Up to a third of these slaves brought to America were Muslim (Curtis, 2009). The history of Islam in America continues with Muslim refugees fleeing war-torn countries in the 1990s and onwards, often due to factors related to American foreign policy. In contrast to Trump's political rhetoric, Muslims have been a part of America's tapestry since its very founding, a point that America's earliest presidents upheld with the Constitution's protection of religious freedom – a cornerstone of America's democracy.

NOTES

1. Although President Trump is the 45th president, there have only been 43 presidents before him since Grover Cleveland served as both the 22nd and 24th president in nonconsecutive elections.
2. To protect the identities of the women we interviewed, pseudonyms have been used throughout the chapter. The same pseudonym was used for each subject throughout the chapter. The IRB Review Committee for New York University Abu Dhabi, where Mubarak served as a research fellow at the time of writing, determined that the subject research protocol is Exempt under Category 2.a. on 29 January 2018. The level of risk was determined to be minimal and no continuing review was required.

REFERENCES

Abu-Lughod, L. (2013). *Do Muslim women need saving?* Cambridge, MA: Harvard University Press.

Ahmad, D. (2009). Not yet beyond the veil: Muslim women in American popular literature. *Social Text, 27*(2 99), 105–131.

Bailey, S. P. (2015, September 14). A startling number of Americans still believe President Obama is a Muslim. *The Washington Post: News*. Retrieved from https://www.washingtonpost.com/news/acts-of-faith/wp/2015/09/14/a-startling-number-of-americans-still-believe-president-obama-is-a-muslim/?noredirect=on&utm_term=.5d9 d84d1010e

Bakali, N. (2016). *Islamophobia: Understanding anti-Muslim racism through the lived experiences of Muslim youth.* Rotterdam, The Netherlands: Sense Publishers.

Beckwith, R. T. (2016, June 13). Read Donald Trump's speech on the Orlando shooting. *Times: Politics*. Retrieved from http://time.com/4367120/orlando-shooting-donald-trump-transcript/

Bilge, S. (2012). Mapping Quebecois sexual nationalism in times of 'crisis of reasonable accommodations.' *Journal of Intercultural Studies, 33*(3), 303–318.

Blair, G. (2000). *The Trumps: Three generations that built an empire.* New York, NY: Simon and Schuster.

Bullock, K. (2002). *Rethinking Muslim women and the veil: Challenging historical and modern stereotypes.* Herndon, VA: International Institute of Islamic Thought.

Curtis, E. (2009). *Muslims in America: A short history.* New York, NY: Oxford University Press.

Donald Trump, President of the United States et al. vs. Hawaii et al. (no. 17-965). (2018). Supreme Court of the United States. Retrieved from https://www.supremecourt.gov/oral_arguments/argument_transcripts/2017/17-965_3314.pdf

Emerson, S. (2002). *American jihad: The terrorists living among us*. New York, NY: Free Press.

Full transcript: Second 2016 presidential debate. (2016, October 10). Retrieved from https://www.politico.com/story/2016/10/2016-presidential-debate-transcript-229519

Gates Jr., H. L. (n.d.). How many slaves landed in the U.S.? *PBS.* Retrieved from https://www.pbs.org/wnet/african-americans-many-rivers-to-cross/history/how-many-slaves-landed-in-the-us/

Henley, N., & Pincus, F. (1978). Interrelationship of sexist, racist, and antihomosexual attitudes. *Psychological Reports, 42*, 83–90.

Johnson, J. (2015, November 16). Donald Trump would 'strongly consider' closing some mosques in the United States. *The Washington Post: Politics*. Retrieved from https://www.washingtonpost.com/news/post-politics/wp/2015/11/16/donald-trump-would-strongly-consider-closing-some-mosques-in-the-united-states/?utm_term=.c584a3a387d6

Krieg, G. (2017, November 30). Trump's history of anti-Muslim rhetoric hits dangerous new low. *CNN: Politics*. Retrieved from https://www.cnn.com/2017/11/29/politics/donald-trump-muslim-attacks/index.html

Kumar, D. (2012). *Islamophobia and the politics of empire: The cultural logic of empire.* Chicago, IL: Haymarket Books.

Medium.com. (2018, April 19). 86 Times Donald Trump Displayed or Promoted Islamophobia. Retrieved from https://medium.com/nilc/86-times-donald-trump-displayed-or-promoted-islamophobia-49e67584ac1

Milbank, D. (2018, June 1). The fight against Trump is a battle for freedom. *The Sacramento Bee: Opinion.* Retrieved from https://www. sacbee.com/opinion/op-ed/article212379749.html

Mogahed, D. & Chouhoud, Y. (2018). *American Muslim poll 2018: Pride and prejudice.* Washington, DC: Institute for Social Policy and Understanding.

Perry, B. (2014). Gendered Islamophobia: Hate crimes against Muslim women. *Social Identities, 20*(1), 74–89.

Pew Research Center (2017, July 24). U.S. Muslims concerned about their place in society, but continue to believe in the American dream. Retrieved from http://www.pewforum. org/2017/07/26/findings-from-pew-research-centers-2017-survey-of-us-muslims/

Said, E. (1979). *Orientalism.* New York, NY: Vintage.
Sheehi, S. (2011). *Islamophobia: The ideological campaign against Muslims.* Atlanta, GA: Clarity Press.
Sidanius, J. (1993). The interface between racism and sexism. *The Journal of Psychology, 127*(3), 311–322.
Spellberg, D. (2017, May 21). Why Jefferson's vision of American Islam matters today. *The Conversation: Articles*. Retrieved from http://theconversation.com/why-jeffersons-vision-of-american-islam-matters-today-78155
Sullivan, K., & Wan, W. (2016, June 17). Troubled. Quiet. Macho. Angry. The volatile life of the Orlando shooter. *Washington Post: National*. Retrieved from https://www.washingtonpost.com/national/troubled-quiet-macho-angry-the-volatile-life-of-omar-mateen/2016/06/17/15229250-34a6-11e6-8758-d58e76e11b12_story.html?utm_term=.4cb8221f0a05
Taylor, E. (2009). The foundations of critical race theory in education: An introduction. In E. Taylor, D. Gillborn, & G. Ladson-Billings (Eds.), *Foundations of critical race theory in education* (pp. 1–16). New York, NY: Routledge.
Telhami, S. (2015, December 9). What Americans really think about Muslims and Islam. *Brookings Institute: Blog*. Retrieved from https://www.brookings.edu/blog/markaz/2015/12/09/what-americans-really-think-about-muslims-and-islam/
Zine, J. (2006). Unveiled sentiments: Gendered Islamophobia and experiences of veiling among Muslim girls in a Canadian Islamic school. *Equity and Excellence in Education, 39*(3), 239–252.

CHRISTINE SALKIN DAVIS AND JONATHAN L. CRANE

DIALOGUE 6

Jon asks, "are either of you surprised at the degree of divisiveness? You all clearly pay a lot of attention to politics. Did the division at the time of the election and since then, did that surprise you?"

Andrea laughs, "It was there before. The divisiveness was there prior to this election."

"Oh, absolutely," Larry says, "You can go back several elections, I think it's been growing.

Andrea says, "There's no way to make everybody happy. There's going to be some group that's going to have an issue with something no matter what. Before, with the prior administration, it was with gay rights, where gay couples can become legally married. And now I feel like since there's a different administration, maybe they feel more threatened that some rights are going to be taken away. And the only reason I bring that up, I have a relative who is in a gay marriage, but I know he and his friends are very much against Trump. So I could be more aware of that divisiveness. In the Obama administration, I felt like they felt heard, listened to, there was more of an inclusion. And now I feel like there is more of a division with that particular group. But, I don't recall Trump ever saying anything about gay rights, period. I feel that history was made in the last administration. We had a first Black president, it gave hope to our African-American population and now they feel like the steps forward that they took in that last administration is now with the whole 'Make America Great Again.' I don't know if they feel like there's not as much focus on minority, that they're starting to feel like we're taking two steps back. But I don't think that it has."

"To me the divisiveness always been there, with the 24-hour news cycle," says Larry. "With social media, it's fueled the fire. Like, people are commenting on social media about tax things. And I'm like, no, this really didn't happen. You've got to understand the whole picture. So I think the divisiveness seems to be more now than it used to be because it's …"

"… in our face all the time," says Andrea.

DOI:10.1163/9789004436329_012

“In our face 24/7,” says Larry. “And people are more fueled up because they’re getting everybody’s opinions every day, all day.”

“And,” Andrea says, “I think the media adds fuel to the fire and stirs the pot a lot of times. However, they put a spin on it so the story will go over better. I think that media is the majority of our problem in the divisiveness because I feel like as a community as a whole we have improved leaps and bounds from when my parents were in school and there was still segregation. And there’s more opportunity now than there was then. So, we can’t say that we have not moved forward. Do we still need improvement? Yes, but I honestly feel we would be closer, if it wasn’t for media, because I think that we have learned as a population. Even in the workplace, around diversity, race, gender, sexual orientation, all of it. There’s been so much more of a focus in so many more outlets. People are going to have a particular perception and it’s easy to look at things through this same lens. Perception versus intent, someone’s intent may not be to make me feel a certain way, but if I’m am looking at it through a lens of having been discriminated against, I might view it a certain way. So, I think for some people’s experience, they’re going to go through life a little bit jaded. When that may not be the person’s intent at all. So, where, how can we break that cycle? If you always go through life thinking that you are treated differently because you’re a woman. Because you were treated differently because of your race. Because I grew up in a lower income neighborhood. If you are overweight. Those things you experienced in life, if you can’t get out of that, if you felt like you were treated differently for a certain reason, you always look at things that way. It’s very easy to perceive things that aren’t intended.”

JILLIAN A. TULLIS

5. NECESSITY, UNCERTAINTY, AND THE ACA

Health Insurance Coverage in the Age of Trump

Seventy. More than 70 times the United States Congress attempted to repeal or undermine President Barack Obama's signature legislative achievement (Riotta, 2017). The 44th President of the United States signed the Patient Protection and Affordable Care Act into law in 2010 making it the first significant healthcare legislation in the United States since the creation of Medicare and Medicaid in the 1960s ("CMS' Program History," 2018; "Summary of the Affordable Care Act," 2013). This new law, frequently referred to as the ACA, included several provisions designed to make health insurance and subsequent care more accessible and affordable. A central component was the creation of a health insurance marketplace, a clearinghouse where individuals could shop and sign up for health insurance coverage. The ACA also included several provisions, such as subsidies that would help make insurance more affordable, access to birth control and annual well-woman check-ups with no co-pay, and the ability for children to stay on a parent's health insurance until age 26. Individuals with a preexisting health condition could also no longer be denied coverage and annual and lifetime caps on coverage were prohibited (see, "Summary of the Affordable Care Act," 2013, for list of provisions). Despite technical glitches when the insurance marketplace on HealthCare.gov debuted in 2013 (Woodruff, 2013), Americans were successfully enrolling each year and the number of uninsured decreased from 44 million in 2013 to 28 million by the end of 2016 ("Key Facts," 2016). Some who had private, employer-based insurance saw premiums increase (Abelson, 2017), yet it seemed as though the major elements of the law were working. The success or popularity of the ACA, however, did not lead to widespread acceptance among Republican lawmakers and voters.

Repeal and Replace. This clever alliteration became a popular refrain of Republican lawmakers and candidates for office, including then presidential candidate, Donald Trump. Over the course of about seven years, the

 | DOI:10.1163/9789004436329_013

Republicans attempted and failed to repeal the law an average of ten times a year (Riotta, 2017). Shortly after taking office in January 2017, Trump and the Republican-led House and Senate, now had the legislative and executive branch control needed to revoke the law as promised once and for all. In July 2017, however, Republican Senator John McCain stood with two of his party colleagues, Senators Susan Collins and Lisa Murkowski, to cast the deciding votes that halted efforts to fully revoke the ACA (Killough, 2017).

While Republicans were unable to repeal or replace the ACA, they did eventually pass legislation to eliminate the individual mandate, which required all Americans to have insurance or a pay a tax penalty. While requiring insurance was unpopular, especially among Republicans and Libertarians who saw this as a threat to individual liberties, it was a necessary component to ensure enough healthy people were covered to help spread risk and costs. This change to the law went into effect in 2019, although at the time of this writing, it is not yet clear how it will influence the cost of insurance premiums or availability of subsidies (Mukherjee, 2017).

Since health insurance is necessary to access and afford most healthcare in the United States, this chapter considers the lived experience of Americans who receive, or at one time, used the health insurance marketplace to secure health insurance. By conducting interviews with beneficiaries of the ACA's marketplace, I learned what effect the 2016 presidential election and the new presidential administration has had on these participants. To understand this experience, I spoke with a dozen women and men across 11 states[1] about what prompted them to use the marketplace, learned about their experiences with the program, and discovered their feelings about the politics of the ACA. I also inquired about the affordability of their insurance and what they wished the general public understood about the ACA. Participants described general anxiety about the fate of the law during the presidential election and overwhelmingly believed that of the two major party candidates, Hillary Rodham Clinton would have been a better option for building up, rather than dismantling the ACA. They also felt the program was far from perfect, yet it was certainly better than having no insurance at all. Interviewees were eager to address misconceptions in the public discourse about the ACA and who benefits from the provisions in the law. Who enrolls in insurance through the healthcare marketplace, and how to talk about this aspect of the law quickly became salient topics during interviews, which is where this chapter begins.

LANGUAGE OF THE ACA

How to talk about the Affordable Care Act, specifically what terms to use, was one of the first revelations during recruitment and upon beginning interviews. The program has many names, too many possibly, including the ACA, the Affordable Care Act, and Obamacare. Yet, none of these terms accurately describes the mechanism millions of individuals use to secure health insurance. The "healthcare marketplace" is a more appropriate term for the site individuals use to secure non-employer-based insurance coverage facilitated by the healthcare law. Once interviews commenced, I understood the individuals I spoke with had general, non-specific knowledge of the ACA. As such, I had to adjust the way I posed questions, asking interviewees to describe their experience enrolling in and using the coverage they signed up for through the marketplace, so as not to confuse their knowledge of law with their experience navigating the program. After I corrected my language it was evident during interviews that beneficiaries of the marketplace recognized the issues the ambiguity of the language created and its consequences.

Nearly all participants noted that how the ACA is talked about in the public sphere created political problems and contributed to stigma. Early on, Republicans were able to use the imprecision of the language to frame the ACA in negative ways. The term 'Obamacare' emerged in an effort to leverage any opposition to the president and deride the initiative. The ACA sounded gentle and vague, Obamacare was an evil epithet, un-American because it was synonymous with government control.

Randy, from North Carolina, described his feelings about the ACA and its name this way, noting how politicians took advantage of the more tarnished term:

> I felt like [Trump] was only doing it [attempting to repeal and replace] because it was Obamacare .... I wish it didn't have the stigma it does and I think many people didn't like it because it had the tag line that it was Obamacare, it could have been Clintoncare or Reagancare, but it had a stigma.

Eventually, once the major provisions in the law were rolled out and people began to sign up, some having insurance and access to healthcare for the first time in years, the program became more popular and Obamacare became celebrated shorthand for access to life-saving insurance. Yet, interviewees felt politicians in particular took advantage of any disdain for President Barack Obama and the public's ignorance of the intricacies of healthcare policy.

Michelle, a 35-year-old academic who lives in Maine, said:

> My mother is ACA-eligible and goes through an insurance agent who just navigates ACA for her. [My mother] doesn't recognize she's on an ACA plan …. People who are massively opposed to the ACA are going through an agent and are not realizing they are on the ACA system.

In addition to general confusion about whether the ACA was the same as Obamacare, Donald Trump called for repeal of the ACA 68 times and consistently used the more loaded term 'Obamacare' (Koronowski, 2017). Interestingly, each claim that he would repeal the ACA was accompanied by the assertion that its replacement would be better and cheaper, yet no details about how this might happen followed. This was not lost on participants. Consider this observation from one participant when asked about the topic of repeal:

> And it's like Trump is saying we're going to repeal Obamacare and they could never agree on a replacement. He's repealing it, but there's no replacement for it, which is almost worse.

Another interviewee said,

> Repeal and replace is good campaign rhetoric, but the reality is a repeal would mean a lack of replacement given the context. So the idea of repeal and replace is a patently false claim, there would be no replacement and everyone who needs ACA is just screwed. 'Screwed' being the most polite term I could use.

Participants felt politicians knowingly contributed to confusion about the program's name, and then used these misunderstandings to advocate for repeal without a new plan. The language, however, was just one element. Other factors contributed to negative public sentiment.

PLENTY OF BLAME TO GO AROUND

Citizens unable to understand there was no difference between the ACA and Obamacare and those who did not understand how the exchange worked, like Michelle's mother, were complicit in allowing opponents of Obamacare to perpetuate ignorance and misconceptions that contributed to a sense of shame for those who needed the healthcare exchange. Lisa, a 33-year-old dancer living in Texas noted, "There is a stigma of not having an employer-based plan. People think you're 'a poor' and can't afford real insurance."

Christine, 51-year-old stay-at-home mom and small business owner observed:

> Part of the frustration to me was just the ignorance. The misconceptions and the misinformation about what it's about. This isn't people getting free health care, this is people like me. I pay plenty for my healthcare. I'm sure I pay as much as anybody, but I don't pay more than my share. I pay my share. And I think that the ignorance that is perpetuated by this administration about what the ACA is and what it means to people is very frustrating to me because ignorance is frustrating. About this whole thing that I really have a hard time with, and I feel like people don't understand it, [is that] certain lawmakers are very attached to the insurance companies and a have financial incentive to spread misinformation. And put their own financial gains ahead of their citizens. But that's maybe getting a little more political than I need to be. It's very very frustrating for me to hear this misinformation spread and perpetuated and to think that it's very much like a lot of things, very much about how the lawmakers benefit individually than it is about actually helping people.

Michelle, who attempted to access insurance through the exchange after her employment was terminated, also made a connection to insurance companies, but described the misconceptions this way, noting the role of the media, not just politicians:

> A lot of my colleagues made really negative comments about the ACA because our personal costs for insurance had skyrocketed. In the news was the linking of anyone who saw their health insurance go up due to the ACA or because of Obamacare, and I think the news narrative that has been out there has perpetuated that and misplaced the blame on Obamacare. When in reality, the blame or responsibility should fall squarely on the shoulders of greedy insurance companies that used this as an opportunity to increase costs under the guise that they would need to accommodate a larger risk pool. And in many cases that was not true, or was only true based on the limitations, because it didn't encourage everyone to get insurance because it wasn't [as] affordable as it should have been. As insurance companies increase their costs overall and simultaneously perpetuate a narrative that it's because of the ACA, the lack of clear understanding of how that works in the broader public is just a massive problem. It disadvantages the population as a whole

and privileges insurance companies and those who work for insurance companies.

People who enrolled in insurance plans through the healthcare marketplace were branded by politicians and the media as taxing the entire insurance system with little attention given to profit-driven insurance companies. While no one I interviewed kept their use of the exchange a secret from family and friends, many recognized they were members of a stigmatized class. Participants wanted to counter misinformation about who accessed the marketplace.

WHO USES THE MARKETPLACE

Employment status was among the misconceptions participants most felt needed to be addressed among politicians, the media, and the public. There were three employment categories among the participants, which I have labeled *transitional* (unemployed and between jobs with employer-based coverage), *retired* (unemployed but waiting to become eligible for Medicare), and *employed*, but without employer-based insurance. The latter group consisted of contract workers, part-time employees, and individuals who own or work for a small business that does not offer insurance. With the exception of one participant, who opted to forego insurance and pay the penalty because it was cheaper than having coverage, all participants felt the risk of being uninsured was too high, whether or not they had a pre-existing medical condition. Only one participant described their insurance as unaffordable. And more than half of the participants had a preexisting medical condition, such as heart disease, diabetes, cancer, and epilepsy, that put them at high-risk for potentially expensive medical care, especially prior to the passage of the ACA.

One of the interviewees, Jason, a 65-year-old retired utility worker from Tennessee who previously had open heart surgery, used the marketplace to secure insurance until he became eligible for Medicare. He noted that if he needed to be hospitalized, insurance was a must or he could face financial collapse. Others had health conditions that required regular medication and durable medical equipment, such as diabetes, sleep apnea, and anxiety. Still others needed preventive care and birth control, all of which would be unattainable without a doctor's prescription and unaffordable without insurance. Overall, participants were not willing to assume the risk of living without insurance coverage and the ACA made accessing insurance through the marketplace possible. And while subsidies helped those who were underemployed afford insurance, it is important to note that nearly all of the participants had some form of income and paid monthly premiums and co-pays just like their peers with employer-based insurance. While four participants were driven to the exchange because they were retiring or unemployed and looking for work, the remaining participants were working at the time they signed up for insurance coverage. Employment status, however, is only part of the equation. Participants described needing to meet an income threshold that created uncertainty.

THE ISSUE OF DOLLARS

A sweet spot of poverty to become and remain eligible for healthcare through the exchange was necessary for participants. Several of them reported having anxiety about making too little to be eligible for the exchange, and worried that if they overestimated their income they would be penalized later. To avoid Medicaid, which was perceived as providing lower quality care, one participant intentionally overestimated her earnings from her small business to qualify for insurance through the marketplace and another had anxiety about not making enough to be eligible:

> How do I put this? Going into tax season I was worried. You can only make so much to qualify for ACA, so one of the questions I asked my tax preparer was, "Will I pay a fine if I make less than what than what I said on my form?" And she said she didn't think there would be a penalty if I didn't make that much. But I know to qualify for ACA, if you didn't make enough, I don't know if it's 10, 11, 12 thousand dollars – I don't know what the amount is – but if I don't make that then I also worry about it. She [the tax preparer] relaxed my fears about the penalty. But I do worry if I'll make enough money this year to qualify for next year. A friend of mine pointed out that if you make $18,000 or less you're considered working poor. I agree and disagree on some level, but right now I'm working part time work and I can't do much more. (Grace, 49, Nebraska)

Aaron from North Carolina, a state that did not expand Medicaid,[2] was hired as a part-time caregiver by his mother who has lupus in an effort to bring his income up so he would be eligible to enroll in a health insurance plan through the marketplace. Another participant, Nadine, a self-employed 62-year-old in Florida, when asked what she would want people to know about the health insurance marketplace, said:

> I would want people to understand that you have to have an income, [and you have to make a minimum of $12,000]. So I think people need to know that from both angles – that you can't sit around and do nothing – but it seems kind of silly that you are required to make that to get any kind of coverage.

Participants opted to use the healthcare marketplace because insurance was finally accessible – the subsidies and tax credits they received through the ACA made affording insurance possible. Participants shared:

> At the time, I was paying as much as my husband and my son combined for less coverage because I have a preexisting condition. So I sought out the Affordable Care Act as a way to no longer be burdened by my preexisting condition.

> I have epilepsy and my seizures have been controlled for many years, I guess I was considered a risk, and I lost my drug coverage. I spent four years finding medication that worked for me. I have night seizures, so my seizure disorder doesn't cause a danger to others and I'm a low risk patient. I was suddenly unable to get my medication. Seven-hundred dollars a month for my medication. It (the ACA) really was life changing. It's an imperfect system, everything is, but it's far superior to what I had before. It is affordable because we don't pay for my pre-existing condition and we are self-employed and get the tax credit. I don't know if everyone gets the tax credit at the end of the year. It makes a big difference for us. I would be very sad to see it go, if it does.

While accessing a plan was relatively easy, the site was simple to navigate, and the cost was generally affordable, there were other facets of the law, such as income minimums and lack of state-to-state portability, that made the experience of securing and maintaining insurance complicated and nerve-racking. Those who access their insurance through the ACA marketplace are not getting a free ride, despite what some, including politicians, might assert. Gretchen, an interviewee from the Pacific Northwest with Type-I Diabetes highlights this issue of the cost of care and pushed back on the notion that ACA beneficiaries are a drain on the system:

> I did not struggle with what pharmacy I could use, I mean it was like accepted everywhere, that type of thing. I did struggle with the brand names, I have an actual localized skin reaction to a certain medication and I needed a different, apparently more expensive type of medication,

> and the insurance didn't want to cover that, and then they were going to charge me pretty much cash price for it. I did have to have my doctor issue a statement that this wasn't a choice, that it was literally an allergy to the one brand. It took a long time, it took probably four months, and I was actually using samples from my doctor's office to just get the exchange [sic] to accept the medication that I needed so, at the time, I was very unsatisfied, but once they covered it, they covered it at 100% .... My, what they call DME or Durable Medical Equipment, it's my insulin pump supplies, like the tubing and stuff like that, was not covered, they only covered 20%, and so that was literally a thousand-something dollars per month is what I had to pay. And you know that's a lot of money .... There's nothing you can do, [$1500 a month DME needs] I have to have insulin. I have to do this to survive. So you just have to find the best way to do it.

Access to healthcare, whether preventative, for the management of chronic illness, or in response to an emergency, requires health insurance. Few could afford care without it. Consider Lois, who described the ACA as a "life saver." At the age of 55 she was laid off from her corporate job after more than 25 years of service. "I figured my next hope [for insurance] at 55 was Medicare at 65." The passage of the ACA just a few years after being laid off meant she had access to insurance again. She continued, "I had a high deductible, but I could at least afford the premiums. [For] anyone pushing 60, [lack of insurance] can destroy you. And even if you don't have an illness there are other things that can happen to you at any age really." Health insurance is not optional, but a necessity, and this made the outcome of 2016 election more fraught.

POST-ELECTION ANXIETY

Not having health insurance in the United States is risky, as Lois noted, and ACA provided a welcome solution. Yet, the prospect of repeal created uncertainty. The election of Donald Trump in 2016 ratcheted up the stress and anxiety experienced by all but three of the participants. Of the three, one participant admitted to having no knowledge or interest in politics, including the future of healthcare, and therefore, did not experience any adverse effects because of the election. A second participant was of the opinion that Congress mattered more than the president when it came to repeal, and was not worried about the outcome of the presidential election. And a third participant, a healthcare practitioner in Wisconsin, who was diagnosed with cancer after enrolling in an insurance plan through the marketplace, offered a more nuanced perspective, and opined that repealing the ACA was too politically risky to be viable. He felt eliminating one of the widely popular provisions of the healthcare law, prohibiting health insurers from denying coverage to people with preexisting conditions, would amount to political suicide for many legislators. For most participants, however, a new Republican president and a GOP majority Congress was a tremendous source of anxiety and felt like an existential threat. Lois said, "I finally had coverage but then they [the GOP] started talking about plans to repeal. I couldn't believe how uncaring they were about such a huge number of people."

One participant had this to say about the outcome of the 2016 presidential election:

> I found out I lost my job the day after the election. It was the 5th or 6th worst day of my life. I booked a bunch of doctor appointments. Stockpiled prescriptions. I had an IUD inserted. I had a medical procedure I would not have had [if I knew I would continue to have insurance]. You end up making medical decisions you might not otherwise make [because of fear of repeal].

Another participant said, "I had anxiety on election night. [I thought] it's going to get worse before it gets better. I was worried about women's health and it worries and upsets me for others since I am healthy."

Nadine, a 62-year-old self-employed woman in Florida, said this about Trump:

> When he was first elected and he first started talking about creating his own program and getting rid of this one I was really living in fear. Like, I was speaking daily to friends and then I finally thought how long it would take him to [repeal the ACA], and that he would have some opposition and that it wouldn't be something he could easily do. So, I went ahead and signed myself up for the [insurance] next year and decided not to let that be in the forefront of my mind. At first, I thought about it daily and I dealt with a lot of anxiety about it because I'm 62. And you know, I could come off and say, 'screw it I'm not gonna have insurance' but that's really not funny at age 62. It's not funny at any age, but you know I couldn't even imagine with the friends I have with significant health issues who are younger than I am, I can't even imagine what they are doing.

Lois and Nadine both noted the adverse risk, stress, and anxiety of being without insurance as an older adult, sentiments only made more intense when GOP policymakers pushed for a repeal, as when President Trump called for the demise of the program:

> Let Obamacare fail; it'll be a lot easier .... And I think we're probably in that position where we'll just let Obamacare fail. We're not going to own it. I'm not going to own it. I can tell you the Republicans are not going to own it. We'll let Obamacare fail, and then the Democrats are going to come to us and they're going to say, 'How do we fix it? How do we fix it?' Or, 'How do we come up with a new plan? (Pramuk, 2017, paras. 1–2)

This call and others like it felt like a direct threat to the well-being of the ACA. Aaron, a decade younger than Lois and Nadine, experienced a long hospital stay. Although he never received an explicit diagnosis, his symptoms were eventually controlled, and he was able to afford all of the tests, treatments and hospitalization because of his ACA health insurance. Also able to get two surgeries for carpal tunnel under his marketplace insurance, he said:

> As someone who has felt his life has depended on this, at times it felt very much like a personal attack, and almost a threat on my life. When someone says, 'I want to take away your ability to have healthcare,' that feels like a threat on my life. It's hard not to sound hyperbolic, but at the same time that's how it feels. It really feels like someone is saying, 'I want you to suffer and die.' Just to put it as bluntly as possible. That's how it feels.

He continued to talk about the anxiety he felt because of the threats to repeal the ACA:

> They certainly aren't lowering my blood pressure and I certainly don't sleep better than I used to. I get less sleep and I am more stressed out than I used to be. My baseline, not like I've ever been the easy-going poster child, I haven't felt this level of anxiety before. And that seems to be, that is a real thing now. When you combine less healthy living with less ability to have healthcare, it feels like somebody wants me to die. I feel bad saying that because it sounds like I'm just being melodramatic … I don't think these people personally know I exist, but I do and I'm living this and it feels like I'm under attack. You take away my joy and

> my rest and add stress and pain and tell me you don't want me to have healthcare, and this is where they start piling on.

Aaron also noted that Trump's reform efforts at other agencies parallel his efforts to blow up the ACA:

> We have an EPA (Environmental Protection Agency) that wants to undo regulations on clean air and water, they want to take away fundamental protections. There is an Education Department that wants stupid people, that wants to not teach. There is a Housing Department that wants to put people on the street. All of it. They want to make sure that we are existing in the least healthful world with no way to address that. No tools. Yes. Again, I know on the one hand I'm putting all of these things together as if I'm describing some evil conspiracy and not to say that is true, but that's how it feels. And I can't deny what it feels like as part of my experience. If someone were to write this as fiction these are the parts that would go into the story.

The threats to repeal the ACA combined with Trump's attacks on the program during the campaign and after the election, left many interviewees with the impression that their health and wellbeing mattered less than those who had employer-based insurance, and less than those privileged enough to afford treatment and medication without subsidies. Participants were ultimately grateful for the program and saw it as a positive step towards a single-payer system or Medicare for All. Nadine noted:

> I would say, to be honest, I'm really grateful it's there. Picture me: my company is closing, I'm paying $650 a month [for insurance through my employer]. I don't know what I would have done without it [the ACA], I would have had no insurance. So yeah, I'm grateful it's there, I'm grateful it's an option …. I think it's a valuable thing. I think it could have been better. But shit, we didn't have anything before, so I think the fact Obama passed something that was greater than any other option we've had. And hopefully some day we get a really enlightened political system that shifts us over to where we should be before I'm gone [laughs]. Well you know, I'm a very hopeful person.

CLOSING REFLECTIONS

All participants acknowledged the system was imperfect, but the ACA was a step in the right direction towards improving access to healthcare and improving the overall health of the country's citizens. The threat of eliminating the ACA was a major concern, but so were the ways in which participants perceived politicians and the press as contributing to misinformation campaigns that perpetuated ignorance about who benefited from the ACA and how the program worked. The people I spoke with were hopeful that our national sense of humanity will succeed and we will eventually provide healthcare for all. Most were buoyed by the prospect that if enough stories about people's real experiences with the ACA enter the public sphere, the wisdom of access to healthcare would take hold. This was especially important even though the threat of repeal had subsided. As Aaron observed, just because the ACA is not appearing in the headlines much anymore does not mean it is not still a concern:

> The discussion of healthcare and its related costs may have quieted in the immediate news cycle because there's so much wrong every day that people are up in arms about, and I dare say rightly so. It [the ACA] might not be today's top headline, but it still is a topic in my household. It is still a daily issue for me and for my parents and for my partner. It remains a daily concern as my father has cancer, my mother has lupus, you know? There are discussions of the cost of healthcare that have not gone away because there are refugee children in cages, there are just more topics to discuss. Just because they are not covered on the news; they are absolutely day-to-day household conversations.

Regular talk and attention about healthcare and the ACA remain necessary to change perceptions. Christine ended her interview with optimism about this goal:

> I've kind of come to a point where I just have to surrender part of my anxiety and just hope, at this point, that the people will prevail, and hope that good common sense will prevail. I saw that in that vote that evening when those three lawmakers [Collins, Murkowski, & McCain] stood up and said 'no.' That was a big relief that delayed some of my anxiety and fears, but I just I feel like there is so much to be anxious about that it's just a constant state of crisis. [And the day of the vote, I saw] those people sitting in the Capitol Building saying, 'I will die if you take this away from me, I will die and you're okay with that.' … And I don't know how any decent human can look at those people and vote against them. I just have to hope that decency takes hold.

The Affordable Care Act not only gave uninsured people access to health insurance, but it provided the participants in this study with a sense of security. They could access physicians to diagnose and treat their illnesses. They could afford their medications. Yet, the peace they felt knowing healthcare was within reach did not last. Calls to repeal and replace emerged and persisted through the 2016 presidential election. Since failing to rescind the ACA in 2017, Donald Trump has been relatively silent on the law. Other than ending the individual mandate, he and other GOP Members of Congress appear to have halted any efforts towards out-and-out repeal. Several of the participants did feel as though they could take a deep breath and relax again. Yet, despite the absence of a direct attack, opponents of the law did little to promote the program and drastically reduced the budget for navigators who help enroll individuals in marketplace insurance (Galewitz, 2018). With two weeks left to sign up, early reports indicated enrollment for 2019 benefits were down in several states including Maine, New Hampshire, North Carolina, Ohio, and Wisconsin (Galewitz, 2018). So, while Trump and the GOP have apparently placed their focus elsewhere, these two actions could eventually serve their ultimate purpose, to decimate the law, to "let Obamacare fail" by undermining all of its key provisions (Mukherjee, 2017).

The ACA has remained on the minds of those who have most to lose; people who are underinsured, or chronically ill, or those who recognize that health is not a static state, but a dynamic one. Assuming the changes to the law result in minimal disruption to the ACA and the insurance marketplace, there is a reason for hope. The mid-term elections in 2018 perhaps signal that a change is on the horizon.

NOTES

1 California, Washington, Wisconsin, Nebraska, Texas, North Carolina, Florida, Tennessee, Pennsylvania, Maine.

2 Several GOP controlled states refused to expand Medicaid, which would have allowed more low-income access to health insurance. This created a gap where thousands of people were not poor enough for Medicaid, not old enough for Medicare, and yet did not make enough income to quality for insurance through the marketplace.

REFERENCES

Abelson, R. (2017, September 19). While premiums soar under Obamacare, costs of employer-based plans are stable. *The New York Times*. Retrieved from https://www.nytimes.com/2017/09/19/health/health-insurance-premiums-employer.html

CMS' program history. (2018, June 20). Centers for Medicare & Medicaid Services. Retrieved from https://www.cms.gov/About-CMS/Agency-information/History/

Galewitz, P. (2018, November 30). Short on federal funding, Obamacare enrollment navigators switch tactics. *Daily Harold*. Retrieved from https://www. dailyherald.com/article/20181130/business/311309954

Key facts about the uninsured population. (2016, November 29). Kaiser Family Foundation. Retrieved from https://www.kff.org/uninsured/fact-sheet/key-facts-about-the-uninsured-population/

Killough, A., & Stafford, D. (2017, July 25). John McCain returns to Senate, casts vote to advance health care bill. *CNN*. Retrieved from https://www.cnn.com/2017/07/25/politics/john-mccain-votes/index.html

Koronowski, R. (2017, March 24). 68 times Trump promised to repeal Obamacare. *Think Progress*. Retrieved from https://thinkprogress.org/trump-promised-to-repeal-obamacare-many-times-ab9500dad31e

Mukherjee, S. (2017, December 20). The GOP tax bill repeals Obamacare's individual mandate. Here's what that means for you. *Fortune*. Retrieved from http://fortune.com/2017/12/20/tax-bill-individual-mandate-obamacare/

Pramuk, J. (2017, July 18). Trump: 'We'll just let Obamacare fail.' *CNBC*. Retrieved from https://www.cnbc.com/2017/07/18/trump-well-just-let-obamacare-fail.html

Riotta, C. (2017, July 29). GOP aims to kill Obamacare yet again after failing 70 times. *Newsweek*. Retrieved from https://www.newsweek.com/gop-health-care-bill-repeal-and-replace-70-failed-attempts-643832

Summary of the Affordable Care Act. (2013, April 25). Kaiser Family Foundation. Retrieved from https://www.kff.org/health-reform/fact-sheet/summary-of-the-affordable-care-act/

Woodruff, M. (2013, October 1). The new Obamacare health care exchange site has already crashed. *Business Insider*. Retrieved from https://www.businessinsider.com/obamacare-health-care-exchange-site-has-crashed-2013-10

CHRISTINE SALKIN DAVIS AND JONATHAN L. CRANE

DIALOGUE 7

"So I have to ask," I say. "I know you all are conservative Christians and Trump has said and done some things, he had a lifestyle that some people question how can Christians support him? So, I'll go there. How can Christians support him?"

Larry says, "It almost feels like being a white male Christian in today's society, you're on the defensive. It's like, you're racist, you don't want to help anybody. I'm supposed to be privileged because I'm white, American, Christian male. But to your point, there's a lot of stuff that's out there in the news, social media, there's a lot or people saying, you know, you wanted to attack President Obama, but it's like, how can you attack him as a white, Christian, conservative, how can you attack someone who has had one wife, he had these kids, and no issues going on in life and he was this great person? And I think he was, and I think he is. But yet, how can you support Trump when he's said all these things about females and his multiple marriages and all that. And, so for me, I've always viewed Christianity not standing from judgement. We all fall short of the glory of the Lord. Now, I'm not a person that was taking shots at President Obama, so you can't say I'm two-faced because now I'm not saying anything bad about President Trump. To me, that's not my place to rebuke him. Is there part of him that I don't think is great? Absolutely. But that's for him and his judgment. Now, you hope and you pray that somebody is going to be a certain way, do a certain way and, and do those types of things. So the question is, how can I be a conservative Christian and vote for somebody who has done the things that he's done. To me it goes back to what I said in the beginning and that I kind of separate the two; I was looking at it from a policy standpoint. And so maybe is that one of the reasons I don't wear a MAGA hat, maybe I don't feel he is somebody worthy of me wearing his hat. Maybe, I don't know, but I think it's not my place. I think what you do is you share the gospel, you pray for the person that you know. He is the president, I care about policies and what he's doing."

Andrea says, "I was going to say the same, I don't have a lot to elaborate. The first two things that came to mind was forgiveness, which that kind of

DOI:10.1163/9789004436329_014

goes along with not standing in judgment as well. Because when it comes to politics, when it first came out about the things that were said about females, as being a female should I be offended? Yes, but at the same time, I try to also separate things. Can you still do your job as a president and keep my best interest in mind as an American outside of what you have done? This whole digging up skeletons in people's closets, there's not a person out there that's perfect."

Larry says, "Oh, my gosh. I don't care who you are. If you can dig and some people think some bad choices is like, oh, your life's over if you did something in college 50 years ago."

Andrea says, "So there's that forgiveness factor, you know, we're not perfect. I'm not perfect. Being a Christian does not mean that I'm perfect by any stretch. I do think that another thing from Christianity is love and caring. So, you might ask, if it's about love, then why aren't we loving our neighbor and letting our neighbors come into the country? Okay, that's fine, come here, but be here legally. The wall I don't think is to keep people out, it's to keep people here legally. His intent, I mean, let's face it. The drug and the opioid issue is a big issue. We've got to get a handle on it somehow, be it the border or whatever. There's got to be a way to protect Americans."

"I saw a meme from a gay friend," Andrea continues, "and it said, 'You care about the lives of individuals until they're gay, transgender, Mexican, whatever.' So their perception is, as a Christian you preach this, that you want to protect someone's life, but at the same time you, from my perspective, you don't love us if we are gay, transgender."

"How did you respond to that meme?" I ask.

"I didn't," she laughs.

"Well, respond to me," I say.

Andrea says, "It would kind of be responding as a question. What makes you feel that a transgender, gay, Mexican, isn't loved? Help me understand how you are seeing that you are not loved?"

Larry says, "Or what is the president doing to show you that? What's the President doing to show that he doesn't care about this?"

Andrea says, "Right. Yes. That would be the question."

I nod.

Andrea continues. "Because when it comes to abortion, yes I am a Christian, and I struggle with that in terms of myself. Because it's kind of like, okay, well as a Christian you should be against that. Well, at the same time, I'll just say I'm not against it."

"Mm-hmm," I say.

"I'm definitely against the late term thing. That's another issue. Late-term abortion is just a whole other thing. But first trimester, in terms of the woman being able to make the decision to do that, I'm not saying that I'm for it, but I'm not saying you absolutely can't have one either," Andrea says, "You know, there's situations that arise where I feel like that decision should be that individual's, period. It is you. It is your body. Again, that is between you and God. You'll have to answer for that later, one way or the other. And just that, that is your decision. That is your decision, you'll have to live with it. I'm not going to judge you for it. That's your decision. That, that is personally how I feel. As a Christian should I feel that way? I don't guess I should, but," she laughs. "I mean, if you were to listen to the public, as a Christian, you should be against abortion. When it comes to gay rights, people bring up all the time the verses from the Bible. At the same time, love, it also preaches love. You can love whoever it is you love, I am not here to tell you who you can love, period. I guess because to me it's all about forgiveness and love."

"Right."

Andrea says, "So, how can a Christian support him. I think, there's not a person that's perfect so I don't think there's any President that would be in office that a Christian wouldn't have an issue with, from a Christian perspective."

"Oh, okay," I say.

"Yeah," Larry agrees.

Andrea says, "I mean, from a Christian perspective, there's not anybody that would hold any office …"

Larry jumps in, "that might not have done something that a Christian wouldn't say that's not a good thing."

"So, therefore, that's where you have to be able to forgive. Forgiveness doesn't necessarily mean not recognizing the fact that they did something wrong or that wasn't acceptable," Andrea says.

"Right," I say.

"But it's recognizing the fact that they're not perfect so why should I expect them not to do a certain thing? I mean, I just try to, I guess, it goes back to the whole publicity thing, I just would hope that they would make the best decision from what …"

"Okay," I say.

Andrea says, "I would just have to sum it up with forgiveness and love, period. How can a Christian support him? Just as I would anybody else, with forgiveness and love and there's lots of it in our heart."

ANA X. DE LA SERNA

6. RESILIENCE ISN'T A SINGLE SKILL

International Students Cope with the Trump Rhetoric

INTRODUCTION

In 2017, for the first time in years, the number of incoming international students in the United States dropped (IIE, 2017). Some studies suggest that due to the rhetoric during the election and subsequent immigration policies, a significant number of students changed their views of the United States. This in turn, influenced their decision not to apply to U.S. institutions. However, there are still more than one million international students in the United States. With this in mind, I set out to better understand how international students and their families were experiencing the current political climate, the Trump presidency, and the surfacing xenophobic rhetoric. I interviewed 33 participants from 12 different countries. Those who shared their experiences were either international students or married to one.

During the interview process I was often surprised by participants' narratives. Some international students and their dependents engaged in a meaning-making process that not only excused Trump's behaviour and the work of his administration, but even preferred it to other alternatives. After my first interview where participants agreed with Trump, I thought it might be a mistake; how could any educated person agree with such behaviour? After a couple more interviews, I began to realize that my participants made sense of the political climate in the U.S. by using diverse coping mechanisms.

Some participants coped by thinking that none of what was happening or being said applied to them. In order to build their identities, people needed to differentiate themselves from others. Individuals who are similar create an in-group and those who are different become the out-group (Palfreyman, 2005; Moore & Hampton, 2015). This separation is also known as Othering. Othering is a powerful process; it is a resource that helps us make sense of the world. Othering allowed international students and their dependents to separate themselves from those whom Trump spoke of with pejorative terms.

 | DOI:10.1163/9789004436329_015

I understood that people's worldview did not begin when they arrived in the United States. Individuals were often enculturated in societies that had long traditions of sexism, racism, and xenophobia. Stereotyping and hate speech were not unknown to foreign students. Participants had diverse ways of making sense of the new presidency.

For those temporarily in the United States, who planned to return to their home country once they or their spouse obtained their degree, avoidance was the coping mechanism of choice. "Avoidance is often conflated with fear" (Servatius, 2016, p. 1). The Trump presidency inspired fear. Therefore, not thinking about the possible repercussions at all was preferable to the stress of facing a new and uncertain future. For them, it was better not to know anything about the tense climate. They avoided media and even conversations that might threaten their stay in the U.S.

The disassociation that other participants used to cope was similar to avoidance. However, they recognized that there was a certain danger in the views supported by the new government. They just found it easier to believe that they could not possibly be the target of threats and xenophobic language. They did not actively avoid news or information. Some of them were well up to date with current political events. For them, it was other Latinos, or other Muslims, or other immigrants who definitely needed to worry. Not them.

In contrast, there were some participants who recognized the changes and it reminded them of difficult times in their own countries. The experiences they had gave them a point of comparison. This inspired the feeling that whatever was coming could not be worse than what they had already experienced. Many had gone through hardships in their home countries, having lived through wars, corruption, and totalitarian regimes. Therefore Trump did not seem like such a terrible choice. They accepted the new President and his ideas. In this way, several participants supported the new President. In the end, international students, like anyone else, had cultural baggage that could not be easily shed.

Finally, there were those who allowed themselves to go through the emotions created by these events. They shared their fears and how they impacted their daily life.

The new government did have a direct impact on the lives of everyone in the U.S., including immigrants and sojourners. Some participants felt they were easier targets of discrimination. Others found it difficult to disclose their views and to participate in conversations about politics, given their status as outsiders. Some found that the harsh regulation of dependents (their spouse and their children) made them anxious. Dependents of international students in the U.S. are often not allowed to work or study. For many, this new role represented a great loss of freedom and independence. Although the regulation had been in place for a number of years, new proposals by the government suggested even more limitations for the dependents of visa recipients. Students expressed uncertainty and noted having to be more vigilant of volatile immigration laws and restrictions.

In this chapter I present contrasting sides of the experience of international students and their families in the age of Trump. I want to share the voice of the latest arrivals to join a nation of immigrants.

I AM NOT *THE OTHER*

Othering has been considered a subtle discursive practice enabling behaviours that create discrimination and exclusion by evaluating *others* as essentially inferior (Cohen, Krumer-Nevo, & Avieli, 2017). I was confounded when Othering began to appear in my interviews. It first surfaced as I interviewed Edgar and Lidia, a couple from Colombia who had lived in California for ten years, moved back to their original country and finally returned to the United States. Edgar had obtained a fellowship as a maxillofacial surgeon and Lidia got a job as a theatre nurse at the university hospital. The couple described themselves as conservative Judeo-Christians. They travelled for hours every weekend to another state, in order to attend the church that fit their beliefs. When I asked them about the current political climate, Edgar explained:

> From a global perspective, the election of Donald Trump, or any other President, based on our interpretation of the Bible, the United States is going to decay and it's going to face many challenges. This saddens me but it is going to happen no matter who is in power. This is happening because the United States as a nation has turned its back on the Judeo-Christian principles on which it was founded. If you look at history, Jefferson and all of them were convinced that God was behind everything, but today, people are convinced of the opposite. The nation is straying and the more it does it will only get worse. I am worried about that, but eventually things will get back on track.

Edgar's worldview was largely shaped by his religious beliefs. He and his family belonged to a Judeo-Christian church. He described his religion as something separate from Christianity or Judaism and believed the Bible should be followed as literally as possible. In his worldview, everything was predestined to happen. In this sense, he believed that the Trump presidency was something inevitable. For Edgar and his family, Trump represented the return of religious values to government. With conviction, Edgar spoke of the need to follow Judeo-Christian principles. He did not address the fact that he and his family were immigrants, and as such they were also a target of the rhetoric of hate. Edgar and Lidia avoided the thought that they too belong to the faceless group of those immigrants who Trump said are "bringing drugs. They are bringing crime. They're rapists" (CSPAN, 2015).

For Manuel, a 39-year-old guitar Ph.D. student from Chile, Othering was not related to religion. Although he and his family had been active members of the Adventist Church, his agreement with Trump's view on immigration came from his own struggle to obtain and maintain his legal status in the United States. Manuel believed that if a person enters a country without having the necessary visa, they should be held accountable for their actions. Manuel's wife Paty had a different opinion. She said that undocumented immigrants exist because people have to flee poverty, violence, and suffering. Asylum is not always possible due to the tough regulations of the Department of Homeland Security. On this issue, Paty and Manuel could not find middle ground:

> We do talk about these things, but we disagree on many issues, for example illegal immigrants, we have different opinions about that and it's not that we can't talk about it, but sometimes we have to stop that conversation because I have my point of view and he has his. So, we don't agree.

Othering is not exclusive to Latin-American students; I ran into it again when I interviewed Mahmud and his wife Aaisha. Mahmud was a 39-year-old Iraqi doctoral candidate in agriculture. Mahmud travelled to the United States by himself at first, to attend a required English course before starting his coursework and Aaisha was supposed to join him along with the couple's two children. However, their plans changed dramatically when ISIS occupied Mosul. Aaisha was then forced to flee to the United States.

> So my country depends on USA, so when they were going to vote they were more concerned about who is going to be the president than American people. Because they are the leader of the world. For example, if we come to America, they think we should listen to Trump, when he puts in new rules. Our government, they listen to American government. If they say right, right, if they say left, left. So when we have ISIS, they asked them to help the Iraqi government, or if they

> have problems with Saudi or with Kuwait, or with Qatar, they asked them to help make peace or something like that. When Obama started, they were so happy, they said so many things are going to change but after all this time they are the same. For me, Trump is the same but I think that he is right. I think if I am American, I will do like Trump. Sometimes he is doing wrong things, all people do wrong things, but when he says we are going to stop the Iraqi people from coming to the USA, at first I am angry, but then I think, he says the truth, you know? We have ISIL [Islamic State of Iraq] in that place, we have terror, we have horrible people, and if they come here, crime is going to be more. So he is thinking about his place. So I think that sometimes what Trump says is true.

Aaisha was saddened because she had no possibility of seeing her family any time soon, yet, she and Mahmud supported the proposed travel ban. For the couple, the ban would not allow terrorists and criminals from their country to enter the United States. The travel ban therefore, should be applied to the Others. The reasoning was that when there was use of anti-Muslim rhetoric it only applied to terrorists, not to good, law-abiding immigrants like Mahmud and his family.

IGNORANCE IS BLISS

Avoidance has been recognized as a coping mechanism that results as a reaction to life stressors (Holahan et al., 2005). For international students, attending an academic institution in a foreign country meant increased demands, expectations, and stress (Nelson, Dell'Oliver, Koch, & Buckler, 2001). Avoiding other stressors allowed them to remain focused on their families and academic studies. Jasmine, a 29-year-old doctoral business student from China expressed:

> For us it doesn't matter, I would say, because our goal is to go back. Go home. So I don't keep a watch on these things. Generally when we go out with friends, I try to listen, but generally I don't take part in political discussions.

As much as participants wanted to avoid anything related to politics, they were directly impacted by the Trump presidency. Immigration regulations were constantly changing, therefore not being informed came with risks. Vlora, a 36-year-old accounting graduate student from Albania expressed:

> You know, I try to stay out of things. I have so much work already. I don't have time to be thinking about such things. Will this or that change …. We don't know, so why spend time worrying? I tell my husband he should do the same. Worry about our kids now, if something is to happen, they will let us know.

Natalya, from Russia, accompanied her husband Ivan to the United States when he decided to obtain his Ph.D. in family studies. She tended to feel concern over the escalating tension between her country and the United States. She felt that it would not be wise for her to visit her family in her home country because there is always a possibility that she could be denied re-entry. She said she tended to feel anxious because she did not have anything to do other than care for her teenage daughter and attend church.

> The clock is ticking and I am 45 and I am getting older, and I am on visa status, and I am not allowed to work or study or … I am suitcase! I think I would like to do something else with my life but I don't know how or when, so it's more from my side, so I realize that if my husband could do something about that, he would definitely change …. I like the idea of having my own house, and decorating it, and having small garden, and inviting friends, and just imagining the way I used to live. Right now I am just around the house and I am driving him, and my daughter, so I am taxi driver. Sometimes I will be in negative mood and I would try to [grrr] with him. I realize that it's not just about him, and he would like to change it also, but I guess the Lord is teaching me to be more patient.

For male dependents who came from masculine-centered cultures, the idea of staying at home was especially difficult. They had difficulties adapting to their new non-working identity. In order to better cope with this situation, they needed to find activities that filled their time without feeling like their wife was doing all the work. For them, avoidance of the current discourse about immigrants was an important skill. Ajit, a 31-year-old engineer from India, had been living away from his wife Raiha, who was studying for a graduate degree in biology. The couple's daughter was living with Raiha, but it became increasingly difficult for her to take care of the child and spend time in the lab. Finally, Ajit moved to join them and take care of the young girl. Ajit said he didn't want to know much about the government in the United States because it would make him feel more stressed.

> Just that as a character, as a person I am still the same. Just that I don't work here, so I spend most of the time, or at least the weekdays, I spend

> most of the time in the house. I go for a walk, or a run sometimes … and … yeah, I try to keep myself busy with something, like taking some courses through Coursera or something. I need to keep myself updated so I keep myself updated with something. Why would I need to hear that things are changing here? It is already difficult to be on a visa. I'd rather keep busy.

Whether student or dependent, some participants found avoidance to be a relief from the troubles of their everyday lives as immigrants or sojourners. Acculturation represents a difficult time for most individuals (Berry, 2006). Adding more uncertainty to their acculturation process sparked fear for these participants. Avoidance made the fear go away, at least long enough to get through their stay in the U.S.

I'VE HAD WORSE

The United States attracts students from all over the world, from a wide variety of backgrounds and life-experiences. When students arrived in the host country, they were expected to conform to social norms and take on the role of student. There was rarely any consideration given to the lives the students and their families lived before coming to the U.S. Many international students had lived under dictatorships, in totalitarian regimes, under corrupt governments, and through interminable wars. Their experiences made the Trump administration seem like a much better alternative.

Ivan lived in Russia through the times before Perestroika. When Ivan grew up, there was no freedom of speech and access to Western culture was very limited. His fear of another Communist regime made him think that the Democratic Party would turn the United States into a failing system. This shaped the way he saw the Trump presidency:

> I really like one thing. That he has not been purchased by the money-holders, those with a lot of money cannot purchase him. Every other president was purchased, but he was not. Even though he is awkward, he is doing some bad things, like talking too much, somebody should take his Tweeter [sic], that's a bad thing, I don't like that about him. But, entertainment. But I think he is a good President for the United States. The reason I say that is because if another candidate was elected, the Democratic Party would continue ruling the country, and the country would continue to be slightly less free, and with less freedom for the people. I observed that my previous past experiences living in

> the USSR under the Communist regime, under strict regulations of the government who tells you what you should do, otherwise, bang, during the Stalin time they would kill people. During Brezhnev time, in the 60's, 70's, and 80's, they would imprison people, and after Brezhnev, Chernenko, and then Gorvachev, Gorvachev finally brought Perestroika, a change of political system, and then Yeltsin, the President of Russia turned the country into chaotic everything, chaotic relation politics, but if the Democratic Party would remain in power in the United States, the country would be turning Communist! Because it is for the community. To take the wealth of the rich and redistribute it among the poor, that is what the Communists tried to do, and the government has no business in the pockets of the rich. They cannot take it away. But when people receive free money, they become spoiled, and when they receive it from the government, the government will tell them what to do. I just know. A lot of similarities, I sense it, I feel it, I don't like it. So I like that President Trump was elected, even if he is weird, like a circus every day. I'm sorry, I shouldn't say that. But I think he would do a good job for the country. He is in a stage in life where the money is not an issue for him, where he honestly tries to do the best for the country, to the best of his abilities, as much as he understands it, as much as he is given information and he is given the context in which he makes decisions.

Raul's experience bore some similarity to Ivan's. Raul was a 28-year-old guitarist in his first year of his Master program. He had recently moved from Mexico and was enjoying the new experience. Raul said he was constantly comparing his new context with his home:

> I love to listen to how people talk about things here. They complain about traffic, They should go to Monterrey or Mexico City. Now that's traffic for you. Everyone here is so concerned with the election of Trump. They should see our president! He is so terrible he makes it easy to make jokes about him. It's not even a challenge. Seriously, I think that in Mexico we have our problems and nobody is as scared about having such government. Trump is not that bad if you think about it really.

The comparison of Trump to politicians and presidents in other parts of the world allowed some participants to have a different perspective. They had lived through difficult times under their own governments. For some, like Ivan, the experience had been so harsh that he felt that anything that resembled Communism should be avoided. For others, like Raul, living under a less than competent president was not new. For both Ivan and Raul, the U.S. could be worse off.

WE ARE NOT FREE IN THE LAND OF THE FREE

Of course, not everyone agreed with the new President, his rhetoric, or his policies. Trump's messages about immigrants were harsh throughout the presidential campaign and continued following the election. The anti-immigrant rhetoric rallied individuals and groups who held negative views of diversity and immigration. Discussions of immigration and demographic change became more interconnected with discussions of terrorism and crime (Green, 2016). The phrase "Make America Great Again" resonated with a large number of people and portrayed Americans as victims of a foreign invasion (Polleta & Callahan, 2017). International students were not exempted from the stereotype of the illegal, job-stealing immigrant.

Since the 2016 election, many immigrants had a heightened sense of fear of being in a situation where they and their families could be discriminated against. Alondra is 29 years old and came to the United States as a dependent of her husband Elmer, a graduate student working on his Master's in Engineering. Alondra had been fearful and felt people stare at her and her children when they spoke Spanish:

> Ever since there is a new president, it feels like people are more aware of whether you are Hispanic or not. You feel like anywhere you go you could face a situation where you are discriminated against, and when we think about it, we think well, in my country nobody is going to discriminate me for my race, because we are all the same, so I would prefer to go back and be there. Sometimes I think well, not everyone is the same, and ever since he was elected I haven't had any issues, we'll see.

Students often found it difficult to discuss political topics with their peers and faculty members. Many international students practiced self-censorship for fear of being misunderstood or because they felt they did not have the right to express a negative opinion about a country that was not their own. Yusuf, a 22-year-old student from Turkey, said:

> You can talk to some people, but not everyone .... It depends on who you talk to. There are some people who are just really convinced of their decisions, and they think that their opinions are what's right. You can't really talk to them because you can lose the friendship! But with

> others, if they say, I voted for him because I didn't know who to vote for, then you can say hey, when you voted for him, you are doing all this stuff and so on.

International student's academic endeavors had also been impacted. Although academia has been largely known to support diversity, there were areas that had become more challenging for international students. For those who conduct research that involves direct contact with the public, there was a fear of negative reactions from their participants. Xanic, a 33-year-old Master's student in Sociology from Ecuador, shared a story of the conflict she felt when doing fieldwork following the election:

> I was working on a study about health in rural populations. I had invested a great deal of time and effort in that study because it is a very interesting topic for me, you know? I was working with a professor I admire very much and wanted to do really well in this project. The study design involved gathering data from rural areas through in-depth interviews. Unfortunately the interviews were scheduled to take place right after the presidential election here in the United States. I say unfortunately because with everything that was going on, I felt really scared. I did not want to put myself or anyone else from the team at risk. In the end, I talked to the professor and she and I agreed that it would be better if I did not do the interviews. What if people did not want to talk to me? That could have messed up the data, time, and money spent on that data collection, you know?

The experiences of international students who were already in the United States influenced potential international students from around the world. Many were deterred from coming to study in American institutions. This was a loss for them, but it was also a great loss for United States higher education. International students contribute to diversity of thought and culture. They also contribute in financial and reputational terms. It is not in the best interest of colleges and universities to diminish the number of international students they attract and retain. However, the message from the Trump administration seemed to contradict that.

CONCLUSIONS

The international student community in the United States has had mixed reactions to the discourse of the Trump administration. For some, there were aspects of Trump's policy and rhetoric that mirrored their own beliefs. For others, fear pushed them to avoid any information about the new government as much as possible. Others tried to keep up with the news and any messages that could be relevant for them. There were some who did not avoid the information, but exempted themselves from any negative connotations about undesirable immigrants.

Students and their families made sense of the anti-immigration messages by using coping skills like Othering and avoidance. Othering was helpful for those who believed that the xenophobic discourse is true; it just didn't apply to them personally. In this fashion, Hispanic students convinced themselves that the anti-immigration messages only applied to undocumented immigrants. Muslim students believed that the immigration ban would help keep terrorists out of the country. Anti-LGBT students disregarded the anti-immigration message and concentrated their attention on the homophobic narrative.

In the 2016 election Donald Trump won 28% of the Latino vote (Pew Research Center, 2016). How could this happen after the depiction of Latinos as criminals, rapists, and bad hombres (CSPAN, 2015)? It happened because for many Hispanic Americans the idea of feminism, Muslim immigrants, and LGBT individuals presented a frightening amalgam (Pew Research Center, 2016). Many of the Hispanic Trump voters responded positively to his hatred of undocumented immigrants. Why should undocumented people be allowed to work in the U.S. if they had not gone through the gruelling immigration process? Ironically, many U.S. Latinos saw immigrants as a threat and the way to make sense of it was by Othering.

Another sector of the international student community compared the new presidency to their experiences with authoritarian governments in their home countries. From this perspective, Trump's government and proposed policies did not seem so menacing. Relative freedom from dictatorships, totalitarian regimes, war, and terrorism made international students feel safe in the United States. They expressed feeling comfortable with the restrictions and limitations proposed and enacted by the Trump administration.

For another group of international students and their families, their role as sojourners allowed them to avoid any information that would result in added stress. This group tended to focus on their academic work and other activities in order to avoid the negative rhetoric of the Trump administration. These students made sense of their situation by emphasizing that they were in the United States for a limited amount of time after which they would return to their country. They did not find it productive to concern themselves with American politics.

One last group expressed concern over the current administration. These individuals talked about the challenges of living in the United States under Trump. They talked about the difficulties of maintaining interpersonal relationships while avoiding political talk. They expressed concern over the impact of anti-immigration messages in their community and their visa status.

Even within family units, individuals had different reactions to the ideas expressed by the new President. Each person opted to use certain coping skills to make sense of their new reality.

REFERENCES

Berry, J. W. (2006). Acculturative stress. In L. C. J. Wong (Ed.), *Handbook of multicultural perspectives on stress and coping* (pp. 287–298). Boston, MA: Springer.

Cohen, Y., Krumer-Nevo, M., & Avieli, N. (2017). Bread of shame: Mechanisms of othering in soup kitchens. *Social Problems, 64*(3), 398–413.

CSPAN. (2015, June 15). *Donald Trump presidential campaign announcement* [Video file]. Retrieved from https://www.c-span.org/video/?326473-1/donald-trump-presidential-campaign-announcement

Green, D. (2016). The Trump hypothesis: Testing immigrant populations as a determinant of violent and drug-related crime in the United States. *Social Science Quarterly, 97*(3), 506–524.

Holahan, C. J., Moos, R. H., Holahan, C. K., Brennan, P. L., & Schutte, K. K. (2005). Stress generation, avoidance coping, and depressive symptoms: A 10-year model. *Journal of Consulting and Clinical Psychology, 73*(4), 658.

Institute of International Education (IIE). (2017). *Project Atlas*. Retrieved from https://www.iie.org/Research-and-Insights/Project-Atlas/Explore-Data/Current-Infographics

Moore, P., & Hampton, G. (2015). 'It's a bit of a generalization, but ...': Participant perspectives on intercultural group assessment in higher education. *Assessment and Evaluation in Higher Education, 40*(3), 390–406.

Nelson, N., G., Dell'Oliver, C., Koch, C., & Buckler, R. (2001). Stess, coping, and success among graduate students in clinical psychology. *Psychological Reports, 88*(3), 759–767.

Palfreyman, D. (2005). Teachers of English to Speakers of Other Languages, Inc. (TEOSL). *TEOSL Quarterly, 39*(2), 211–233.

Pew Research Center. (2016). *Hillary Clinton won Latino vote but fell below 2012 support for Obama*. Retrieved from https://www.pewresearch.org/fact-tank/2016/11/29/hillary-clinton-wins-latino-vote-but-falls-below-2012-support-for-obama/

Polleta, F., & Callahan, J. (2017). Deep stories, nostalgia, narratives, and fake news: Storytelling in the Trump era. *American Journal of Cultural Sociology, 5*(3), 392–408.

Servatius, R. J. (2016). Editorial: Avoidance: Basic science to psychopathology. *Frontiers in Behavioural Neuroscience, 10*(15), 1–4. doi:10.3389/fnbeh.2016.00015

DIALOGUE 8

"The economy's great," Larry says. "From a foreign policy standpoint, I think that is going fine. I think if you look at the nationalist approach to trying to put people to work, it's really providing people more opportunity for an American dream. And trying to put a platform in place to be able to make people not reliant on handouts, I hate to use that word, but I think it's trying to make people self-reliant and trying to put forth a policy that says you gotta pull yourself up by the bootstraps."

Elizabeth says, "well, with the economy, I'm happy with the stock market and how my investments are doing. And I'm going to retire in a year so that's important to me. There have been some ups and downs in the stock market, but I feel comfortable with how the economy is going."

Larry continues. "Now, there's jobs, and there are so many opportunities for people that have been created. I'm a business guy, so, it's one of those things you can go, okay, well, I can just go to Mexico if it's going to cost me less to make this product than if I made it in the U.S., and I don't have to deal with unions and all this other stuff. The business guy's going to go, yeah, my bottom line's going to be better. But to have somebody as President who is rich, to shame companies from doing that. You've got to remember, when he was first elected, he met with these companies and said they're now going to invest so much money in our country. So he pushed companies not to move their businesses overseas. In some cases, he actually got stuff done shaming them, that's great, we're going to create jobs. And you know what, I want to get you off welfare, I want to get you off food stamps. I want to put you to work and create opportunities for you. I want you to be able to make your choices via healthcare but I also want to realize there are things that are bad about trying to control pricing in medicine."

"So, I think," Larry continues, "I hate to keep coming back to this nationalist approach, but he's kind of built on that. I think there's been some good things when you look at middle-class, income tax credits. Of course, I always want to know who's going to pay for this, but I think it's to try to keep the economy going, to get people working, you provide some tax credits.

DOI:10.1163/9789004436329_016

You do deregulation to stimulate companies to hire people and invest in their companies and build and keep things going. So he's built a platform for those things to occur. So, you end up feeling better about yourself because you've been able to get out of a place. I think he's trying to really push for that, for people to get to a place where they're getting themselves sustained. And also, we're not going to continue to fight these endless wars, things he said on the State of the Union. We're going to pull out. And in some cases, there's been regulations in place and he's going to undo these policies. So, yeah. I think those are some good things that have happened. We're two years in. Government doesn't move quickly, so from that standpoint, I think we're at a good place. I'd say for him, the economic success is the easiest thing to point to."

Andrea says, "I was going to say the economy is his primary success so far. Through lower unemployment. From the interest rate and the change in the tax bracket, I feel he has given it a little bit of a boost."

Larry says, "He doesn't seem to look at things in Presidential terms; he looks at this as a business. He's running a business. So, obviously, he exacerbates some of the lack of the unifying that goes along. I think he wants it, but I think he doesn't know how to do it."

STACY HOLMAN JONES

7. LIVING AND RELATING QUEERLY IN THE POST-TRUMP WORLD

We wake up early after a restless sleep. It's Election Day in the U.S. and voting is in full swing as the sun rises on the other side of the planet where we live in Melbourne, Australia. Despite the creeping dread of the past few weeks, brought into sharp relief by the re-opening of the FBI investigation into Hillary Clinton's use of a private email server just 11 days before the election, we persist in our belief in a Clinton victory, bolstered by the reports of pundits and pollsters and the surety of friends and chosen (though sadly not birth) family in the States. For more than a year, we've been following the primaries and campaigning via international news reports, livestreaming both conventions, and in conversation with other American expats living in Australia. If we aren't certain, we are optimistic when we go to bed the night before the election, hoping to wake up to good news. Or at least news pointing toward more good news.

We are up before the sun rises, making coffee and debating who will log on to Facebook to see if there are any early signs. Strange how these days the best – and worst – news of the world and sometimes our own lives comes through posts on Facebook. Just a few months ago, my partner learned they'd won a prestigious and competitive grant when a friend posted "congratulations" on their timeline in advance of any 'official' notification. And I cannot forget the afternoon I paused my writing to surf Facebook for a few moments and learned that one of my beloved mentors had died suddenly the day before. I felt the "shock" and "profound disorientation" of his loss alongside the jolt of a new "mode of attention" suddenly snapping into place (Stewart, 2007, p. 2). The heavy residue and force of a distinct 'before' and 'after' hit my body and settled there. Kathleen Stewart (2007) terms these sudden shifts "ordinary affects" – an "animate circuit that conducts force and maps connections, routes, and disjunctures" (p. 3). In the days leading up to the election, her description of the push-pull of public feelings and intimate lives feels prescient:

> Rooted not in fixed conditions of possibility but in the actual lines of potential that a something coming together calls to mind and sets in

DOI:10.1163/9789004436329_017

> motion, [ordinary affects] can be seen as both the pressure points of events or banalities suffered and the trajectories that forces might take if they were to go unchecked. (p. 2)

A few days before, we made our own kind of ordinary affect, or tried to, inviting the American expats we knew over to watch election returns and celebrate a Clinton victory. We'd considered whether it was a good idea to invite people to celebrate a victory we weren't certain about, but decided that we would ride the wave of positive signs and ignore voices of concern, negativity, and naysaying. We pressed send, hoping to open up a circuit that conducts force and maps the connections we desire.

On election morning, our first glance at the news reports confusion and long lines at the polls. Early returns have the race looking closer than we'd hoped. We wonder aloud about the party, and whether it is – still – a good idea. It's early. The polls won't be closing for a few hours, we say. It's not time to worry about the shape things might take. Not yet.

We shower and dress in our white shirts, pausing to take a photo together with our dog Murphy, who immigrated from the U.S. to Australia with me just over a year before. We post our photo with the caption "Wearing White for Hillary" and catch the train to work.

By the time we are out of class and meetings, the polls are closing and results are coming in. The news is not what we imagined or want it to be. We take separate trains and meet at home. We turn on the television, silently watching the map turn red. A cavern opens up in the electoral vote tally. We message our friends in the States – What's going on? Is it as bad as it looks on the news here? What do they think? They say things are close but important states are not yet calling the race: Michigan, Wisconsin, Pennsylvania, Florida are still out. There's still hope. We decide to go to the grocery store and shop for the gathering we are no longer calling a victory party. We enter Woolies, grab two shopping baskets and set out separately with our lists. It's hard to move through the aisles and I find myself staring blankly at boxes of crackers and blocks of cheese, unable to decide. I finally put the last of the items on my list into the basket and look around for my partner. I don't see them anywhere. I walk up and down the aisles, searching until I see them in the bakery, basket on the floor, phone in hand. I approach, and they look at me, tears spilling over lids. I look down at the phone. Florida. Utah. Iowa. Georgia, all called for Trump.

We check out and head home. We send a message to our Melbourne friends, saying come over anyway, to commiserate if not celebrate. Some respond that they'd like to, but they just need to stay in. Some say let's get together some other time, soon. Others say they are coming – now is no time to be alone. When they arrive, we embrace, holding on for longer than usual. We pour wine and sit down in front of the television. We celebrate a Clinton victory in Nevada, no matter how little or how late. After a while, though, the news is so sour on our tongues that we turn off the television. We decide to forego dinner and move cheese platters and wine glasses into the dining room. We sit around the table, four Americans, an Aussie and an Irish-Australian, talking. We ask each other why and how and what now? We cry. We sing and hold hands. We cry some more. And when we say goodbye at the door late in the night, after Hillary has conceded, we embrace again and promise to keep on holding each other.

***

The next morning, I log onto Facebook and read the words of friends and colleagues who say they can't work. Or get out of bed. Or wake up from the bad dream of the "weighted and reeling" present (Stewart, 2007, p. 1).[1]

I think about Stewart's words that "It's been years now since we've been watching" and yet, somehow, we've missed it (2007, p. 9). Missed this, until it "surges into view like a snapped live wire sparking on a cold suburban street" (2007, p. 9). Suddenly the world we thought we were living in and the history and future we believed we were making slips away, is lost. Though was it lost – just then? And if so, to whom? Or what?

Something is lost and people begin feeling, begin asking, just who *are* the people who voted for a present reeling with misogyny, racism, exploitation of workers, disdain for human rights and increased armament and violence? Just who *are* the people who voted for a future weighed down by neoliberalism, isolationism, xenophobia?

Something slips and people begin asking: Who are *we*? How did we fail to sense the gathering potential of hatred and violence? Have we shielded ourselves "from the truth by our own isolated form of left and liberal thinking" (Butler, 2016, n.p.)? Have we "believed in human nature in some naïve ways" (Butler, 2016)?[2]

***

Over the next few days, I trade messages with friends and colleagues, our disbelief giving way to sadness and guilt, anger and fear. I am sad I cannot be *there* to comfort friends and sad that I am *here*, unable to enter a meeting or a classroom and speak without someone asking, "What's going on over there?" "and "How could the U.S. elect someone like Trump?" and "Does he represent what Americans think and feel?" and "Should we be worried"? (McArthur, 2016; Vigeland, 2016). Unable to enter a shop without someone saying, "He won't last long – he will say or do something so outrageous or be charged with treason or criminal conduct and be impeached" or "America can't hide its racism or sexism any longer, now; it's right out in the open" or "He's going to destroy entire populations or the planet or both" (Vigeland, 2016).

I feel guilty about not having done enough to contribute to on-the-ground efforts to ensure Trump's defeat and the fear and violence that will come to at-risk populations including women, people of color, the working poor, LTGTIQ Americans, undocumented migrants and so many others in the wake of the election (Beard, 2016). I feel guilty for not being there, now.

I am angry at people for pointing fingers at the U.S. while ignoring the history of conservativism, hatred and violence of Australia and the global tide of right-wing populism and its reliance on nationalism, white male supremacy, racism and xenophobia, evidenced by Brexit and the swearing-in of Theresa May (and later, Boris Johnson) as Prime Minister, not to mention the long tenure of German Chancellor Angela Merkel and other neo-conservative movements worldwide (Castela, 2017; Seidler, 2018). I am angry that so many of the people I grew up with, including members of my own family, are less informed about what's happening in the U.S. – and the rest of the world – than most of the people I meet and talk with outside the States (McArthur, 2016). Even well-meaning comments – "It'll all be okay" and "You're lucky you escaped and don't have to live here under Trump's rule" – leave me feeling frustrated and impatient (Beard, 2016; McArthur, 2016).

I feel the fear rising in my throat as I think of booking holiday travel to the US for my genderqueer family members, deciding we can't risk an airport scan or immigration interview gone wrong. Not this year. I feel the fear rising up and through the messages I receive from LGBTIQ and POC friends and colleagues (though some straight, cis, and white folks write, too) asking how I like living in Australia and if I know of any jobs they might apply for, so desperate are they to escape with their families and their selves because they know the rollbacks in what little protections and rights they'd achieved in the last few years and decades will come. And they do.

***

Just weeks after the inauguration, Trump and his administration make good on campaign threats and promises, signing executive orders, establishing policies, and issuing directives banning nationals from seven countries (Iran, Iraq, Libya, Somalia, Sudan, Syria and Yemen) from entering the U.S. based on questionable 'public safety threats' (Gopalan, 2018). These orders, policies, and directives also legalize discrimination against LGBTIQ federal employees, creating broad exemptions in federal law that encourages discrimination against women and LGBTIQ persons under the guise of religious liberties, as with, excluding LGBTIQ Americans from documentation in the U.S. Census (Siskind, 2018). They ramp up deportation orders and immigration bans, "peeling away protections from women of color, LGBTIQ people and Muslim and Jewish Americans" (Siskind, 2018, p. 51). The days, weeks, and first year following Trump's election provide a mountain of evidence pointing to how minoritarian peoples are living in a 'massacre culture' and where it might lead us if we do not start paying attention and tune into what's happening while there's still time.

Massacre culture is a state in which any known sense of safety has disappeared, despite the material interventions available to us. The impossibility of safety in massacre culture means that in the post-Trump era many of us feel we are living in a near-constant state of hypervigilance. Indeed, there's news of a 'massacre' nearly every day. For example, in 2017, there were nearly 62,000 incidents of gun violence, including 346 mass shootings, which resulted in 15,635 deaths (Gun Violence Archive, 2018). And while 2016 was proclaimed the deadliest year on record for LGBTIQ persons, with more than 1,000 incidents of hate-related violence, an increase of 17% from the previous year (Dastagir, 2017), that record was obliterated in 2017, which brought an 86% increase in hate violence homicides (Bowden, 2018). And of this writing, the number of trans persons murdered in the U.S. may yet again surpass the previous year's number, with the death toll for 2018 now at 29, as it was in 2017 (Human Rights Campaign, 2018; Winters, 2018). Every year is the 'deadliest year on record' (Human Rights Campaign, 2017; Schmider, 2016). And while some argue that in American 'fear culture,' perceptions of fear outstrip actual risk (Glassner, 2010), there's ample evidence that not only did the Trump campaign rely on and exploit fear (Altman, 2017; Ball, 2016; Green, 2017), but for some populations, the risks are real and increasingly alarming (National Coalition of Anti-Violence Programs, 2018). Such embodied and affective sense of injurability and anxiety can swamp interpersonal and cultural connections, perpetuating massacre culture in even the most mundane ways.

The everyday degradations associated with making minoritarian positions, persons and practices visible in contemporary massacre culture pile up, creating a state of mundane annihilation, in which non-dominant subjects not only *fear* backlash against difference (going far beyond the panopticon metaphor of surveillance), but expect it. We see it all around us, every day. We live non-conforming lives in Lauren Berlant's (2007) sense of the "slow death" of precarity, one in which we are "socialized into the intensification of the ordinary work of living" (p. 761).[3]

***

Facebook status post, November 11, 2018:

This from my 18-year-old niece, in response to my comment expressing 'anger' and 'disappointment' about a repost of an article suggesting that while Trump promised to protect the LGBTIQ community in his convention speech, it was his running mate and party's platform that posed risks for LGBTIQ people[4]:

> My beliefs are none of your concern. And don't bring what I'm going to school for into it either. I'm very passionate about what I do and what I intend to do. Which you wouldn't know about because it's not like you talk to any of us anyway. Don't act like you know me and don't comment on my things. Thank you have a nice day.

Statements of support and 'me too' begin rolling in immediately – reproduced conversations with parents and grandparents, aunts and uncles. Screenshots of messages of celebration that allow, "I see how my close friends and family are afraid and sad. Let's show them that you [sic] on their side! That you hear their fears! I know you're gonna kill it! Praise God!" It doesn't take long, though, for my mother to chime in:

> I am so disappointed in your text to your 19-year-old niece. You seem to believe that your views are the only ones that matter. Well they are not and you have no right to project your views onto your niece. Grow up and mind your own business. Your Mother.

And then my sister:

> Just to be clear, our family has ALWAYS loved and cherished Stacy with our whole hearts with no conditions attached and we always will. For whatever reason, she chose to walk away. She hasn't spoken to me

or my family in years and continues to pass judgement. My parents, who raised us and deserve immense respect get nothing, not even a phone call. This is our side of the story and it deserves to be heard. Please respect that and know that we are hurt and confused. We will always, without a doubt and with unending compassion, love her and her family unconditionally. I only wish she could see and know that to be true.

I sit with these messages for several days. I'm sad and angry, though when I think about it, I'm not surprised. It's the latest in a years-long dialogue of blame and homophobia – my birth family's response to my coming out and my relationships with genderqueer family and friends. I decide that while I might not be able to change their minds and certainly cannot undo the hurt of my words or theirs, it's important to claim the public space of Facebook and address the 'Grow up and mind your own business" and "None of your concern" aspects of their posts. I consider my words carefully and post my own message on the thread:

> Racism, xenophobia, white privilege, classism, anti-intellectualism, and homophobia are my business. They are my concern. I make it my business to call out and comment on and work to change these things professionally. I must do the same personally. Indeed, I have taken up the challenge that the personal is political in my work for 20+ years. I have resisted the reduction of the political to the individual and the private and have tried to demonstrate the relational in even the most personal writing and experience. The fear, pain, grief, invisibility, marginalization and the violence wrought in our lives is my 'business.' Let us be concerned about each other.
>
> And today, as a woman, as a queer person, as someone who counts two beautiful trans people as family and as an ally to friends of color, disabled friends, undocumented friends, friends who dare to cover their heads and observe their religious beliefs in an ever-dangerous world, friends who work themselves to exhaustion without proper healthcare coverage, affordable housing, or enough food to eat, I won't stay quiet. I won't mind my own business. I won't tell people it's going to be all right or to get over it. I won't tell the people who have written me over the past three days about their fear and their wish to be anywhere but the U.S. right now to stay put and fight while I root for them in another

hemisphere. I won't go back to my own privileged life and put my head down and pray and wait for the next four years to be over.

I won't accept the 'we will always love you because you are family' as a response to my objection to homophobic and misogynistic comments at the breakfast, lunch, and dinner table. I won't accept the 'no matter who you love, we accept you' as an answer to my questions about why 'family' suddenly remember that they have other commitments and make excuses so that they won't have to share space with queer and trans people in that same family. I won't make another phone call or board another airplane or have another conversation with 'family' about their unending compassion or unconditional love. I won't accept the presumption that making calls and boarding planes and staying in the conversation or keeping silent or minding my own business is MY financial, emotional and intellectual burden or responsibility. I know my queer friends understand that choice. It's heartbreaking, but it's a choice for survival and self-love. And no, I won't keep silent about my disappointment or my anger about the apologias offered as a diversion to the impending violence promised by the new administration when it appears on my Facebook feed. This is public space. Relational space. A space of accountability.

Thank you, friends and chosen family for your compassion. Your love. Your acknowledgement and recognition of my humanity and my right to live freely and with respect in this world. I return the same.

Friends and chosen family continue to post messages of support and solidarity for several days. My mother, my sister, and my niece do not reply. Later I discover that my niece and sister have unfriended me. And while my mother and I remain 'friends' on Facebook, she doesn't mention the exchange and neither do I, until nearly two years later when my partner and I visit.

My partner raises the exchange and how much it hurt and upset me.

My mother says she felt the same.

My partner asks my mother why she chose to scold me publicly, rather than reach out to me privately.

My mother says she was angry and lashed out.

My partner asks my mother why she was defending a post her niece made that contained information clearly damaging (now that the 'evidence' was in) to and about LGBTIQ people, including her daughter.

My mother says she didn't know she'd done that.

My partner asks her why not – it was right there, in a link to the post.

My mother said she didn't read her niece's post. My mother says my sister had called, saying she was angry and feeling defensive about her daughter. In haste and without finding out for herself, my mother says she logged onto Facebook and made her own post. Without reading any of the others.

My mother says she is sorry she hadn't paused, hadn't asked, hadn't waited or wanted to hear my side of the story.

And I? I accept her apology, because I understand that kind of anger, that kind of response to feeling attacked, that kind of push to speak and fight back.

I accept her apology and apologize myself, for causing her hurt and frustration.

It is one of the few times I can remember having such an honest conversation, one in which both of us are willing to say we were wrong, and we are sorry.

***

Berlant writes: Slow death is not a state of exception to the change and crisis of "catastrophe" or "mere banality," but a "domain of revelation where an upsetting scene of living that has been muffled in ordinary consciousness is revealed to be interwoven with ordinary life after all, like ants revealed scurrying under a thoughtlessly lifted rock" (2007, p. 762). As visibly different, we measure the violence of our lives not in 'what-if,' or 'what's worse' scales, but rather the everyday annihilations of having, it seems, to always keep coming to the table, to continue relating reasonably and patiently while (somehow) taking the anger and dismissal of others, and to keep 'making family' with people who'd rather publicly shame you than to face you.

The slow death of mundane annihilation of queer people and other minoritarian people is not seen as crisis and catastrophe, but rather, a slow death by the "structural intractability problem the world can live with" (Berlant, 2007, p. 762). It is an everyday assault, and the accumulation of mundane annihilations is what begins to erode communities of differences both within and without. Mundane annihilations are the 'micro-aggressions' that serve as reminders that we are precarious; they are the 'suggestion' that we are on the 'inside' only at the discretion of the insiders. They begin in families and they are mirrored in the larger culture and the 'what ifs' as the precarity we feel in even the seemingly 'safest' places takes its toll (Harris, Holman Jones, Faulkner, & Brook, 2017; Schulman, 2009, 2016).

***

It's the kind of snapping into attention that happens when we least expect or want it. A state of attunement, when we attend "to what might be happening … to possibilities opening up and not necessarily good ones. But maybe" (Stewart, 2007, p. 6). Like the kind of attention our friend Craig writes about on social media the morning after taking a beloved pet to the emergency vet in the hard hours of the night. The pause and spreading dread of *what-ifs* set off by the *spouse/co-owner* line on the intake form. The form and the representation of kinship and/as sovereignty becomes singular and charged, at once weighty and diffuse like a "headache induced by a shift in the barometric pressure" (Stewart, 2013). Time "speeds and slows"; "space stretches out and pulls in as an immediate surround" (Stewart, 2013). Questions crowd out the alarm bells ringing in the body: Will writing Jonny's name set in motion its own alarm bells – homophobic fear and rage and with it the denial of emergency care for a beloved under the 'right' to refuse service? In what other waiting rooms does such 'intimate terror' reign? What is the calculus of counting which or whose lives matter in such shape-shifting moments of potentiality and loss (Berlant, 2011)?

***

In *When Species Meet*, Donna Haraway (2008) introduces the concept of 'making killable,' to describe the "development of categories to contain those, human and nonhuman, who are dispensable and killable" (p. 38). Making killable "turns people and animals into always already objects ready for violence, genocide, slavery" (Tuck & Ree, 2013, p. 649). The mass production and destruction of beings-as-objects does not happen elsewhere – in some cubicle or cupboard or semi-truck where categories are made and exercised with violent and sometimes homicidal results. It happens, instead, in the boundary materializing work of facing each other. Making killable is a relation predicated on the precarity of an Other, "an acknowledgment of dependency, needs, exposure and vulnerability" (Puar qtd. in Puar et. al., 2012, p. 163).[5]

Butler's (2006) development of the relational nature of precarity draws from Emmanuel Levinas's (1996) notion of "face," which she takes to mean "that for which no words really work; the face seems to be a kind of sound, the sound of language evacuating its sense" (p. 134). To respond to the face, to the sound, to the affective force of that which precedes sense, understanding, and movement means to

> be awake to what is precarious in another life, or rather, the precariousness of life itself. This cannot be an awakeness … to my own life, and then an extrapolation from an understanding of my own precariousness to an understanding of another's precarious life. It has to be an understanding of the precariousness of the Other. (Butler, 2006, p. 143)

A relational and ethical understanding of precarity, Levinas writes, happens in the "face of the other in its precariousness and defenselessness … [and is] at once the temptation to kill and the call to peace, the 'You shall not kill' (Levinas, 1996, p. 167). Of the invocation of the commandment 'Thou shall not kill,' Butler writes:

> Why would it be that the very precariousness of the Other would produce for me a temptation to kill? Or why would it produce the temptation to kill at the same time that it delivers a demand for peace? … [The] face makes various utterances at once: it bespeaks an agony, an injurability, at the same time it bespeaks a divine prohibition against killing. (2006, p. 135)

A case in point: In October 2018, Cesar Sayoc builds and mails 13 explosive devices to Democrats including former President Barack Obama, former Vice President Joe Biden, former President Bill Clinton and former U.S. Senator Hillary Clinton, former CIA director John Brennan, former Director of National Intelligence James Clapper, congresswomen Deborah Wasserman Schultz and Maxine Waters, senator Cory Booker, former U.S. Attorney General Eric Holder, billionaire donor George Soros, along with outspoken critics of Trump, including the actor Robert DeNiro (Sabur & Alexander, 2018). Sayoc, whose van was plastered with images of "my president" Trump, photos of Hillary with a target superimposed over her face and "CNN Sucks" stickers, sent his homemade bombs to people who have been publicly critical of Trump. The 'temptation to kill' that is produced in the 'utterances' of the agony and injurability of some people (those who feel heard and bolstered by Trump's nationalist messages, along with Trump himself), does not, in this case, also voice the 'divine prohibition against killing' described by Butler. Or if it does, as in Trump's condemnation of Sayoc's "terrorizing acts" as "despicable" and call for Americans to unify "in love and peace as fellow citizens," the prohibition of 'thou shall not kill' is *undone* by what accompanying messages that suggest the "bomb thing" is a disruption of Republican mid-term election momentum and claims that it is *he* who is "attacked all the time" by the U.S. media (and thus the precarious one) (Sabur & Alexander, 2018).

Trump's incitement of the "temptation to kill," even as he makes demands for "peace," lies at the heart of Haraway's (2008) discussion making killable. She writes:

> …what my people and I need to let go of if we are to learn to stop exterminism and genocide … is the command "Thou shalt not kill." The problem is not figuring out to whom such a command applies so that 'other' killing can go on as usual and reach unprecedented historical proportions …. Perhaps the commandment should read, 'Thou shalt not make killable.' … Facing up to the outrage of human exceptionalism will, in my view, require severely reducing human demands on the more than human world … [and] require working for the mortal entanglements of human beings and other organisms in ways that one judges, without guarantees, to be good, that is to deserve a future. (pp. 80, 106)

If the industrial complex (and the normative heterosexual orientation that (re)produces it) turns all living beings into objects – 'things' to 'do things' with, we must, as Haraway argues, stop focusing on figuring out to whom the command "Thou shall not kill" applies and instead pay attention to how we make some human beings and other organisms killable – that is, not worthy of a future. In facing up to making-killable, we must reckon with how bodies – both individual and collective – are bounded and entangled, precarious and enmeshed, infinite and ephemeral.

Another case in point: In November 2017, we join the 'victory' march the day after clearing the final in an excruciating number of hurdles in the fight for marriage equality in Australia. After our plans to gather and celebrate with others right-then-and-there were dashed by rain and a long-delayed vote in Parliament, we turn up the day after and join a march through Melbourne's CBD (Central Business District). Already we feel both time-weary and out of time. As we march, we chant in verse with the slogans coming through the megaphone – "We're here, we're queer, we're getting married next year … we're here, we're queer, we're getting married next year … we're here, we're queer …." With each repetition, we become more and more … uncomfortable. What about our queer friends and family who aren't here – because they don't have the time or ability to turn up to a march that began before the working day ended? Because they don't want to wait to get married, next year or ever? Because they are no longer alive, after having waited so long for this day, these [and so many other] rights, to come? We wonder if the time for "we're here, we're queer," has passed; if it is a kind of 'overkill' that overlooks just how hard it's been to imagine such the future, turning it into a "spectre, a pure virtuality" (Fisher, 2014, p. 22).

Though the border between 'life' and 'death,' and 'here' and 'queer,' are not certain or sure; 'making killable' and 'overkill' are intra-active encounters, rather than time-bound happenings. And the fuzzy borders we try to put up around life and death and here and queer can happen "without human bodies present, quite beyond questions of personification" (Chen, 2011, p. 265). In their consideration of toxicity and contamination, Mel Y. Chen takes up queer debates about life and death, proposing the idea of toxicity as "an extant queer bond" (p. 265). Chen considers their own sensitivity to toxins as a way of thinking about not only how queer people are, in many ways 'made killable' in how they are "treated as toxic assets," that also reminds us to "ask after the desires, the loves, the rehabilitations, the affections, the assets that toxic conditions induce" (p. 281).

***

As I try to find a way of 'finishing' my writing about relationships following Trump's first year in office, outrage and disbelief about the continued human rights violations of the Trump administration weighs on my mind. In the first half of 2018, thousands[6] of children were separated from their parents and 'detained' (read: incarcerated) at 15 makeshift 'immigration centers' and 'tender age' shelters in the U.S., suggesting – again – that human-on-human violence has reached yet another unimaginable crisis point. The youngest child separated from parents at the border was 8 months old; each of these "unaccompanied alien children" has suffered – will suffer – from the stress and trauma of forced separation. What kind of world builds such hostile shelters for its most vulnerable inhabitants (Burke & Mendoza, 2018)? Or fails to remember the millions of babies and young children who have been detained or forcibly separated from their parents – in the U.S. and elsewhere – over the course of 'human' history? Or doesn't see how these children, and their parents, are treated as 'toxic assets' that must, if not made killable, be contained so that their contamination does not poison sociality or capital. Indeed, ridding the nation of the toxicity of migrants is necessary to "make America great" by strengthening its "immunity" by erecting emotional, physical, geographic and political borders between 'us' and 'them' (Chen, 2011; Haraway, 1989). And it is those very borders (and both the toxicity of others and the immunity they are erected to provide) that stops the 7,000+ asylum seekers including hundreds of families with children who have traveled more than 2,000 miles on foot from Central America from entering the U.S. at the Tijuana checkpoint in November 2018. That, and canisters of tear gas and rounds of rubber bullets (Olsen, 2018; Rhodan, 2018).

My outrage and disbelief is reflected in the news reports I see and hear and in the social media feeds of friends. We ask each other why and how this can be happening and what can we do about it right now, today, including how we respond to the people supporting the barbarism for one ethically bankrupt reason or another. My friend Devika posts online, "Where you are born, the country and continent in which you are born, the family in which you are born is all a genetic lottery, just the luck of the draw. Which means, we could potentially have been those kids or those parents in those detention centers. No one has a say in where and to whom they are born. Show some goddamn humility."

There are posts that remind us that what's happening to these children doesn't just impact those of us who are parents or immigrants to this country or another; that it isn't happening outside – to someone else, to some other 'category' of people. It is happening to *us*. Why is such relational perspective taking difficult? Is it easier to find love for others than the ones closest to us? Though what is 'closest'? And what or who is 'outside' or 'other' in this equation?

Some would argue that what's closest or intimate or 'family' might be the furthest away – beings and things do not remind us of ourselves too much and so can be located somewhere down the line in the ethical hierarchy of human exceptionalism that allows us to draw boundaries around who or what is worthy of our care and concern and who or what is dispensable. Theories about why and how Trump won the election circulate in metaphors of toxicity and immunity and the borders thrown up between 'us' and 'them' – disenfranchised white and other 'dominant' groups working out identity-based (race, class, sexuality) resentments about the 'rest' of us (Khazan, 2018; Lopez, 2017). Of course, invoking "metaphorical luxuries" like these can and do have complex and "deadly consequences" for the things, bodies, and communities to which metaphors of toxicity/contamination and assets/immunities refer (Chen, 2011, p. 270). Keeping in mind these caveats and considerations, Chen still finds value in viewing contamination and toxicity as not only a process of making killable, but also a performative "asset" that, in the same way that "queer" troubles capitalism, heterosexuality, ability and other normative systems, invites in "loss and its 'losers,' and trespassing containers" of living and dead, human and in/non-human, us and them. In its best versions, queer toxicity "propels, not repels" queer love (Chen, 2011, p. 281).

***

And so, while the death-making policies of the Trump administration and the state and socially-sanctioned violations they authorize, particularly against vulnerable populations (including those to which I belong), feel more transparent and more frightening than they have ever been before, I feel a deep need and responsibility to respond. It's clear, too, that we need a deeper awareness of the intersectionality of all oppressions and how compounded abuses are threatening not only the U.S. under Trump but also global politics and the planet in not just abstract but large-scale, material ways. If the only way forward is *through*, we must look to governments and institutions as well as ourselves to heal the harms we continue to perpetrate against ourselves and others. Doing so means taking a relational approach to both violence and freedom. As Butler (2015), drawing from Hannah Arendt, reminds us: "Freedom does not come from me or from you; it can and does happen as a relation between us, or indeed, among us. So, this is not a matter of finding the human dignity within each person, but rather of understanding the human as a relational and social being … no human can be human without acting in concert with others and on conditions of equality" (p. 88).

Relationships of freedom *and* of protest in the post-Trump era depend on interconnection and intersectionality. Our sense of sadness, guilt, anger and fear must be matched with a demand for equality, freedom and relational humility. Critical autoethnography – the kind of work I am practicing here – offers one way forward for holding a lens up to the business-as-usual of death making politics. It allows us to refuse the banality of 'just another massacre' that mainstream media and corporate /political structures ask us to take for granted. It is also a way for us, as scholars and artists, as activists and citizens, to refuse to remain unmoved by the systematic loss of human and other life, despite (and because of) its ubiquity across the landscapes of our lives. For our own sakes, we must *see* these recurring massacres as unacceptable and that seeing, in its very necessity, must be queer in the sense of the interruption and disruption of queering practices (Ahmed, 2006). As Martha Graham observed, "There is no satisfaction whatever at any time. There is only a queer, divine dissatisfaction, a blessed unrest that keeps us marching and makes us more alive (qtd. in De Mille, 1952, p. 335).

***

Something comes together and people say and feel they can't – work, get out of bed, wake up from one bad dream and into another. But people do – they work, they get out of bed, they wake up, and keep going despite the spectre of cynicism lurking around every corner. Susan Sontag (2003) argues that "Critics of modernity, consumers of violence as spectacle, adepts of proximity without risk, are schooled to be cynical about the possibility of sincerity. Some people will do anything to keep from being moved" (Sontag, 2003, p. 99). And yet to look, to consider – images of violence and the traumas and administrations and presidents that (sometimes, perhaps often) give rise to them – is an "invitation to pay attention, to reflect, to learn" (Sontag, 2003, pp. 116–117). Accepting that invitation, coming together to look, reflect, and learn is how we recognise others and their lives as not only important and worthy, but also *grievable* (Butler, 2006, p. 20).

Something happens and we come together, we look at others and ourselves in all of our precariousness and vulnerability to annihilations both mundane and systematic – and we are moved to be and become differently (Butler, 2006, p. 150). To make work that works to recognize and acknowledge ourselves and a world not as it has always been, but to "solicit a becoming, to instigate a transformation, to petition the future always in relation to [each] other" (Butler, 2006, p. 44).

Something happens and we begin, again.
We ask each other why and how and what now?
We cry.
We sing and hold hands. We cry some more.
We embrace and promise to keep on holding each other.
We organise. In the now. Again. And again.
When something is lost, we look, listen and remember that it is

Not till we are lost, "not till we have lost the world,
do we begin to find ourselves, and realize
the infinite extent of our relations" (Solnit, 2010, p. X).
We tune in to "to what might be happening …
to possibilities opening up and not necessarily good ones.
But maybe" (Stewart, 2007, p. 6).
When losing something gives way
to something "unexpectedly hopeful" (Stewart, 2007, p. 6).

NOTES

1 The writing in this section is inspired by a discussion of the post-election feeling of 'something happening' Anne Harris and I write about in *Queering Autoethography* (2018).

2 In the wake of the 2016 US presidential election Judith Butler (2016) writes: "For a world that is increasingly mischaracterized as post-racial and post-feminist, we are now seeing how misogyny and racism overrides judgment and a commitment to democratic and inclusive goals – they are sadistic, resentful, and destructive passions driving our country" (para. 3). She continues: "Who are they, these people who voted for him, but who are we, who did not see their power, who did not anticipate this at all, who could not fathom that people would vote for a man with racist and xenophobic discourse, a history of sexual offenses, the exploitation of workers, disdain for the constitution, migrants, and a reckless plan for increased militarization? Perhaps we are shielded from the truth by our own isolated form of left and liberal thinking? Or perhaps we believed in human nature in some naive ways. Under what conditions does unleashed hatred and reckless militarization compel the majority vote?" (para. 4).

3 For an extended discussion of 'mundane annihilations,' 'making killable' and 'toxicity/contamination,' see Harris and Holman Jones (2019).

4 The article is Amanda Terkel's "Donald Trump Promises to Protect the LGBTQ Community" (2016), published in the *Huffington Post*.

5 For an extended discussion of 'making killable,' 'mundane annihilations' and 'toxicity,' see Harris and Holman Jones (2019).

6 Estimates are at least 2,500 children have been separated from their parents when the 'zero tolerance' policy for crossing the US-Mexico without documentation was reversed (Gerhart et al., 2018; Rampton & Holland, 2018). These children are being 'detained' in tent cities, military facilities and in converted Walmart stores in 15 US states (Miroff, 2018). Salvador Rizzo (2018) writes, "Some of the most intense outrage at the measures has followed instances of parents deported to Central America without their children or spending weeks unable to locate their sons and daughters" (para. 33). Rizzo also reported, "in other instances, paediatricians and child advocates have reported seeing toddlers crying inconsolably for their mothers at shelters where staff are prohibited from physically comforting them" (para. 33).

REFERENCES

Ahmed, S. (2006). *Queer phenomenology: Orientations, objects, others*. Durham, NC: Duke University Press.

Altman, A. (2017, February 9). No president has spread fear like Donald Trump. *Time*. Retrieved from http://www.time.com/

Ball, M. (2016, September 2). Donald Trump and the politics of fear. *The Atlantic*. Retrieved from http://www.theatlantic.com/

Beard, N. (2016, December 20). International activism and the American expatriate. *Topical*. Retrieved from https://www.headstuff.org/

Berlant, L. (2007). Slow death (sovereignty, obesity, lateral agency). *Critical Inquiry, 33*(4), 754–780.

Berlant, L. (2011). *Cruel optimism*. Durham, NC: Duke University Press.

Bowden, J. (2018, January 23). Report: Anti-LGBT violence surged in 2017. *The Hill*. Retrieved from http://www.thehill.com/

Burke, G., & Mendoza, M. (2018, June 20). At least 3 "tender age" shelters set up for child migrants. *AP News*. Retrieved from https://apnews.com/

Butler, J. (2006). *Precarious life: The power of mourning and violence*. New York, NY: Verso.

Butler, J. (2015). *Notes toward a performative theory of assembly*. Cambridge, MA: Harvard University Press.

Butler, J. (2016, November 10). US Elections: A statement from Judith Butler. *Sexuality Policy Watch*. Retrieved from http://www.sxpolitics.org/

Castela, M. J. C. (2018). *The Trump effect and Brexit: The 2016 United States Elections and the 2017 European elections*. Vida Economica.

Chen, M. Y. (2011). Toxic animacies, inanimate affections. *GLQ: A Journal of Lesbian and Gay Studies, 17*(2–3), 265–286.

Dastagir, A. E. (2017, June 12). 2016 was the deadliest year on record for the LGBTQ community. *USA Today*. Retrieved from http://www.usatoday.com/

De Mille, A. (1952). *Dance to the piper*. Boston, MA: Little, Brown.

Fisher, M. (2014). *Ghosts of my life: Writings on depression, hauntology, and lost futures*. Alresford: Zero Books.

Gerhart, A., Karklis, L., Steckelberg, A., Muyskens, J., Rabinwotz, K., Shapiro, L., Tierney, L., Tran, A., & Davis, A. (2018, June 25). Where are the migrant child facilities? Scattered across America. *The Washington Post*. Retrieved from https://www.washingtonpost.com/graphics/2018/national/migrant-child-shelters/

Glassner, B. (2010). *The culture of fear: Why Americans are afraid of the wrong things: Crime, drugs, minorities, teen moms, killer kids, mutant microbes, plane crashes, road rage & so much more*. New York, NY: Basic Books.

Gopalan, S. (2018, June 27). Donald Trump's Muslim travel ban win may be good law but it's bad policy. *ABC News*. Retrieved from http://www.abc.net.au/

Green, E. (2017, May 9). It was cultural anxiety that drove white, working class voters to Trump. *The Atlantic*. Retrieved from https://www.theatlantic.com/

Gun Violence Archive. (2018). *Past summary ledgers*. Retrieved from https://www.gunviolencearchive.org/past-tolls

Haraway, D. (1989). The biopolitics of postmodern bodies: Determinations of self in immune system discourse. *Differences, 1*(1), 3–43.

Haraway, D. (2008). *When species meet.* Minneapolis, MN: University of Minnesota Press.
Harris, A., & Holman Jones, S. (2019). *The queer life of things: Performance, affect and the more-than-human.* Lanham, MD: Lexington Books.
Harris, A., Holman Jones, S., Faulkner, S., & Brook, E. (2017). *Queering families, schooling publics: Keywords.* New York, NY: Routledge.
Holman Jones, S., & Harris, A. (2018). *Queering autoethnography.* New York, NY/London: Routledge.
Human Rights Campaign. (2017). *Violence against the transgender community in 2017.* Retrieved from https://www.hrc.org/resources/violence-against-the-transgender-community-in-2017
Human Rights Campaign. (2018). *Violence against the transgender community in 2018.* Retrieved from https://www.hrc.org/resources/violence-against-the-transgender-community-in-2018
Khazan, O. (2018, April 23). People voted for Trump because they were anxious, not poor. *The Atlantic*. Retrieved from https://www.theatlantic.com/
Levinas, E. (1996). Peace and proximity. In A. T. Peperzak, S. Critchley, & R. Bernasconi (Eds.), *Emmanuel Levinas: Basic philosophical writings* (pp. 161–170). Bloomington, IN: Indiana University Press.
Lopez, G. (2017, December 15). The past year of research has made it very clear: Trump won because of racial resentment. *Vox.* Retrieved from https://www.vox.com/identities/2017/12/15/16781222/trump-racism-economic-anxiety-study
McArthur, S. (2016, November 18). What Trump's presidency means for expats. *Huffington Post.* Retrieved from http://www.huffingtonpost.com/
Miroff, N. (2018, June 14). U.S to house migrant children in tents outside El Paso as government takes more into custody. *The Washington Post.* Retrieved from https://www.washingtonpost.com/world/national-security/us-to-house-migrant-children-in-tents-outside-el-paso-as-government-takes-more-into-custody/2018/06/14/3dcff87e-7008-11e8-9ab5-d31a80fd1a05_story.html
National Coalition of Anti-Violence Programs. (2018). *A crisis of hate: A report on lesbian, gay, bisexual, transgender and queer hate violence.* Retrieved from http://avp.org/wp-content/uploads/2018/01/a-crisis-of-hate-january-release-12218.pdf
Olsen, M. B. (2018, November 26). Children shot with rubber bullets and tear gas by US troops at Mexican Border. *Metro.* Retrieved from http://www.metro.co.uk/
Puar, J., Butler, J., Cvejic, B., Lorey, I., & Vujanovic, A. (2012). Precarity talk: A virtual roundtable with Lauren Berlant, Judith Butler, Bojaba Cvejic, Isabell Lorey, Jasbir Puar, and Ana Vujanovic. *TDR: The Drama Review, 56*(4), 163–177.
Rampton, R., & Holland, S. (2018, June 20). Trump backs down on separating immigrant children, legal problems remain. *Reuters.* Retrieved from https://www.reuters.com/article/us-usa-immigration/trump-backs-down-on-separating-immigrant-children-legal-problems-remain-idUSKBN1JG27Q
Rhodan, M. (2018, October 23). President Trump threatened to turn back caravan migrants if they don't claim asylum in Mexico. That's not legal. *Time.* Retrieved from https://time.com/5431447/donald-trump-threat-turn-back-caravan-migrants-not-legal/
Rizzo, S. (2018, June 19). The facts about Trump's policy of separating families at the border. *The Washington Post.* Retrieved from https://www.washingtonpost.com/news/fact-checker/wp/2018/06/19/the-facts-about-trumps-policy-of-separating-families-at-the-border/?noredirect=on&utm_term=.c5141263ddbf

Sabur, R., & Alexander, H. (2018, October 27). US mail bomb suspect named as Cesar Sayoc, Trump supporter with long criminal history. *The Telegraph*. Retrieved from http://www.telegraph.co.uk/

Schmider, A. (2016, November 9). 2016 was the deadliest year on record for transgender people [Blog post]. Retrieved from https://www.glaad.org/

Schulman, S. (2009). *Ties that bind: Familial homophobia and its consequences*. New York, NY: The New Press.

Schulman, S. (2016). *Conflict is not abuse: Overstating harm, community responsibility and the duty of repair.* Vancouver: Arsenal Pulp Press.

Seidler, V. (2018). *Making sense of Brexit: Democracy, Europe and uncertain futures*. Bristol: Policy Press.

Siskind, A. (2018). *The list: A week-by-week reckoning of Trump's first year*. New York, NY: Bloomsbury.

Solnit, R. (2016, July 15). 'Hope is an embrace of the unknown': Rebecca Solnit on living in dark times. *The Guardian*. Retrieved from http://www.theguardian.com/

Sontag, S. (2003). *Regarding the pain of others*. New York, NY: St. Martins.

Stewart, K. (2007). *Ordinary affects.* Durham, NC: Duke University Press.

Stewart, K. (2013). An autoethnography of what happens. In S. Holman Jones, T. E. Adams, & C. Ellis (Eds.), *The handbook of autoethnography* (pp. 659–668). Walnut Creek, CA: Left Coast Press.

Terkel, A. (2016, August 22). Donald Trump promises to protect LGBTQ community. *Huffington Post*. Retrieved from http://www.huffingtonpost.com.au/

Tuck, E., & Ree, C. (2013). A glossary of haunting. In S. Holman Jones, T. E. Adams, & C. Ellis (Eds.), *Handbook of autoethnography* (pp. 630–658). Walnut Creek, CA: Left Coast Press.

Vigeland, T. (2016 , May 20). Donald Trump is ruining my life as an expat. *Quartz*. Retrieved from https://qz.com/688242/donald-trump-is-ruining-my-life-as-an-expat/

Winters, S. (2018, November 20). International Transgender Day of Remembrance 2018 [Blog post]. Retrieved from https://transpolicyreform.wordpress.com/2018/11/20/international-transgender-day-of-remembrance-2018/?fbclid=IwAR0KBM88RWr98h63B F4poyWBQ0XrQBXtAuit9lLEitTDCmwA8vyeqUuGOvY

CHRISTINE SALKIN DAVIS AND JONATHAN L. CRANE

DIALOGUE 9

Larry says, "One thing that's been tough is the southern border when parents were being separated from their kids. Those laws already existed but nobody was enforcing them, now he started enforcing them. It might have been better to just turn them away and send their kids back with them, and say, we're not going to separate kids from parents. The laws allowed him to do this, and in some cases, the kids could have been cared for and been in a better situation than running across the desert with no provisions. But keeping parents with children and just saying, not right now, let's figure out how to get you in the right way, would have been better."

Andrea says, "He was just enforcing the law that was already there. But it was reported as what Trump is doing. He was enforcing what was already there. But did he necessarily have to do it that way is the question."

"Yeah," Larry says, "did he have to separate them?"

Elizabeth says, "I think he did have to separate children from families. I know that's unpleasant to hear, but I think it's a necessary message to send to countries in Central America and parents, not to bring their child with them. With immigration, I like that Trump has kept the dreamers from getting amnesty. Some of my friends believe that any person should be allowed to come into our country, whether legally or illegally. That that's the Christian thing to do, and that came up at election time, the difference between Trump and Hillary's illegal immigration policies. I agree with Trump's position on immigration, because I think really, no one should be just breaking the law to come here; they are using our country's infrastructure."

Andrea adds, "I think he's so focused on the next election, and when you look at the government shutdown and his position that he took on the wall, I think he could have compromised and said, it's about border security and the methods of getting border security might differ as long as the outcome is better border security. Unfortunately, I think he put himself in the place of having to build the wall, Mexico's going to pay for the wall, and now he feels like he has to figure out a way to get the wall done in order to get re-elected. And I don't know if he has the ability to get it built. I think he's backed

DOI:10.1163/9789004436329_018

himself into a corner. If it doesn't happen now, for him it's a loss. Politics has become like the Super Bowl, win or lose."

"So now, if Pelosi and Schumer come back with another border security solution, he'll still think he's losing because he didn't get his wall. So he's in a bad spot," says Larry. "I don't think it's going to work out."

"Yeah," Elizabeth says, "I disagreed with the government shutdown. I don't think he should have shut down based on the border wall. I think they're two separate issues, and I think it was bad to have government employees that weren't being paid, working and not being paid. I think it was wrong to stop paying government employees for 30-some days, and some of them had to keep working. Some had to stay at home. And even if they get back pay, that didn't help them pay their rent and buy food. So I didn't agree with his policy on that. I think that was a big mistake."

KRISTEN E. OKAMOTO AND SONIA R. IVANCIC

8. OPPORTUNITIES TO UNSILENCE

Walking the Political Line at Home

From conversations we have with friends to articles in popular media outlets, it has become clear that this election, unlike any other in recent history, has significantly impacted family relationships and friendships. For instance, Sonia listened to a friend narrate the experience of her young son who refused to leave her side after the Trump election for fear his mother would be taken away. Another friend discussed the decision not to allow family members who voted for Trump to attend her wedding, citing her discomfort in mixing these individuals with her LGBTQ friends. Not only did the election prompt people to re-examine their relationships, but it prompted new and different conversations. Following the election, McGill (2016) wrote in *Vox* that, "after Trump won, we [my father and I] had our first true talk about politics – ever" (para. 14).

Through the use of autoethnographic narrative accounts, we explore how the election of Donald J. Trump was navigated with family members of differing political beliefs. As Koenig Kellas (2005) stated, "not only do our family stories shape us, but we also shape our family stories and our family identities together" (p. 386). Research conducted to this point centers primarily around stories that families tell jointly to overcome difficult situations (e.g., Trees & Koenig Kellas, 2009). However, this chapter examines the inverse: how do larger cultural narratives and events (i.e., a political election) impact family identities and relationships?

To answer this question, we relay our personal experiences. Both of our stories illustrate the contentious conversations that took place with family members following Trump's election and provide an opportunity to contemplate what it might mean to move forward. Kristen had always viewed her father as apolitical. In the November following the election, her dad revealed that he had voted for Trump, catching Kristen off guard. Her dad had never voted until that point. Sonia's in-laws are sixth generation cattle ranchers who consistently vote Republican. She was not surprised

DOI:10.1163/9789004436329_019

when she found out they voted for Trump, however, she struggles to enact and maintain a positive relationship with them post-election. In this chapter, Sonia discusses her embodied response to staying with her in-laws for the holidays and her challenges engaging them in political conversation. Amid her efforts to ask her in-laws to understand how Trump's hateful rhetoric impacted certain people, she can still hear her mother-in-law saying, "But I try to be a good person and I'm nice to everyone."

The election of Trump demonstrates how the feminist ethos – the personal is political – has become central to examining the impact of this election. In narrative terms, the 2016 election served as a "rupture point" that caused us to rethink our relationships with family members and friends. That is, until the election, we recognized that differences existed, but we did not know how deep the divide actually was. Lorde (1984/2007) argues: "too often, we pour the energy needed for recognizing and exploring difference into pretending those differences are insurmountable barriers, or that they do not exist at all" (p. 115). We found, through the revelation that our family members voted for Trump, that we had been guilty of misdirecting our energy into burying and obscuring our differences. The election demanded a response – we could no longer ignore such differences and we could no longer keep our opinions quiet. This chapter explores the role of silence, un-silencing, and difference at home, as we ask: what was it about this election that prompted these first time, intentional, political conversations? To explore such a question, we narrate our embodied responses through autoethnography with particular attention to how the election impacted our familial relationships. Specifically, we attend to intersectionality in terms of our subject positions as women and early career scholars, as well as our identities – regional (rural vs. urban) and/or multiracial.

By conveying these autoethnographic accounts, we subscribe to the underlying assumption that subjectivity is constituted in and through the body, not just the mind. Bodies are marked in ways that carry "cultural freight" (Selzer & Crowley, 1999, p. 362). No body is "disinterested" (Selzer & Crowley, 1999, p. 363). Alongside Kruks (2001), we argue that attention to the body moves us beyond thinking about the body as solely a symbolic entity enmeshed in discourse. We felt and experienced the election – and the results of it – with and through our bodies. Thus, the need for an embodied approach to understanding is necessary for a project exploring the familial relationships in a post-Trump world.

Further, this chapter understands lived experience as *a*, not *the* way of coming to knowledge. In line with Merleau-Ponty (1968), this exploration of personal narratives assumes that each perception is mutable and only probable – "it is, if one likes, only an opinion; but what is not opinion, what each perception, even if false, verifies, is the belongingness of each experience to the same world, their equal power to manifest it, as possibilities of the same world" (p. 41). Thus, the reflections and meditations expressed here do not speak for familial experiences writ large, but do illuminate the meaningful ways that politics play out at home during this cultural moment. Through allowing others to witness these moments in our lives, that first year after the election, we aim to speak our truth, find commonalities with others, and cultivate moments of wisdom about the politics of "families and disagreement." Our stories were separated by a continent, and occurred nearly a year apart. However, we experienced striking similarities. Below, we tell our stories in tandem rather than separately. Ultimately, we hope that the act of writing itself serves as a form of healing and reconciliation for us and others.

HOLIDAY GATHERINGS AND RISING POLITICAL TENSIONS

Kristen

Thanksgiving 2017 was the first time I had seen my dad since the election. Living more than 3000 miles apart made our visits sporadic. I had just begun a new job as an assistant professor and looked forward to sharing my new life with him, one that I had worked diligently towards creating for myself for many years. I was anxious with both excitement and fear and my body let me know as much. For several days before my dad's arrival my stomach was in knots as I nervously paced back and forth through the house trying to prepare for my dad's arrival. Knowing my dad's political identity as a staunch conservative, I had anticipated some uncomfortable conversations and tense moments, but nothing like what eventually transpired, which left our relationship strained and in disrepair.

I am my father's daughter. A single father, my dad raised me; I am an only child. Much of the time it felt as if it was the two of us against the world. I inherited his love of music, food, and wine. I still remember fondly the spur of the moment road trips we used to take when I was a kid, driving down the highway and listening to everything from Heatwave's *Boogie Nights* to Alice in Chains' *Man in the Box*. I wanted to be just like my dad growing up. I make this point in order to emphasize the deep chasm that the most recent presidential election has opened, to illustrate that not even close bonds, such as those between my dad and me, were immune. Sonia also felt a similar anxiousness about seeing her in-laws for the holidays, an anxiousness she had been anticipating since before Trump was elected.

Sonia

My chest felt tight as I sat on the Alaska Airlines flight from Seattle to Missoula, en route to meet my husband and in-laws for the Christmas holiday. Just over a month had passed since our country had elected Trump as the next president. Imagining being in the same room with my husband's family – who had all voted for him – made my skin itch and my pulse race. A tear rolled down my cheek as I thought about this holiday trip, which we had planned before the election, and how it meant staying in their home for 16 days. I wondered if the passengers next to me sensed the tense energy radiating from my body. As the holidays crept closer and people reconvened with their families during this tumultuous political moment, I wondered how many others were having a similar experience.

As the plane neared the mountains of Western Montana, the pilot's muddled voice came over the intercom. "We are experiencing low visibility because of fog that has settled into the valley. We are going to circle the area, and if we are not able to find a clearing, we will have to turn back to Seattle to refuel," he said. *Back to Seattle*, I thought. As I sat crammed into my seat on the puddle jumper, I envisioned the conversations I wanted to have with my in-laws. I thought about feeling stranded in a place where I had little autonomy and no easy means of escape. I was fully aware that they wanted me and my husband to pretend that everything was fine. If we go *back to Seattle*, where I grew up, where my progressive parents and sisters live, who are also angry at Trump and Trump voters, I thought, *there is no way I am getting back on this plane*.

My social media took a political turn in 2016 – I posted various things about Trump's xenophobic rhetoric – his sexism, racism, and anti-immigrant fear-mongering. I needed to express myself, find pockets of solidarity, and I wanted my feelings about Trump to be ardently clear to everyone – particularly those who might vote for him. Derek's parents were not part of the Trump stronghold. They did not go to rallies, put signs in their yard, or wear "Make America Great Again" hats. But they are unwavering members of the Republican party. We knew his parents and grandparents were going to vote for him. They did not need to tell us. We were right. I frequently said to Derek during the closing months of the election, "I don't know if I can go to Montana if Trump wins." When I said this, he said nothing, letting the statement hang in the air. We both, for many reasons, hoped it would be a non-issue, hoped that Trump would not win. For both Kristen and me, these confrontations had been years in the making.

WEAVING POLITICS WITH FAMILY HISTORY

Kristen

My dad is the first son of Japanese-American immigrants. Their parents, my great grandparents, fled Japan to freely pursue their Christian faith. On February 19, 1942, Franklin D. Roosevelt signed into action Executive Order 9066, which authorized the relocation of people of Japanese ancestry, among others, to internment camps. Under this order my grandparents were sent from their homes, their birthplaces, in Watsonville, California and Tacoma, Washington to an internment camp, or "relocation center" in Southern California. They eventually made their way to a makeshift community for Japanese-Americans in Bridgeton, NJ. My father was born there, in a cobbled-together home thrown together in ad-hoc fashion to house the newly released internees.

Work was scarce for the *Nisei*.[1] My grandfather began his own business sexing chicks for large commercial hatcheries. The job was dirty and demanding, requiring the handling of excrement, and putting in long hours for little pay. My grandfather's exposure to the abject in this way served to further marginalize his body. His work was necessary for his family's survival, but detrimental to their identity. By the time my father was in second grade, my grandparents moved the family to a small town in central North Carolina for my grandfather's new job at a poultry plant. They were the first Asian family to live there. Their presence was newsworthy. A local headline read, "Oriental meets Occidental," and pictured my grandparents, my father, and uncle seated on a couch inside their home. In the photo, my grandfather was clothed in a double-breasted suit, my grandmother in a sleeveless, dark navy dress adorned with pearls. The photograph is a reminder of what philosopher David Kim (2014) terms identity assimilation, which is concerned with an agent's self-formation of identity, values, and abilities. Bodies become the canvas upon which this assimilation takes place. The body is always a contested site of power. Conforming to the culture that confined and interned your body is evidence of this. I cannot help but wonder if identity assimilation plays into my dad's political beliefs. My grandmother, his mother, would often refer to her time in the internment camps as "summer camp." Is part of, at least what I consider to be, the disconnect for my dad due to the impact of assimilation? Is this why he cannot empathise with immigrants and those labeled as "other?"

Perhaps this has to do with narratives related to the myth of the "model minority." Within this myth, Asian bodies often stand as examples of upward mobility through thrift, education, and strong familial ties (Li & Wang, 2008). The term was first coined by William Peterson (1966) to describe the Japanese-American population. In his 1966 publication of a *New York Times Magazine* article titled "Success Story: Japanese-American Style," Peterson (1966) asserted that, "by any criterion of good citizenship that we choose, the Japanese Americans are better than any other group in our society, including native-born whites" (p. 21). Other publications from the period served to reveal the ways in which Asian-Americans were "outwhiting the whites." The Model Minority Myth is problematic for many reasons. As philosopher Kim submitted, the myth "offers the polity a way to maintain racial hierarchy by partially incorporating Asians while deftly normatively containing them in ways that make them seem non threatening" (Kim, 2014, p. 110). Due to various socio-historical factors, Asian-American bodies are often treated as "honorary Whites," while at the same time being denied access to full acceptance into mainstream society.

More than a year after Trump's election, there are many chilling parallels between my grandparents' early experiences and today. Pictures of immigrant children living in cages, nursing children separated from their mothers, parents desperate to locate their displaced children, dominate the nightly news. In a recent op-ed, former first Lady Laura Bush (2018) compared the current immigration events to those my grandparents experienced. A sobering reminder of our collective history. For Sonia, understanding her history with her in-laws is also vital to her story.

Sonia

By the winter of 2016, Derek and I had been together for over nine years and married for two – I had known his family for about nine years. Derek is one of the kindest, most thoughtful people I know, and is a complicated mix of identities that can be, at times contradictory and incompatible, but are also what make him beautiful. Derek is a poet and comes from six generations of cattle ranchers. Parts of his childhood were ordinary – he played in the backyard with his brother, joined soccer teams, and went on camping trips.

But he also grew up riding horses, branding cattle, building fences, floating rivers, and taking family trips into the wilderness with pack mules. Stories of raucous, independent, and financially sophisticated cowboys create the brick and mortar of his family narrative. Derek's family is also ardently conservative. Hence, my introduction into the family was complicated. A progressive Seattleite with strong convictions was not exactly their first choice for the person who was to be their son's partner. And to be frank, my experience with rural conservatives was limited. I was a city girl who knew few conservatives and I could count on one hand the number of times I had been to church.

Nine years took Derek and me many places. We experienced the tumultuousness and scarcity of the Great Recession, worked random jobs, enrolled in master's degrees in different states, got married, and moved to the rural Appalachian town of Athens, Ohio to complete Ph.D.s in separate programs. Our honeymoon was spent in a 26-foot moving truck, towing a car, as we made the trek from Missoula to Athens. Over these years, my relationship with Derek deepened and we both changed in significant ways. Although many things about us changed, one of the alterations relevant to this narrative is that Derek's political beliefs became increasingly different from the ones he grew up with.

On Thursday, November 10th, 2016, the night after Trump won, I wrote my in-laws a two-page single-spaced letter that I would never send them. The next night, I talked to Derek on the phone from the National Communication Association Conference in Philadelphia. As I ran around my hotel room, changing clothes before I met friends for dinner, I had Derek on speakerphone. He explained that he had spent over three hours on the phone with his mom the night before. She had been deeply upset in the aftermath of the election, feeling that people on social media were "being mean" to those who voted for Trump. She mentioned a post from our close friend who was soon to deliver a mixed-race child. Our friend – an Indian-American and daughter of immigrants who was ardently against Trump – mentioned in her post that she vowed not to raise her child in "a house of hate." "Do you feel that you were raised in a house of hate?" Derek's mom asked him. Derek told me that she was hurting and, although he disagreed with her vote, he felt sympathy for her pain. I snapped back – "Well she should have thought about that before she voted for Trump. Actions have consequences. These are the consequences of voting a hateful man into office." I talked about how the consequence of her "feeling bad" were minimal to the pain, fear, and lack of safety that many people of marginalized identities are feeling right now.

RUPTURES: UNABLE TO REMAIN SILENT

Kristen

The first few days of my dad's visit were pretty textbook. My dad would jokingly refer to me as a "leftist," and I would respond in kind with some sort of parodic Fox News soundbite. At first we could agree to disagree and simply ignore the "elephant" in the room (pun intended). I had strategically deleted all of the cable news channels from my television to avoid conversation about anything remotely pertaining to politics. We made it through the day performing all of the traditions of a typical American Thanksgiving. We cooked a big meal, ate until we were stuffed, and watched the Dallas Cowboys play their annual Thanksgiving Day game. We talked about the weather, but it soon became obvious that even neutral topics were politically charged. Even something as seemingly innocuous as a movie. All of my thoughts and emotions came to an abrupt head on Thanksgiving night. We were preparing to watch *Miracle on 34th Street*, a tradition that my dad and I have observed every Thanksgiving for as long as I can remember. Unlike the days of my 1980s childhood, I began to cue the move for internet streaming. This act in turn prompted a comment about net neutrality, which at that point was facing an imminent vote for repeal in the following month. The flood gates opened and raw emotion spilled over the embankments.

Our conversation revealed several things. First, I confirmed that my dad had in fact voted for Trump. Up until that point I was not certain. I assumed, but had no confirmation that he had even voted in the 2016 election. The confirmation somehow made it worse. I think I would have rather have lived with being uncertain. At least then there was some room for denial. Now the fact was starting me straight in the face and I could no longer be quiet. Second, I also found that this was the first election my dad had ever chosen to vote in. Until the 2016 election, he was not even a registered voter. Why now, did he choose to break his neutrality?

If my dad and I shared one commonality during this election period, it was that we both could no longer remain silent. This is the impact the Trump presidency has had on many – the illusion of impartiality has disappeared. Prior to the 2016 election, my dad and I simply agreed to disagree, carefully avoiding all conversations that may be considered in any way "political." Now the topic was unavoidable. These revelations sparked an anger in me unlike anything I had ever felt, which converged into a perfect storm. The question flew out of my mouth like venom, "how can the son of immigrants vote for Trump?" I screamed, no longer able to keep my silence. How could my dad vote for someone so intolerant? Has he not heard what Trump proposes? Does he not know Trump's stance on immigrants? The juxtaposition of my family's history and our country's current events made the realization that my dad had voted for Donald J. Trump feel like an act of betrayal – a personal attack on everything our family had been through. The question hung there for what seemed like forever. My dad did not have an answer. All he could say was "I'm too old to be lectured!" and then told me that I would understand when I "got older."

My dad's response seemed patronizing. I cannot help but think that my positionality as a woman plays into my relationship with my dad in a post-Trump world. I had grown up playing the role of "good daughter." Because I saw so much of myself in my father, I wanted badly to please him. While this may certainly be common among many parent-child relationships, the role of daughter is particularly significant in my story. As women, we are taught to be agreeable, to never disrupt the status quo. In fact, female bodies are taught to take up the least amount of space possible. As Young (2005) offers, "feminine existence lives space as enclosed or confining, as having a dual structure, and the woman experiences herself as *positioned in space*" (p. 39, original emphasis). Much like the image of water being held in a glass, the female body becomes positioned in space, rather than being space itself. As a child, I would get notes sent home from school. "Kristen has a hard time sitting still in class. Please work on this at home." I was sent to the principal's office in fifth grade for failing to raise my hand in class, where I was told to sit with my legs together, lower my voice, and, of course, raise my hand before speaking.

I remember taking my dad to the airport the next day. The silence was palpable. Neither one of us wanted to address what had taken place the day before. I felt relieved that he was leaving, but also sad given the unresolved tension between us. As I dropped him off at the curb for his flight back to California, I reached up to give my dad a hug. Living on opposite coasts, the act of saying goodbye has come to feel routine for my dad and me. Normally when we say goodbye he gives me a kiss on the cheek. This time there was no such display of affection. I deeply felt that omission. Instead, he gave me a quick hug and said he loved me. As I watched him walk through the sliding doors of the airport, I wondered what this would mean for our relationship.

I experienced this confrontation with my dad in a visceral way. The experience left me feeling drained and lethargic. So much so, that the week after he left, I came down with the flu – the only time in my life that I have contracted the virus. It was if my body was giving up. My own body was attacking itself, and I was powerless to stop it. Whether or not the two were related, I do not know. But being bedridden for the better part of two weeks brought a certain clarity and calm. I knew I could not change what had happened, but I was glad that I had expressed myself. While what had transpired between my dad and me felt like a direct betrayal of my father, it also felt like I was standing up for and defending the rights of so many others – the immigrant community, those who belong to the LGBTQ community, my fellow women, and many others. At what price, though, did my stand take place? Was I, in effect, choosing these brothers and sisters over my own family? I am still trying to figure out my answers to these questions.

Sonia

When I got together with Derek's family, we mostly attempted – but often failed – to avoid political conversation, as it took ugly turns and left people angry. We had developed an unspoken agreement, that because of our known differences, we would "not talk about politics." However, during visits, we were often together for long periods of time and it was challenging for us all to keep our opinions stifled. When contentious topics arose, I tended to feel isolated and discounted. Because I was the odd one out – and Derek is a skilled peace keeper – I felt that my in-laws were able to speak freely while I was expected to "not cause problems." Women are raised with an intense pressure to be likable – likability, for us, is often equated with morality. I felt the continual tension between the desire to be liked and the need to express myself.

With Trump's win, I made a commitment to speak my truth, not avoid political discussion, and approach life with an increased ethos of confrontation. I aimed not to be hostile, but upfront, honest, and bold. The more time I spent with people of various backgrounds and upbringings, the more I realized that we are simultaneously living in different realities, with different notions of truth, morality, love, and (in)justice. We are getting different news, listening to different music, watching different things. And when we are watching, listening, and seeing the same things, we are taking completely separate meanings away from them. I feel that part of how we got here was by deciding that political conversation was impolite, rude, and disruptive. I decided I would go to Montana, but I would only do so if people were willing to have political conversations with me. In doing so, I aligned myself with feminists who took risks and acted "difficult." Feminism, Ahmed (2017) explained,

> brings to mind loud acts of refusal and rebellion as well as the quiet ways we might have of not holding onto things that diminish us. It brings to mind women who have stood up, spoken back, risked lives, homes, relationships in the struggle for more bearable worlds. (p. 1)

I wanted to make my body and speech ardently political. In a symbolic act of this commitment, I acquired three pins before my trip. They said: "This is what a feminist looks like," and "Black Lives Matter," and the third was a small rainbow ribbon in support of the LGBTQ community. That winter, I wore them everywhere, along with a steely expression on my face, and waited to see how people responded.

The day my flight got in, Derek and I arranged to have 'the Trump conversation' in the afternoon before heading to a basketball game. We sat in the small TV room, which opens up to a large kitchen. Derek sat next to me on the couch and his mom, Carol, sat across from me in a La-Z-Boy chair. I asked that Derek's dad Doug also join us – he was currently up at the barn, working, and said he would come down later.

Derek set the stage for the conversation – that we were both upset by this election and that we had some things we needed to say. I started by laying out some of my concerns – how the person they voted for sexually assaulted women and bragged about it; how his rhetoric had racist, sexist, and xenophobic implications; how my friends who are immigrants, people of color, or LGBTQ are feeling increasing hatred. "The personal is political," but simultaneously, the political is also personal. What I wanted to convey was that this election was deeply personal. This was about my body, my friend's bodies, my sister's bodies, my colleagues' bodies, my neighbor's bodies. Bodies that are black, brown, gay, or have had their "pussy grabbed." Bodies of people that I do not even know, but who deserve to be safe and loved. I told Carol that I always knew we had political differences, and that in many ways that was okay and was probably good for all of us. I explained that this election revealed a chasm between us that had maybe always been there, but was far wider than I had thought.

Carol listened. When it was her turn to speak, she countered by bringing up something about Hillary Clinton. "But what about Hillary Clinton's [xyz scandal]?" she asked.

"I am willing to talk about Hillary, but that needs to be a separate conversation," I said, creating discursive brackets. I reiterated that this conversation was about Trump and the fact that they supported him: "Trump's policies are hateful. I don't know how you can support Trump and his policies."

"Well I don't know how you can support abortion," she said.

"Gladly, proudly. With joy," I responded curtly.

Things were starting to unravel. Derek jumped in. He suggested we not talk about abortion at the moment. Carol then went down a winding road explaining her religion and describing her views on sin and humanity. To me it felt out of context, but for her I knew it was not. I listened and struggled to understand how it related to the present conversation. She said that the world is a difficult, sinful place. She talked about how people make good and bad choices, choose sin, and that everyone is sinful.

Derek tried to bring up systems – how we are thinking in terms of structures, systems, and power, not just the 'personal choices' of an individual. How a person's life is influenced by complex forces that go beyond whether or not they make 'poor choices.'

Responding to the sentiment that Trump was hateful, Carol explained that she does not hate people. "I try to be a good person and I'm nice to everyone. I don't support transgenderism, but I don't hate them. I'm nice to the checker at Target."

I took a deep breath, trying to remind myself to meet people where they are. Derek's family knows little about the circumstances (or terminology) regarding people who transition. But I also felt angry and frustrated. "It's not something you do or do not support," I said, "And it is not enough to *be nice*. They *know*. People know how you really feel."

"How do they know?" She asked.

"People can tell." I said, thinking of my own ability to sniff out the slightest whiffs of sexism, even in someone I hardly know.

She asked "Then where is the place for my Christian beliefs?"

"*Everywhere*. Constantly, all the time. Because nearly 80% of this country is Christian," I said in a stern voice.

Carol revealed her frustration with the toll the election has taken on our family. "I'm not going to let Donald Trump, someone we've never even met, divide our family," she said.

Late in the conversation, Derek's dad came down from the barn. Carol said, "Doug, get over here and talk with us. You need to be part of this too."

He sat down reluctantly. I re-explained some of my feelings from before. He said "I don't know why we're having this conversation. I have some good ideas, I have some bad ideas. You have some good ideas, you have some bad ideas. We're not going to agree. Why are we doing this?" Doug indicated that this disconnect could not be helped and he had little interest in trying.

"Then I can't be here," I yelled.

Carol interjected, looking at Derek's dad. "Doug, if Sonia needs to have this conversation to feel comfortable being here, then we need to have it." Wiping tears from her face, she explained, "It breaks my heart that my daughter-in-law doesn't feel comfortable in my own house. Doesn't want to come to my house. We need to figure out how to make this better."

At some point Doug asked me what I was doing to fix these problems. "What are you out doing?"

I said "Well, I write, research, and teach things related to these issues. I call my politicians."

He replied, "that's not doing anything."

I explained that Derek and I would be going to DC in January for the Women's March.

"Marching isn't going to change anything. That isn't *doing something*. I'm out there *doing things*," he said, referencing his cattle ranching business which involves physical labor – building, branding, shipping tangible things.

Carol told Doug he was making things worse. Doug became increasingly uncomfortable. Unable to stay seated, he got up and started making a cup of tea. He asked if I wanted any, I declined. Trying to lighten the mood, he said, somewhat sarcastically "So do you feel better?"

I did not feel better, but I snapped back at him, saying, "Yes, this was an important conversation to have."

The night of 'the conversation,' we went to a college basketball game at the University of Montana. The game was intended to be a distraction, a fun thing we could all do together that relieved tension and did not involve heated disagreement. But after the election, and especially while in Montana that December, everything around me felt intensely political. All I could think about was how many people in this audience voted for Donald Trump? How many of these people are against the Black Lives Matter movement, as they sit here eating hot dogs and snow cones while being entertained by two teams of predominantly black bodies? How do they not sense that disconnect? The message they seemed to be sending, I felt, was "we are okay with your black bodies when they provide us with entertainment, but they are also disposable. We will not advocate for them. We will not be made to feel uncomfortable by them. We will become angry if they disrupt our fragile white realities." At one point, I got up from the bleacher seats and went to the bathroom, holding my head in my hands, trying not to cry with frustration.

That year, Derek's Grandmother said that no one had to go to church on Christmas Eve if they did not want to. This was a big step, an olive branch. However, it became clear to us that other family members felt differently.

This was Christmas, after all, and it was decided that this was one thing Derek and I "would not make into an issue."

So I went to church on Christmas Eve – a church that still does not allow women to read scripture from the lectern. Trump bumper stickers adorned pickup trucks in the snowy parking lot. That night, the pastor gave a traditional Christmas homily, speaking about Jesus' love and God's gift to humanity. His sermon, though positive and well meaning, felt disconnected from the lived experiences of many people today. I could not help but think of the global refugee crisis or the way Trump portrayed immigrants as criminals and rapists while calling for a "total and complete shutdown of Muslims entering [our country]." The people around me rejoiced in the happiness of the Christmas spirit, wanting to dwell in hope and light. For me, that year, in the company of many Trump voters, the festive sentiment felt disingenuous. But the pins on my jacket gave me solace. No one asked or wanted to hear what I had to say, but my body spoke for me. And much to Derek's Grandmother's credit, she boldly introduced us to their church companions. "This is my grandson Derek, and his wife Sonia," she said confidently, fully aware of my buttons. I remember one man in particular, who shook my hand enthusiastically only for his gaze to meet the buttons pinned to the left collar of my pea coat. His eyes grew wide and his head jerked up in shock.

I became sick that winter and had to visit Missoula urgent care on New Year's Day. An infection that I often get during times of stress became the worst version of this infection I had ever had. Days of discomfort, pain, low grade fever, and the inability to keep many intimate details private,[2] followed. Stress tends to find a way to express itself on the body. According to Anzaldúa (2015), "We must bear witness to what our bodies remember" (p. 21). *This is my body speaking to me*, I thought. This was a reminder that confrontation, difficult discussions, and activism are important, but this needs to be balanced with self-care, the ability to take breaks, and escape – which is emotionally and materially difficult for me to do while visiting my in-laws in Montana.

I felt intense relief leaving Montana that winter. At the small Missoula airport, Derek and I lifted our checked bags onto the carousel and said our final goodbyes. I reached up to hug my tall father-in-law. I moved to hug my mother-in-law and she squeezed me hard. She whispered in my ear, "I know it was really hard for you to be here this year. Thank you for coming. It meant so much to me," her voice quivering. I said that I was glad that I came, and then paused.

"If I send you some articles, will you read them?" I asked.

She said "Yes." When we pulled away, I could see tears welling up in her eyes.

Several years ago I wanted so badly for Derek's family to like me. I could not help indicating my disagreement with the racist/sexist/homophobic things that were sometimes said. But, I also chastised myself for 'being difficult' and 'making things an issue' when I felt these responses – sometimes ungracefully – leap out of me. Now, post-Trump, being 'likable' is not something I am aiming for. Culturally, we are in the middle of what Ahmed (2010) called a "happiness turn" where the pursuit of happiness has become a primary object of people's attention. This is what I experienced Trump voters wanting after the election. "Can't we all just be happy and get along?" Clinton voters were accused of acting like "babies" and of being unable to handle "losing." Why was it so hard to allow others to "just be happy" that their candidate won? Clinton's slogan that "Love trumps hate" was even used by Derek's mom as a reason for why we should simply ignore how people voted and "love each other" – a reason we should not "let" this man divide us. I thought about Ahmed's (2010) argument that "happiness" is used to justify oppression. Her words about the importance of feminist killjoys gave me the fuel and conviction I needed to have these conversations with Derek's family (and others) and to point out problems even if it meant, that I too, would be singled out as a problem. I no longer cared. "The feminist killjoy 'spoils' the happiness of others; she is a spoilsport because she refuses to convene, to assemble, or to meet up over happiness" (Ahmed, 2010, p. 65). I refuse to let 'love' become weaponized, to mean a passive sort of friendliness, keeping other people comfortable and 'happy,' when that happiness marginalizes others.

INCOMPLETE RESOLUTIONS

Kristen

My conversations with my father are like an ellipsis – rife with things unsaid. My dad and I do not talk as much as we used to. He remarked to me recently that it is painful for him to call me. It is painful for me to know that the one person in the world with whom I once felt completely secure, no longer feels safe. Perhaps this ellipsis is as good as it will ever get, and to some extent I have come to terms with that. Perhaps full healing is not possible and agreeing to move on is the best option. However, remaining silent now, especially in the face of even more injustice in our country, feels like complacency, and complacency feels like remaining complicit.

Sonia

In January 2017, my husband and I, along with a slew of our friends, made the trek to D.C. and marched. The year following Trump's election, we had more bold and confrontational political conversations with our family members than we had ever had in the past. Through our actions we made it clear that our votes would have consequences – we could not continue on as family with any expectations of complicit silence. I sent Carol an email about refugees and immigrants. In it, I appealed to her faith with an article that uses a Christian perspective to advocate for the importance of welcoming refugees into our country. I framed it as an invitation to dialogue and learn more about each other. Months after I sent that email, she told Derek she had printed it out and was planning to read the attached articles. That was over a year ago. I never heard back.

I am still trying to understand what Trump's presidency has meant for my relationship with my in-laws. In having these conversations, I remind myself that we will not, and cannot, know where they will take us. I cannot expect that agreement or transformation will occur as a result. But un-silencing myself is an important and radical act.

MAKING SENSE OF THE RUPTURES

In many ways we are still struggling to make sense of how Trump's election has and will impact our relationship with our family members. Our idealized and perhaps even culturally dominant ways of talking about family align it with home. Home connotes a place of refuge. A place that writes itself onto our bodies and becomes engraved in our memories. Home might be somewhere that we – or someone we loved – came from or somewhere we yearn to return to. The events that transpired in the 2016 presidential election complicated and ruptured our sense of being 'at home' with our families. National political events occupied our homes in ways we were unable to ignore. In both of our cases, homes became the site of emotionally charged political altercations. Before and after the election, we struggle to feel at home in our own country. For Bhabha (2003), the *unhomely* is a conjoining of home and world. It is a postcolonial space that connects the "traumatic ambivalence of a personal psychic history to the wider disjunctions of political existence." It is "the shock of recognition of the world-in-the-home, the home-in-the world" (p. 11). The reality that our family members voted for Trump – and the conversations that ensued as a result – represent our experiences of the unhomely.

The "silence" of politeness and civility that had previously regulated our interactions with our families was ruptured by Trump's victory. In writing these experiences, we felt an empowered sense of relief, release, and catharsis. We cannot guarantee a safe, just, or fair world, but we can talk and write about the injustices that we see. Upon receiving a breast cancer diagnosis that forced her to reckon with her own mortality Audre Lorde (1984/2007) said, "what I regretted most were my silences. Of what I had I *ever* been afraid?" (p. 41). We do not know what will happen with our family relationships as a result of our insistence on bringing Trump's election "home" – but in having these confrontations, we will at least not regret being silent.

Having difficult discussions is not an easy task and requires genuine commitment from all parties. Our preference would be for dialogue in which disagreement is acceptable and people continually work to understand the other person. In these contentious moments, we both wonder if this is possible. We look back at these conversations and wonder what we could have done better, what we will do better in the future. Did I listen well? How can I express how I am affected by this election without attacking my family member who voted for Trump? Are they feeling heard? Why am I not feeling heard? What does it mean, in practice, to actually "hear the person, not just the opinion?" (Mathes, 2016, para. 23) How can I work to be both direct, honest, but also compassionate? bell hooks (2010) explained that "conversation is always about giving. Genuine conversation is about the sharing of power and knowledge; it is fundamentally a cooperative enterprise" (p. 45). This is what we are looking for and this is what we will keep trying to do.

NOTES

1 The Japanese name given to children born to Japanese immigrants in America.
2 Privacy with illness is challenging when one is a visitor at someone's house.

REFERENCES

Ahmed, S. (2010). *The promise of happiness*. Durham, NC: Duke University Press.
Ahmed, S. (2017). *Living a feminist life*. Durham, NC: Duke University Press.
Anzaldúa, G. (2015). *Light in the dark/Luz en lo oscuro: Rewriting identity, sprituality, reality*. Durham, NC: Duke University Press.
Bhabha, H. (2003). *The world and the home*. Durham, NC: Duke University Press.
Bush, L. (2018, June 17). Laura Bush: Separating children from their parents at the border 'breaks my heart.' *The Washington Post.* Retrived from https://www.washingtonpost.com/opinions/laura-bush-separating-children-from-their-parents-at-the-border-breaks-my-heart/2018/06/17/f2df517a-7287-11e8-9780-b1dd6a09b549_story.html?noredirect=on

hooks, b. (2010). *Teaching critical thinking: Practical wisdom*. New York, NY: Routledge.

Kim, D. H. (2014). Shame and self-revision in Asian-American assimilation. In E. S. Lee (Ed.), *Living alterities: Phenomenology, embodiment, and race* (pp. 103–133). Albany, NY: SUNY Press.

Koenig Kellas, J. K. (2005). Family ties: Communicating identity through jointly told family stories. *Communication Monographs, 72*, 365–389.

Kruks, S. (2001). Going beyond discourse: Feminism, phenomenology, and 'women's experience.' In S. Kruks (Ed.), *Retrieving experience: Subjectivity and recognition in feminist politics* (pp. 131–152). Ithaca, NY: Cornell University Press.

Li, G., & Wang, L. (2008). *Model minority myth revisited: An interdisciplinary approach to demystifying Asian American Educational Experiences*. Charlotte, NC: IAP.

Lorde, A. (2007). *Sister outsider*. Berkeley, CA: Crossing Press. (Original work published in 1984)

Mathes, B. (2016, July 27). How to listen when you disagree: A lesson from the Republican National Convention. *Urban Confessional*. Retrieved from https://urbanconfessional.org/blog/howtodisagree

McGill, C. (2016, November 15). My scary, awkward, hopeful conversation with my dad about why he voted for Trump. *Vox*. Retrieved from http://www.vox.com/first-person/2016/11/15/13623694/trump-voters-understanding

Merleau-Ponty, M. (1968). *The visible and the invisible*. Evanston, IL: Northwestern University Press.

Peterson, W. (1966, January 9). Success story, Japanese-American style. *The New Yor Times*. Retrieved from https://timesmachine.nytimes.com/timesmachine/1966/01/09/356013502.html?pageNumber=180

Selzer, J., & Crowley, S. (1999). *Rhetorical bodies*. Madison, WI: University of Wisconsin Press.

Trees, A. R., & Koenig Kellas, J. K. (2009). Telling tales: Enacting family relationships in joint storytelling about difficult experiences. *Western Journal of Communication, 73*, 91–111. doi:10.1080/10570310802635021

Young, I. M. (2005). *On female body experience: "Throwing like a girl" and other essays*. New York, NY: Oxford University Press.

CHRISTINE SALKIN DAVIS AND JONATHAN L. CRANE

DIALOGUE 10

"How has this election affected you all? How have you been affected in the last two years?" I ask.

Andrea says, "My 401k has increased."

Larry adds, "Yeah. That was great. Taxes were good this time. There's so many things that people look at, not just outcomes from stocks. Corporations are doing well, but people say, 'that's the rich getting rich.' Well, you know what, if corporations do well, that's good for us. I don't think it's a bad thing when corporations do well."

Andrea says, "I'm middle class, and our tax bracket did decrease, so our income was taxed less, so we had more income throughout the year. Now, granted, we actually had to pay this year, but throughout the year we actually made more. So, I had more money to spend. Even though steel tariffs increased the cost of certain goods, the offset is I've had more money in my pocket to pay for those goods so it's, I think, so far, a big win."

"And, you know, as long as it's across the board and not just a certain group, yeah," says Larry.

Larry continues, "I'll be honest, I don't live in any kind of social issue lane, you know, I'm blessed. I've got a great job, I have insurance, so some of these other things that might be there where somebody might be looking for something more, whether it's on the healthcare side, I haven't had to experience it. Fortunately, I have a company that pays for my insurance so for me personally, I haven't seen premium increases, but my company's had to pay a little bit more to provide medical insurance for everyone. But for some of the social issues, I think he's honestly trying to stay away from social issues. I don't think he was going that way, I don't think he was really looking like, 'I'm going to overturn Roe v. Wade.' I think what's happened now is this legislation that's come out with these late term abortions, now all of a sudden he comes out saying, now we're going too far. I don't think that's a hill that he wants to stand on. I don't think social issues is something he really wants to go down. He's trying to run a country like a business, so I don't think social issues are really a lane that he wants to go down. And

DOI:10.1163/9789004436329_020

maybe that's why the other side thinks that he maybe doesn't care about them but again, and I'll say we're blessed in the fact that we don't live in a time where we're seeing negative effects of any of his policies."

Andrea says, "I would say overall, I've been pleasantly surprised. I had more reservations to begin with, and now two years in, I've been pretty satisfied and pleasantly surprised with what he's done."

"Yeah," Larry agrees.

"But, I still would say he's a little rough around the edges," Andrea says. "I would say that I've been pleasantly surprised with him. To begin with, he had a little bit of nervousness, and I thought, look out, oh my God, President Trump, are you kidding me? Out of all of these candidates," Andrea laughs, "how did we end up with Trump as President? Anyway. Donald Trump as President, so how did this happen? So, you know, I would say that there was a level of nervousness, but I would, I'm pleasantly surprised with how, with overall how he's done."

Larry says, "Would we vote for him in the next election?" He laughs.

"Would you?" I ask.

Larry says, "I think it's going to come down to who he's running against. It will be very interesting to see."

"And a lot could happen in two years," Andrea adds.

"I think the office needs to be held to a higher standard than some of the things that he's put out there," Larry says.

ROBYN R. JARDINE AND BETHANY SIMMONS

9. NOT/MY PRESIDENT

Presidential Race in Southern Black/African American and White American Families

DONALD TRUMP: THE DOG WHISTLE SOUNDS

Prior to Trump's Election

Pulling into the driveway, I was flooded with a mixture of anticipation, excitement and uncertainty. As I've driven through the rural South for the past two years, interviewing Black/African American and White American families regarding their experiences of race, my feelings have been intense and emotional. I got out of my car and was promptly greeted by my host. As I set up my equipment, the familiar and welcome smells of traditional Southern meat pies and peach cobbler permeated the room. I instantly felt at home with the comforting Southern hospitality rituals of food and connection. During my two years of being on the road studying multiple generations of Black/African American and White American families' perspectives on race relationships in the Southern United States, I was frequently fortunate to sample plates of fried chicken or fish, hot water cornbread, and greens. Although I didn't expect such generosity, I never turned down heaven on a plate.

This morning, as the interview began and the bowls of food were passed around, conversation turned to politics and the political climate. This visit was held during the run up to the 2016 presidential election, and Black/African American families expressed their concerns to me about Donald Trump, the potential Presidential candidate, as they discussed their perspective on race relations. For Black/African American families, Donald Trump's language, anti-immigrant policies, and racist Birther Movement rhetoric were dog whistles signalling what to expect should he be a nominee for the President of the United States. Even before Trump's selection as the Republican nominee, it was clear that many families viewed him as a White male supremacist. His

DOI:10.1163/9789004436329_021

emerging popularity was seen as a reaction to having had a Black/African American president. Black/African American participants told me:

> You hear Trump on TV saying that he wants to send the Black people back to Africa, and then, you have … Trump … talking about the Blacks, I don't even watch it anymore, but why you wanna get rid of the minorities? When you boil it all down, … they don't understand, and they don't even know how to treat people as people.

> You see, we in …, an adversary society here. You think you got to take sides. And you know, the Republicans is good at playing this sides game. And Donald Trump, oh, he just having a ball clowning with people with sides. Yeah. [Laughs] I mean, make an absolute fool out of him …. Now, he know better. But he's playing other people for a bunch of nuts, and they are a bunch of idiots, sitting there listening to that crap. Said, boy, this is intelligent looking people, you can sit there and buy into that? Yeah, this thing of sides. No, we don't have to do that, but there's a way you can subjugate people into thinking that this is how things have to be. And that's just not true …. The whole society leads you into that.

> Donald Trump saying some stuff, like, people actually listening to what he says. We all know it's pure ignorance, but they listen. And it affects some people. But it's not my problem that you ain't got the sense to understand that this ain't right, you know?

One of the most profound and prophetic moments for me was when one study participant, a middle-aged Black/African American, proclaimed: "Racists gonna really show up in 2016. I mean worse. It's gonna be worse."

As I left the interview, this statement troubled me, but I quickly dismissed it. It would not be until one year later that I realized how profound and prophetic this participant was. But for this informant, it was foreknowledge based on a deep-rooted fundamental understanding of the nature of the cultural and political context of the presidency, and the effects it has on our country and her people.

In contrast, White American families I spoke with focused on President Obama and what his presidency as the first Black president meant to them. They also talked about intersectionalities of race, power, and the meaning of the presidency. Most White families didn't take Trump seriously, but many wanted a White man back in office. It was obvious from the interviews that, to all participants, having a Black/African American man in the White

House demonstrated how narratives of race and power are embedded in the historical, social, political, and familial contexts that structure American relationships.

NOT/MY PRESIDENT: REACTIONS TO TRUMP'S VICTORY

Participants shared a broad range of reactions, experiences and opinions related to Trump's presidential election and first year in office that often varied based on race and social status. Their stories demonstrated how the system, structure, and culture of race is embedded within the historical, social, political, and familial contexts into which we are born, and particularly how those narratives inform and are informed by the highest position of power in this country. It is evident how this nexus continues to impact people's everyday experiences in all facets of their daily lived realities. One of the most powerful things that this research revealed was just how forcefully the political translates into the personal. For this reason, we showcase the voices of those living under Trump's presidency and highlight the significant impact his administration has had on the lives of Southern families.

Hopes and Fears

Expressions of hopes and fears regarding Trump's election differed according to the race and ethnicity of participants as well as by their expressed support or opposition to Trump's presidency.

All families expressed either hopes and/or fears regarding Trump's election. Participants against Trump's election had strong negative, fearful reactions, while participants who supported Trump expressed both hopes – notably with less fervor – and fears, regarding how he would be received and treated.

None of the Black/African American families interviewed expressed hope, but rather strong fears about Trump's election.

> It [will be] as close to hell on earth, I can imagine, if everything that he has attempted to do were actually come to pass.

> Oh yes, my fears have come true. The man was telling you who he was all during the campaign, he was showing you who he was. All of that vulgarity he was talking about to women, this is the man running for president. People didn't pay it any attention. He said he could go out there and kill somebody right now and people would still vote for

> him. He told people on the campaign "Get'em out of here, if anything happen to ya'll I'll pay for it. That is the President. White supremacist, skinheads, all of these different organizations came out to support him. I don't let it get me because I know God is in control, not Trump. I get aggravated but I don't let it get me down.

> … a lot of them [fears] did … [come to pass] …. My biggest fear was that I didn't feel like he was in touch with the basic common average American person, the day to day working citizen, and he has proved that to be so. That his mind is not really on us, it is as though we don't exist, he's proven that. Or that our needs are not important.

> Impossibility. I thought it would be a cold day in hell when Donald Trump could end up sitting in the presidency.

The White American families interviewed included people who supported Trump and those who were against Trump. All of these participants expressed both hopes and fears about Trump's presidency.

> It's been hopeful because I think we see that he [President Trump] is trying to make some changes … I believe probably most likely that he's [President Trump] getting our country back on track as far as financial programs that were being offered to … citizens that may have seemed like maybe when Obama was in office … that maybe one class of people being catered to more, and Trump is more across the board going to get things better for everyone, from a financial standpoint, any kind of programs, from health insurance to, I guess you would call it welfare, to food stamps and any other kind of government assistance that's available …. Lower income class people, probably people that abuse the system. I'm not going to help those who abuse the system, you know his goal [President Obama] was probably to help all lower class people, people that struggle, but I think it ended up being a lot of people that are just freeloaders who took advantage of it … you know, I'm a teacher, so I teach all races of children; [they all] also take advantage of the system too. Not just Black people but it tends to be that class of people identified with welfare and getting the monthly check, food stamps and things like that …. Going in a better direction …. Just hopeful, at the same time I've had moments I'm like 'Oh can the man just shut up!'

> I think one of my fears was that people weren't going to accept him. It was going to continue to split the country. I pointed out that he was a

> White, dominant, powerful man and after a Black man, not that a Black man can't be powerful and wealthy and called those things too, but I just feared that he would be a negative thing who wasn't going to bring the nation … together.

> Yes, fears. Afraid that he [Trump] would promote vitriol …. There are a lot of things that are important to different areas of our societies, different groups of our society that he is removing. Gone way backwards with equity for all. We are being conditioned to ignore and just go on with our lives.

Stress & Dangerous Consequences

It is clear Trump's election has been stressful for many of the families interviewed. Some of the words and phrases used when they expressed these reactions and experiences were "trauma/traumatic," "in mourning," "stressful," "fear/afraid/scared," "numb," "dangerous," "disappointment," "frustration," "embarrassing" and, "aggravated." With the exception of one pro-Trump family, participants both for and against Trump shared strong physical and emotional reactions to Trump's election.

Many Black/African American families discussed how Trump's victory has not only been stressful, but has also had serious, dangerous consequences for them, their loved ones, and others within their communities. For Black/African American participants, Trump's victory heightened long-standing daily lived challenges and concerns, particularly after experiencing racial aggression and dangerous situations that exacerbated existing fears for personal safety. Participants recounted having to be cautious when they were out in the community. They described being kept from living in certain areas of the community, of having been called derogatory names, and of having received verbal threats from White Americans.

In one Black/African American family, only the daughter agreed to be re-interviewed after the election. The mother and other family members declined out of

> fear [of] not remaining anonymous. Even though I [daughter] explained I would be doing the same thing, she [my mother] said 'no, I can't have my name getting out there and it get back to me and something happen to me.'

The participant's family members were unwilling to be re-interviewed after Trump was elected, because they had encountered dangerous, personal experiences of racism after the election. Those experiences brought back memories of older racist encounters that had resulted in the loss of life and physical, emotional, and financial harm.

Another Black/African American mother and daughter were driving in a White community after the election when a younger White male in a truck shouted racial slurs and tried to run them off the road.

Yet another family shared a story about how a Black man in their community almost lost his life and has to live with permanent injuries after talking to a White woman in a public establishment. According to the family, the perpetrators in this incident directly linked their attack to Trump's presidency, stating, "We've known someone that [was] beat up for going into a place and speaking to a White girl. They beat him to a pulp and told him 'Trump is your president now boy.'"

Not a single White American family voiced concerns or fears for their safety, nor shared any stories of experiences of dangerous consequences after Trump's election.

Social & Relational Challenges – Familial, Friendship, Community & National

It is clear that the election had a direct impact on personal relationships and the community. All participants said they were mindful about who they talk to about the Trump presidency due to concerns about others' reactions, yet, as we've shown, the consequences and reactions were often diametrically different for Black/African Americans and White Americans.

Moreover, all participants discussed how the presidential election impacted their family dynamics and relationships with each other. In many cases, the election amplified existing tensions or illuminated long-standing, polarizing beliefs, creating conflict. In other cases, some families described increased feelings of solidarity and cohesion. Overall, families discussed the impact of the political discourses on their relationships. Not only did the election impact relationships within families, but also between White American families and Black/African American families, and with interracial friendships and casual interactions.

In addition, many Black/African American participants saw Trump's election as an extension of and promotion of White supremacy that supported aggression toward people of color, in an attempt to maintain the White supremacist status quo. Trump's election exposed racial challenges and divides that are often discounted by White Americans.

This isn't just things I've heard, but people we actually know experience a lot of racism … because of the tone and the attitude of our President. It was like giving permission to behave this way. So, we no longer have to respect you as a race or as a person because our president doesn't. We don't have to like you. We don't have to pretend, none of that anymore …. I think it gave people the boldness to act on what they really felt. [It] gave you the boldness and the permission to be a fool. There is no other way to say that, to be a fool. If you were not already thinking that way or behaving that way, I don't think that it has caused people to be that way, or to become that way. It might have given you the boldness to act out, but you are acting out on what you already felt.

I have some really good acquaintances, since Trump has been in office they feel it's okay to say nigger, or post certain things, and I just have to reiterate to them that at the end of the day, I am Black and there are some things that you can't say and do around me. So, they tend to forget, and I have to give them a reality check. In my mind, I say that this is not really their personality and that's how we manage to stay friends.

The effects of his presidency, media coverage, people's reacts [sic] to [his presidency], I am seeing its effects on individuals in the public. Insecurity. A majority of the people. Like riding a ship. Big tidal waves. Doesn't ever feel like that ship is going to get level again …, you don't even feel like you are going to a safe place anymore. Insecurities have increased. There is this paranoia, freaking out until something relieves you as a distraction … from the anxiety.

Oh yes, even with colleagues … the very first thing that I noticed is we were never allowed to wear political shirts on campus but when he [Trump] got in office there were Trump shirts everywhere …. It was on the news on another campus that students showed up in pickup trucks with Confederate flags and those students were not reprimanded for their behaviors; it was just overlooked. It's gotten worse.

In everyday communication with people in stores when you are interacting with people in business. The automatic looks that are on their faces, they're actually seating you in the back corner of the restaurant as opposed to any other place, when the entire restaurant is open, 'we are just going to sit you back here.' No, we are not just going to sit right back here, in the corner, in the dark.

White American participants discussed the personal and social impact of Trump's election. Some focused on defending Trump, and on their distrust of the media, while others discussed White privilege and acknowledged discrimination and racism. These participants were hopeful that Trump might unify Americans, and encourage needed conversations and dialogues.

> Other members of my family voted for Trump – it has caused a rift in our family, my brother is dead to me.

> [In light of Trump's election], it is more important to me to continue the diversity role I have on this campus, in my family, wherever I go. Because I'm White, I'm talking from a White privileged position. It makes the conversations that we have with each other so important. It has strengthened the support system on this campus. I'm hoping the conversation keeps going.

> My boyfriend has family members that don't like Trump. We have friends that don't like Trump. You know there is always that debate at some point, even in the White community about him .... I have to tell my [boyfriend] to put a filter on it, pause, think about what you are saying, there is time and a place, don't discuss sex, politics, and religion in a mixed crowd of people, unless you can really represent yourself and do it eloquently.

> [The election gave us] something to complain about, disagree ..., it intensified .... [In the end], Trump has been extremely good for our family, because we had to set aside our differences, we had to make the decision to come back and we did. That has made us a tighter unit and more compassionate group of people and a stronger family. It's a trauma the family went through.

> I feared that it would be just like a joke to people, people from other countries going to think 'oh what a joke, look who they have in office.' I think he [Trump] has a really good heart. I think he doesn't know how to express it. People take him the wrong way .... Yeah, I do think people take him the wrong way. He says things that he doesn't [mean], that people take out of context. People are so good at twisting words now .... A lot of it is the media. I don't know why the media have gotten as [bad as they have] .... They like to play up that he is a bad person, make him a negative in the world.

> I think Donald Trump will be an incredible unifier. I can't listen to media, mainstream media .... I distrust the media .... They are going to do whatever they want to in Washington. [We have to] build ourselves up .... We've been forgotten, the middle class .... The people in Washington are only looking after themselves, not listening to their constituents. The middle class is getting screwed.

Race Is Personal Is Political Is the Presidency

The presidency of the United States carries significant symbolism and power as it relates to race. This power is exhibited on social, political, cultural, and historical macro levels, and also at the micro interpersonal level, shaping, influencing, and amplifying family dynamics. The presidency both constructs and magnifies racialized societal dynamics that are political and personal. Both Black/African Americans and White Americans noted the power of the Presidency to affect their everyday lives and shape their politics, relationships, and their emotional, cognitive, and physiological reactions to oppression and danger.

There is a mutual relationship between culture, racialized social structures, racialized social norms, and race relationships. All participants shared experiences and stories which connect the power of the presidency to race relationships in America, and illustrate how the polarizing politics of the Trump administration have affected social, business, and personal relationships between White and Black/African Americans.

Trump's election came as no surprise to Black/African American participants. Trump's political success was seen as a backlash to the first Black/African American president. Black/African American families reported daily experiences of racism and microaggressions have increased since the Trump administration took office. For Black/African American participants, Trump and his politics resulted in an escalation of their oppression, and a promotion of systemic White supremacy.

> It was payback for having Obama in. That's exactly what it is, it was rigged [Trump getting the presidency]. I wholeheartedly believe this is payback.

> Trump was raised by his daddy and his daddy was a businessman ... those people know how to play the game, how to game the system. To game the system you have to understand the system. And Trump has been on several interviews over the years ... he had mentioned some

> things that let you know that he understood the game. One of the games that can be played is this race game, and playing to that group of White men who want their position back. They think they are entitled to be the head of the food chain. And this is what Trump has played into, because we got at least ⅓ of the country that has that mentality. And he knows that .... Sometimes when people are getting the benefit, they render themselves, call it cognitive dissonance, to not allow themselves to know what they fear will cause them to lose the benefit. At least on one level, deep down inside they [White people] know. They are just playing dumb or render themselves dumb because it is convenient for them or beneficial to pretend they don't believe something or don't know something. As long as it doesn't cost them anything, that works for them. But if you turn the table, they wise up real quick. Some are genuinely ignorant, and some are ignorant by choice.
>
> I knew it was there, but I didn't know the percentage. Such a large number of White women would not vote in their own interest. They voted for a White male supremacist. They [women] are conditioned to do that by White men.
>
> In all honesty, it [Trump's election] shed light [on] what African Americans have lived through throughout the years. It's just made it more visible to other individuals that live in a bubble.

White American families, particularly pro-Trump families, seemed to disconnect both themselves and Trump from his racist rhetoric, not identifying themselves or his coming to power as a symbol of racism, while at the same time making racist statements themselves. Nevertheless, they did recognize the significance of the race of the president as fundamental to political power that impacts them from the macro to the personal level. For example, White American Trump voters expressed a sense of hope for "balance and fairness" for all citizens, citing their belief that President Obama catered to Black/African Americans, and didn't like how Black/African Americans responded to his presidency.

> [Saying] 'I'm not a racist,' makes it [support of Trump] come across ... like we are racist, but we are not. There's always been a need for that debate within the White community.
>
> I always felt scared when Obama was in office. He really didn't know what he was doing, and maybe he was halfway doing it, I can't find

> one thing that he really accomplished, that made him this awesome president. I don't think it has anything to do with that he is Black; in a way it does because people made such a big deal of him being Black. So as the Black president, if it was such a big deal, what did he do? I never felt like he connected to the White people of the country.
>
> I think it [Trump's election] caused a split and a division .... I wondered why Black people are so against a White, wealthy man that's educated, who has some good ideas. Are they fearful that he will take away welfare? Are they fearful because he's doing it because they are Black and he is picking on them? I really have thought about that .... Why don't they [Black people] really like him? Why? I did not, not like Obama because he was Black, I didn't like the reaction to when he became president. I didn't like that I never got what his presidential goal was. What was his whole objective as president? His platform? I just never did.

One White American participant, staunchly anti-Trump, became visibly distressed as he realized during the interview that while he considered himself to be a White ally advocating for equal rights, he actually supported some of Trump's policies, which were racist in nature. The election of Trump challenged families' notions of what it means to be a racist and a White American.

These perspectives describe the experiences of both White Americans and Black/African Americans living within the structure and culture of racism embedded at the highest level in our society. It seems that the racist platform of Donald Trump, and his subsequent election victory, was no coincidence following on the heels of the first Black/African American president. Both Black/African American and White American families' responses suggested that the election of Trump and his "Make America Great Again" platform was a homeostatic response to maintain the White power structure. All participants discussed how the Trump presidency embodied a power struggle between White Americans and Black/African Americans.

CONCLUSION

Through the use of galvanizing political rhetoric, theater, and policy, the first year of the Trump administration impacted many facets of American lives. Racial antagonism was center stage in the country in the wake of the Trump presidency. Mistrust and divisiveness between White American and Black/African American families increased as a result of the election.

In addition, Trump's rhetoric encouraged racialized violence, which heightened safety concerns for Black/African Americans. Increased racial bias also impacted their social mobility, such as where they could buy a house. They had to deal with harassment and address racism at work. Overall, Black/African American participants reported an increased need for hyper-vigilance to avoid being caught in an unsafe position.

Participants who voted for President Trump (only White families in this study) reported being supportive of his agenda, but did not consider him or themselves racist. They felt hopeful that the future will be more egalitarian in terms of the distribution of resources for everyone, based on their belief that during the previous administration, the poor and minorities were taking advantage of the social system at the cost of the White American middle class. Participants did not always agree with Trump's presentation, behavior, and communication, but that did not undermine their support of his program to "Make American Great Again." In addition, White American participants voiced their mistrust of the news media, citing reporting on Trump as selective, exaggerating, and/or inflating stories about him for the purposes of ratings and to win a partisan political war. Trump was described as a victim who was treated unfairly by the press. White American families did not want to be perceived as racist simply because they were pro-Trump.

The election of Trump to the presidency was attributed by both White and Black/African American participants to be a reaction to his African American predecessor. In addition, it was perceived by Black/African American participants to bolster a White, patriarchal, racially structured system. In conjunction with America's historical and present-day experiences of race, White supremacy is culturally ingrained in American race relationships, and also in the political structure and foundation of the country. The Trump administration's polarizing, racially charged, political platform challenged American identity for both Black/African American and White American participants and divided some families to the point that relations were severed.

These experiences of all participants in Trump's first year in office highlights the perpetuation of systemic oppression and racism. The stories in this chapter also illustrate the denial and minimization of continual challenges in our present-day interracial relationships. In the eyes of Black/African American participants and some anti-Trump White participants, his presidency both reflects and promotes continuation of this country's racism. On the other hand, Trump supporters denied his (and their) racism, and disconnected Trump's racist, White supremacist platform and policies from themselves. In part, to identify Trump as racist would also implicate themselves as having a racist or White supremacist ideology, which they strongly refuted. They were unable to articulate self-awareness of White privilege – how they themselves benefit from the oppressive system and structure itself.

It is clear that it does matter who the President is, as well as the race and ethnicity of the office holder. The power of the presidency lies in its ability to influence who we are in relation to one another. In addition, the President of the United States clearly affects all our daily lives as our country wrestles with acknowledging systemic racism, creating equity/equality, and abolishing white suprepremacy.

CHRISTINE SALKIN DAVIS AND JONATHAN L. CRANE

DIALOGUE 11

"Russian interference in the election?" I prompt.

Andrea says, "So far, they have found none, nothing, so I believe there's nothing."

Larry says, "is it possible that they had a desire to want Trump elected? Sure. I mean, are there lobbyists that want certain presidents because they see their views? Sure. So they're no different to me than any lobbyist firm that is trying to push their candidate. If it's the NRA that's pushing something out there, that's no different than pushing an agenda. So, did they influence me? No. Do I think there was any kind of meddling? Somebody got on social media and said things about Hillary. Well somebody put up the recording of what Trump said on the bus, on *Entertainment Tonight*. I feel like people should be able to look past all that and go down to some of the issues. And in the end, I think it's all to be weighed. Do I think they actually put things out there and made things known to try to influence? No more than anybody else does, certainly."

Andrea says, "Does it hurt my ears? Yes. You know, because it makes you wonder, holy cow, that would not be cool to have Trump and Russia in cahoots with each other."

"Okay," I say. "But you don't think they are?"

"Not in the election," Andrea says. "Now he'll want to build a Trump Tower there, I mean, you know. And, honestly, could it really boil down to a Trump Tower somewhere? I just, I don't. I would like to hope that that would not be any type of influence."

Larry says, "Nothing surprises me. Any party, any candidate would use any information to their advantage to try to do what they needed to do to secure an election, and, yeah, information is power. I like to have as much information as possible. How I get it, it's still information I was able to get."

Andrea adds, "On the one hand, if that could be a good relationship with Russia, then it makes you feel good. Just like North Korea. If we could put ourselves out there and have a better relationship with those countries, that's good. But then, on the flip side, it's been so much bad for so long, is it really

DOI: 10.1163/9789004436329_022

a relationship that you could trust? So, with North Korea, don't tweet, 'Oh, he could become a good economist and a good this and a good that.' No. That could be a deal breaker. Don't start promoting somebody who you called Little Rocket Man to begin with."

"That's a great point," Larry says. "We're this way with one person and then we're immediately this way with one person. I think he has this real big thing about loyalty and people who support him, and you could be at war, if he got into a room and Kim Jong-Un went over and said, 'Oh, you've got cool hair. I like your hair,' I think, for Trump, it feeds his ego. I think people with that kind of power, in that kind of position, have tons of ego or they wouldn't be where they're at. He just feeds off that. But he takes it to the level of, this person's a great person and I think they're going to do all these great things. And it's like, did you forget that he killed his uncle or brother or whoever it was? Had him executed. Did you forget about that? You know."

"I mean, yeah, that's where I would have reservations a little bit," Andrea says.

"What does it mean that white supremacists supported Trump, and racial violence has increased since the election?" I ask.

Larry says, "What I would say is that, have white supremacists ever not come out in favor of a candidate? So, go back to Charlottesville, and I think it's what was said immediately after. Was it rebuked in a strong enough manner? Because I think at the end of the day, you have to look at the people he's surrounding himself with, you have to look at his past and the way he's been recognized for certain things. I don't think racists are people that he wants to associate himself with, but, I don't know. If it's stoking his base. Yeah, it's a horrible thing, and I think he could have handled Charlottesville, obviously, a lot better. I think he should have immediately come out and rebuked a little bit stronger than he did. What his endgame was, I'm not sure. I don't think it's support for white supremacists. I don't think he's a big supporter of that."

"Okay," I say.

Andrea says, "And I think it goes back to who feels comfortable to be more vocal at the time. Things that stood out to me, at the State of the Union the other day, maybe this was a political game. But, the black lady who was in prison for life over some drug charge. I mean, we've got people who kill people on DUI's and spend six months in jail and they're out. Whereas this person does whatever kind of drug, I don't know what her specific drug offense was. I just know it was a drug offense and she was supposed to be serving a lifetime sentence. And she was pardoned. A black lady. And then there was a black gentleman, same thing. He was also pardoned. So, to me, you can get into a lot deeper in terms of looking at the population of people who are sentenced to that, and what their race is. But the fact that it was two black people he pardoned. Also, he recognized a Jewish man who was at a shooting. So I was thinking, wow, he's recognizing a diverse range of people."

Andrea continues, "I would like to have a conversation with people who don't support Trump. I work with an African-American lady, and she and I have some conversations from time to time. We try to stay away from politics, but I can definitely tell she is not a Trump supporter. I feel like I'm an open-minded person. And I really like to put myself in other people's shoes and see how they perceive things to really get a true understanding. But I don't, I truly don't understand. Maybe some people would say that it's ignorance on my part. I don't know. But I truly don't understand what Trump has done to make them feel like he's racist. I don't understand."

Larry adds, "I don't, either. I think maybe he handled something poorly, maybe, in how he communicated right after Charlottesville but, I don't know. But I don't sit in their shoes. Maybe something was said somewhere and it didn't resonate with me, but it resonated with them. That's very possible."

Andrea says, "Even with the NRA, I don't think that's something that he's been standing heavily on."

"You don't see him out touting. I mean, he's talking about building a wall. I don't see him every day going, 'keep your guns, twenty round magazines,'" Larry says.

Larry says, "So, I don't, from my own perspective, I don't know what ..."

Andrea interrupts, "he has done to make ..."

"... certain minorities feel he is racist and against them."

"I don't," Andrea says.

"I think I'm a realist," Larry says. "I think I'm a rationalist. I'm a conservative Christian who is willing to vote for a Democratic president if I felt that was the best candidate. I will not agree with some of the dialogue that's being put out there, the things that are being said by a president that we actually voted for. I'm conservative but I'm more moderate. I'm not a tea party guy."

Andrea says, "And I think a lot of it is just simply, if you feel like if your party didn't win, then your best interests, your interest is not going to be kept in mind."

"Yeah. Mm-hmm," Larry agrees.

"So, in terms of white supremacy, I think a lot of it is who supports him. And then I think maybe it is fear, concern, that now that this president, who is Republican, who believes in x, y and z, well then, now I'm going to be put on the back burner."

"Something's going to happen," Larry says, "Like entitlement programs. You know, I can speak to situations where somebody drove to a grocery store in an Escalade, bought a wedding cake, several hundred dollars using food stamps, and then had their party reception at an expensive venue."

"That's a problem," Andrea says.

Larry says, "And I can tell you of people who have come in this country and used documentation to seek employment, fill out a W-4 and put 20, 25 dependents on there to pay the least amount of taxes, and then never file taxes on that information. So, sometimes you go, yeah, there's things that need to be done so that we know whether or not there's a certain party that could get elected that might want to enhance those entitlement programs and, as a country, it's breaking us. Gotta figure something out."

"Yeah. There's people who need it," Andrea says.

"Absolutely."

"Of course, there are so many people abusing the system."

"Yup. And some of them more than others," Larry says.

"And I saw something recently about, well, just because I have an EBT doesn't mean that I can't have nice things, too. Okay. I get that concept. I understand that everybody likes to feel like they need to have something, but she had mentioned, yes, I drive a 2015 Maxima. Yes, I have an iPhone. And she had three kids and uses her EBT card for whatever purchase. Okay. That's fine. I totally get that. But, at the same time, if you're having to use that, just be a better steward of what you have."

Larry says, "Yeah, I mean, my tax preparer can tell you stories about how they manipulate the number of children that each one will claim in order to manipulate taxes and receive $11,000 refunds on their taxes. You hear that and you just go, 'what?!' We're out here working hard. We're trying to do what we need to do. We pay our taxes, and it's just not right. So when I hear someone that's gone extremely left and trying to push an agenda where we're going to take care of everybody. We want everybody to, you know, all have free healthcare. It's a 'we're going to take care of you' kind of mentality; I think we have a president now that's saying no. You're going to work. We're going to put people to work and we're going to do what we need to do. It needs to be there but it doesn't need to be a crutch. Able-bodied [people] who can work, there are jobs, there are things you can do, go find a job, and do something. And it might not be what you want, but maybe it's a stepping stone to something else. And so, that's the conservative side of me coming out. I think that's what he wants. That's what I believe in, and I think that's the good side. Just get off Twitter."

Andrea says, "that's the truth. Get off Twitter."

JENNIFER L. ERDELY

10. INTERCULTURAL RELATIONSHIPS IN A POST-TRUMP WORLD

Mediating and Mitigating

INTRODUCTION

This autoethnographic essay looks at intercultural relationships since Trump's 2016 presidential run. The relationship between my spouse and I has not existed in a Trump vacuum. This chapter uses narratives from the distant and more recent past to contextualize our relationship within the recent political environment. Bringing awareness to these incidents serves as a plea for people who have privilege to engage in what Kelly Oliver terms witnessing. It is imperative for those of us who can, to discuss, stand up for, and testify against what happens to brown bodies in the United States. This chapter witnesses how Donald Trump's election has contributed to a surge in nativism and instilled a fear of immigrants and people of color, and, in response, generated a fear of being Othered among immigrants and other vulnerable populations.

RACE AND RACES

The Personal

Growing up as a white female in the Southern United States, I often *heard* the words that people of color were called. *Cigány* was the first derogatory racial term I heard. It is a Hungarian word for gypsy, and Hungarian was my grandparents' first language. In my family vernacular, this word was used to describe any person of color pejoratively. I later learned that my family name is from the Transylvania region of what is now Romania. In this portion of Romania, people from the Indian diaspora migrated and are collectively called Roma.

I read as a cis-gender, able-bodied white woman. I grew up in a predominately white neighborhood outside New Orleans, Louisiana, and

 | DOI:10.1163/9789004436329_023

I moved to Houston, Texas to live with my partner in 2010. My partner's parents immigrated to the United States from India, and he is a naturalized citizen of the United States.

When my partner and I first moved to Houston, a city of six million people, we laughed at the stickers on the backs of Mercedes-Benz sedans with "Secede" in black letters over a Texas flag. We chuckled at the improbability of the Republic of Texas having an independent trade agreement with Germany to import Mercedes-Benzes. We amused ourselves thinking about how a Mercedes would look driving on roads that weren't paved with a smooth stream of federal transportation funding. That was in 2010.

In 2015, the stickers began to fade when former Texas Governor Rick Perry initiated his run for President of the United States, not the Republic of Texas. When Trump became the Republican Party's nominee, we started seeing fewer Mercedes sedans with stickers and more pick-up trucks with flagpoles built into the truck's bed. Sometimes their flags would say: "Don't Tread on Me" with a snake and a yellow background, sometimes the flags would repeat the "Secede" mantra, other times we saw American flags, the Texas State flag, the Confederate battle flag, or some combination of the three.

As the pick-up trucks passed us, they also passed miles of storefronts in strip malls filled with the latest in Mexican, Tex-Mex, Indian, Pakistani, Chettinad (South Indian), Honduran, Filipino, Nigerian, Jamaican, El Salvadorian, or some fusion of these cuisines. Also, Hooters, Chili's, McDonald's and other national chains peppered the strip malls.

We, too, participated in the peppering of Houston's population. As a white and Indian American couple, we fit into Houston in ways we did not fit into other parts of the South. In other parts of the South, my partner and I were often the only people seated in the dark corner of a restaurant or behind a wall dividing the serving sections. White couples and families occupied one section, people of color were seated in the section where we were seated. When we are out together, people often ask my partner where he is from. Sometimes, strangers guess he is Latino, Middle Eastern, or Southeast Asian.

My partner politely responds to queries about how "good" his English is with, "I guess it's because we grew up watching the news and *Sesame Street*." Though born on opposite sides of the world, we actually grew up the same predominately white neighborhood. His dad took out a high-interest loan to live in a middle-class neighborhood. Most of the other parents in the neighborhood had a good-paying job at one of the two oil refineries or the chemical or nuclear plant located nearby on the Mississippi River. Our parents worked at none of these businesses, but they were determined to live in an area with some of the best public schools in the state. My partner and I knew of each other as children and attended the same schools growing up. Through a series of circumstances neither of us could have predicted, we encountered one another by accident ten years after we lost touch. At the time that we reconvened, I was pursuing my doctorate, and he was pursuing his second bachelor's degree.

My partner enjoys American movies, television, and video games. I enjoy speaking French and learning Spanish and Bengali (his first language). We both love to travel. We both love punk rock. We both love to learn, and we love our dog. My partner and I joke that the voice recognition software on our phones understands him better than me even though English is my first language. Having a partner who is both non-white and an immigrant has made me aware of racial issues he's had to endure his whole life.

My partner and I are news enthusiasts – we follow the news with constant attention. We cross-check sources – public radio, Twitter, network broadcasts, newspapers, news aggregators, and online news sources such as *Vox*, *Vice*, and *The Huffington Post*.

The purpose of this chapter is to provide a perspective on how the political affects the personal. This essay serves as a window into a relationship caught between and through worlds (political, social, cultural, familial, national, and spatial). My partner and I are both citizens of the United States. We're grateful that we both have good careers and are educated. These circumstances provide me the opportunity to write about issues of intercultural relationships in a post-Trump era. My aim in writing this is to bring further awareness to matters of race in relationships and serve as a call to action for those of us with white privilege to bring awareness, and ultimately, change the way we view people who may not look like us.

I think about race, religion, and culture a lot, but in this chapter, I struggled with writing about something as important as my relationship with my life partner. Equally important, I grappled with how my partner would feel about episodes in his life being a part of this piece, and with documenting the rituals that are a part of his family traditions. I also wrestled with confronting our fears and how they are a part of our daily lives and how they affect the ways in which we move through the world.

After expressing these concerns to my partner, he said, "I think it's important to publish these issues."

"They're not just applicable to us," I added.

"Absolutely."

With his permission, I wrote about our experiences. These aren't just his experiences, or my experiences, or our experiences as a couple. Experiences such as these are shared across a broad spectrum of the U.S. population. We do not desire to leave this country, but instead we desire to witness to our stories so that individuals with white privilege can have some insight into the lives of people of color.

The Political

When Donald Trump announced he was running for president on June 6, 2015, he said:

> Our country doesn't have victories anymore …. When have we beat China…When have we beat Mexico at the border? They're laughing at us at our stupidity, and now they are beating us economically. They are not our friend, believe me, but they're beating us economically. The U.S. has become a dumping ground for everyone else's problems. It's true. When Mexico sends its people, they're not sending their best. They're not sending you [points to crowd above]. They're sending people that have lots of problems, and they're bringing those problems with us [sic.] They're bringing drugs, they're bringing crime, they're rapists, and some, I assume, are good people …. It's coming from all over …. They're sending us not the right people. It's coming from more than Mexico. It's coming from all over South and Latin America, and it's coming probably, probably from the Middle East, but we don't know because we have no protection and no competence. We don't know what's happening, and it's got to stop and it's got to stop fast. (*PBS Newshour*, 2015, n.p.)

Early in his candidacy, Trump began establishing a platform for policies that would marginalize Muslims. On November 16, 2015, Trump called into *Morning Joe* after ISIS attacked several locations in Paris. He said, "We should watch and study the mosques because there's a lot of talk going on at the mosques." On the same broadcast, he discussed past surveillance programs at New York City mosques (*Morning Joe*, 2015). In December 2015, Donald Trump stated that borders should close to Muslims (Johnson, 2015). He followed this with a tweet stating, "Just put out a very important policy statement on the extraordinary influx of hatred & danger coming into our country. We must be vigilant!" (Trump, 2015, n.p.).

Families without Borders

The first time I went to India was six months into my marriage with my new sister-in-law and her son, my nephew, who was five years old. As an avid traveler, I dreamed of going to India. I was excited to experience the cultures, the streets, the people, and the music. I never imagined that I would be going to South Asia as the new bride of the only son of the oldest son in the family to participate in the immersion rituals on the Ganges. I cried when his family accepted me into theirs – a *bideshi* – a foreigner who did not speak Bengali or Hindi. I fell in love with my husband's family, just like I fell in love with my husband. I feel a strong connection to my husband's roots. His grandmother, aunt, and I cried the first time we met. Our connection was palpable. As we traveled through India visiting family, my sister-in-law taught her son and me about the traditions, customs, and dress, as well as how to greet Indian family members.

WITNESSING

Trump's presidency has emboldened individuals to act in racist ways, and technology and the press have allowed stories of these acts to be widely circulated. Witnessing enables people to see what is happening, and it can be a tool for us to better understand and support those around us who suffer discrimination. By recounting these incidents and their implications to others, we bring awareness of these incidents to those who may not have experienced them. The most effective way of bringing awareness to these issues is through telling and retelling these stories. Autoethnography serves as a particularly powerful tool for witnessing through narrative. Giorgio (2013) discusses her own impetus for utilizing autoethnography. She states, "We write autoethnographies to make sense of the seemingly senseless, to deepen our understanding of self and other, to witness lived experience so that others can see it, too" (p. 407). Giorgio (2013) describes how autoethnography helped her to "build community and collective memory" while processing her grief, trauma, and losses (p. 407).

Telling stories is an important tool in building communities in which individuals' experiences are better understood. As Ellis states, "Narrative truth seeks to keep the past alive in the present" (p. 745). Many other scholars have written extensively about the impact of narratives (Adams, 2011; Boylorn, 2013; Chawla, 2014; Davis & Breede, 2015; Ellis & Bochner, 2000; Harris, 2014; Holman Jones, 2016; Langellier & Peterson, 2004; Madison, 1998; Park-Fuller, 2000; Spry, 2016). Storytelling disarms the listener. Rather than listening to a lecture, the listener listens to an incident, an episode, or an experience in someone's life. These incidents, when recounted in detail, are difficult to refute and cement a connection between the teller, the listener, and the subject of the narrative. Stories of experiences give tangible evidence of racism and xenophobia. Personal stories of these larger societal issues can provide the listener different perspectives and recontextualization.

Using autoethnography and Oliver's concept of witnessing to testify to the racism and xenophobia that people of color experience in the United States, serves as a sort of double-witnessing. This chapter uses Oliver's concept of witnessing to link the role of solidarity with the act of storytelling. Witnessing is a way to activate the public, as Kelly Oliver (2001) states, "witnessing has the double sense of testifying to something that you have seen with your own eyes and bearing witness to something that you cannot see; there is the juridical sense of bearing witness to what you know from firsthand knowledge as an eyewitness" (p. 18).

White privilege protects many of us from experiencing hateful acts because of our race. White privilege does not alleviate the responsibility of white people to testify about hateful acts we have witnessed against people of color. Although targeted individuals do not *need* white people to witness for them, claims Oliver (2001), white people's witnessing is necessary to their own need to see and hear the injustices happening around them. Oliver is not calling for a white savior; she is calling for white recognition, translation, and support of individuals' struggles as a way to promote change. As a person with white privilege, suggests Oliver (2001), it is critical for me to recognize and acknowledge the oppression of individuals who do not share the same status, "in order to reestablish subjectivity and in order to demand justice" (Oliver, 2001, p. 90). Change is only possible through listening and striving to understand the painful struggles of others.

With each telling and retelling of stories, listeners learn the nuances and difficulties of others' lives. Each recounting provides an opportunity to obtain *some* semblance of an understanding of the injustices that people of color still endure to varying degrees today.

Oliver's second point is that acts of witnessing should run parallel to and in conjunction with the stories of people of color in the United States. While witness accounts do not substitute for first person narratives of another's ordeal, Oliver (2001) reminds us, too often

> victims' experiences of discrimination are explained away as imaginary, the product of paranoia or hysteria, or the result of some physical problem or illness. Their experiences are pathologized, and they are made to feel as if there is something wrong with them rather than the social institution. (p. 161)

Oliver's third point is that it is a moral imperative to attest to the injustices that we see happening around us.

> The performance of witnessing is transformative because it reestablishes the dialogue through which representation and thereby meaning are possible, and because this representation allows the victim to reassert his own subjective agency and humanity into an experience in which it was annihilated or reduced to guilt and self-abuse. (Oliver, 2001, p. 93)

Finally, witnessing empowers people who have experienced oppression and gives them a safe platform to discuss these incidents. As a white person who has witnessed injustices, it is essential that I attest to the subjugation of people of color. Oliver (2001) further explains that we have obligations to those who have been targeted: "response-ability is the founding possibility of subjectivity and its most fundamental obligation" (p. 91). As witnesses, we are required to respond, assist, and collaborate on solutions.

Answering Oliver's call to make repairs and serve as agents of change, finding solutions requires recognizing, accepting, and embracing dissimilarities. Yet, as in my relationship with my partner, it's important to focus on our commonalities as well as our differences. Although we are from different cultures, love and commitment drive me to fight for him. As Oliver states:

> Relations with others do not have to be hostile alien encounters. Instead, they can be loving adventures, the advent of something new. Difference does not have to be threatening: it can be exciting and the source of the meaning of life. (p. 224)

To look at my husband and me is to see opposites – dark and light skin, tall and short stature, curly and straight hair, but the same cores. We are caring people who want everyone to get along, accept others for their differences, and find what which unites us.

Infamy

The glow of the television lulled me to sleep on Tuesday night at 11:00 pm central standard time, just as reporters and pundits were sitting around a semi-circular table with matching gray semi-circles under their eyes. CNN's (2017) crawl flashed Michigan: Trump 47.6%, Clinton 47.4% with 97% of precincts reporting. Donald J. Trump appeared on the screen and stated, "Thank you, thank you very much. Sorry to keep you waiting. Complicated business, complicated business. Thank you very much. I've just received a call from Secretary Clinton. She congratulated us – it's about us – on our victory" (CNN Staff, 2016).

I awakened at his voice, my right hand flat against my right eye. I was not dreaming. I got off the futon in the living room where I fell asleep before Michigan and Colorado's election results came in. I shuffled my way to the bedroom with my spouse and followed him to bed. My eyes closed and abruptly opened on Wednesday, November 9, 2016, at 2:46 am. My partner was awake. "Did you see?" he asked.

"I cannot *fucking* believe it," I responded.

"I can't either. What are we going to do?" he asked. I was hoping he was asking this rhetorically because I had no idea. I was scared for him, for us.

"I can't believe I have to get on a plane in three hours," I responded as usual with my most immediate, pressing work event, which happened to be a national conference in Philadelphia, Pennsylvania. We said an unusually tearful goodbye, and I arrived at Houston's Hobby Airport refusing to look at the televisions lining the terminal. Betrayed. Assaulted.

After a three-hour flight, I stepped off the plane, and the chills of Philadelphia immediately confronted my body. These visceral chills matched the chills of hate, the chills of fear, and the chills of state-sponsored racism. I called my spouse upon arriving at the conference hotel in Philadelphia, "What's it like there?" I asked.

"It's so weird."

Dejected, I sat at the desk in the hotel room with my hand supporting my forehead, the phone pressed against my ear. I heard chants from below, and I looked out of the window onto the street. People moved through the streets carrying signs and punching fists in the air. I heard their cries seven floors up with the windows closed. I wanted to be on the street with them, but I also wanted to try and comfort my spouse. I couldn't calm him. I stayed on the phone. We cried. I reiterated that I was okay leaving the United States for a while, giving up my job, and moving anywhere that he would feel safe. But where? My spouse was born in India, but he came to the United States on his mother's passport at nine months old. He is an Indian-born naturalized citizen who took the oath of citizenship at age six. He walks like an American; he speaks Bengali with a Midwestern accent.

"When Trump says he's going to ban Muslims, he's really saying that he's going to ban anyone who is brown. What's so frustrating is that people refuse to see that Muslim is code for brown. Why don't people get that?" I lamented to my partner.

"People think he's a 'straight shooter,' and he's 'telling it like it is. It's disgusting," he said with exasperation.

As we fell silent, I thought about the circumstances in which my father-in-law immigrated to the United States. He was invited to come to this country in the 1970s due to his job. My father-in-law and other immigrants like him followed the same steps as many immigrants at the turn of the 19th century. They were inventors. They ran businesses, served as physicians to rural areas, attended and taught at universities, cleaned houses, cooked and served food, and raised children here. People once welcome in the United States were now being targeted.

Eleven Days Earlier

On October 29, 2016, my spouse of almost three years and I sat cross-legged next to each other on a *mandap*, a small square stage, in the Hindu Worship Society in Houston, Texas. The ceremony fulfilled our promise to my late father-in-law. In the month before his passing, we promised him we would have a Hindu marriage ceremony. He told us that the service was for our ancestors. Because of his untimely passing, my father-in-law was now our ancestor.

I still find it hard to believe that my father-in-law accepted me without question. Only 15% of Asians marry non-Asians (Larsen & Walters, 2013). The first time I met my father-in-law, he offered to throw us an engagement party. I was shocked. I barely knew this man, but he knew I loved his son.

In the hours before my husband joined the ceremony, my parents sat next to me on the carpeted floor of the Hindu temple and participated in the rituals to bless me as I symbolically left their family and moved to my husband's family. My parents sat patiently listening to the chants in Sanskrit. When the *pandit*, or priest, instructed them to put water over a small representation of the god Vishnu, they did so even though they didn't know the meaning. Their patience lessened and their bodies tired with each instruction over the three-hour ceremony. I reminded them that we were keeping a promise to my late father-in-law, whom they also loved dearly. My mom nodded and continued to listen to the chants. I smiled and thought about the beautiful marriage between cultures and families. Here, in Houston, this was a reaffirmation of love and commitment between two people who came from different parts of the world to find one another.

Reality

Under the sacred, dried garlands that we exchanged during our wedding ceremony (now hanging from our mantle), with tears streaming from my face, my husband and I watched the election results.

The tension in Houston was palpable. When driving south of our neighborhood on November 15th, I saw “Impeach Trump” scrawled on the perimeter of a school’s construction site in black spray paint. The local news media told a different story. Dan Schiller (2016) of the *Houston Chronicle* reported that Kartick Venkatachalam, “an India-born scientist,” said he was harangued in downtown Houston by a panhandler who told him he would be glad when Donald Trump started deporting foreigners” (para. 1). Venkatachalam reported this happened “just moments after a divided discussion with colleagues about whether there had been an increase in racial clashes. He said he’d been cursed before in other cities in the United States for not sharing his change but that this was a different type of anger” (para. 20).

Venkatachalam continued, “The fact this happened establishes, at least in my mind, that there is a huge swath of this country which – incorrectly or not – thinks they can get away with this stuff” (Schiller, 2016, para. 21). Venkatachalam was right. They can. They have.

Rays of Reality

This incident called to mind Ray, the woman who painted henna, or *mendhi*, on my arms and feet the evening before our Hindu wedding ceremony. She came over at 4:00 pm prepared with a blue cloth-covered pillow to prop up my arms. She pulled out two plastic tubes made from Ziploc bags. A greenish-gray paste of tea tree oil, water, and dried and crushed henna leaves filled the tubes. Dressed in a traditional *Hijab*, she was from Iraq and, along with her father, mother, and sisters, was granted asylum in the U.S. She explained the differences between Hindu *mendhi* designs and Muslim designs. “The Hindu designs include more paisleys and mandalas whereas the Muslim designs include more circles.” We talked about other topics too. We talked about how much we loved Houston. We loved the diversity that could bring together a Muslim woman who was preparing a white woman, raised Christian, to marry a man who was raised Hindu.

Ray held my hands and arms for six hours. She marked the center of my inner forearm with a dot of henna paste. Using that dot as a center, she made a ring of dots. Then she drew two curved lines, forming a paisley of paste on my arms. She told me to remain still, and she created another and another. She covered my arm with paste. She turned my arm over and drew designs on the other side. She moved to my other arm and repeated the design flawlessly. While kneeling, she took my right foot into her hands. She drew complementary designs on my feet for another hour. The smell of eucalyptus perfumed the air.

Ray incorporated the tattoo that I got over twenty years ago into her design. She was patient; she was kind. She powdered my arms with sugar to preserve the color. She gave me detailed instructions on how long to wait before I could wash off the sugar to reveal a red-brown tint that highlighted my white skin. Her talent, her story as an Iraqi refugee, and her grace enamored me.

With every turn of my palm, every careful instruction, every time she checked in with me to make sure I was comfortable in the six hours it took, my affection for Ray grew.

More Tension – More Awareness

While scrolling through my Twitter feed, I saw a headline from Houston's NBC News affiliate, "Man says two men threw something in the car to start a fire on Katy Freeway." I clicked on the link and saw a local reporter, Brandon Walker, appear on the screen. "A Katy man was discharged from Memorial Hermann Hospital Wednesday, two days after his car caught fire on the Katy Freeway" (Walker, 2016, n.p.).

The reporter continued, "Syed Raza has second- and third-degree burns on his right arm, and a first-degree burn on the right side of his face. He told KPRC2 he felt his arm burning and knew he needed to get to safety."

"They were asking me to roll down the window. I did that. I thought they were asking for directions," Raza said. Instead, Raza said the two men began to laugh before throwing an object into his car. It landed on the floorboard near the back passenger's side seat.

My heart hurt for Raza. He was trying to help someone out, and he got firebombed. No one has been found or prosecuted for this incident, and Raza was hoping it was not a hate crime (Walker, 2016).

I continued to scroll through the comments. As the commenters suggest, there's no way one can know why this happened. Why was a Muslim man firebombed three miles from our house on the heels of the election?

Love and Languages

I became enamored with Bengali culture and I decided to learn the language. To know people, you must know their language. I started going to Bangla school. Bangla school taught written language to children and adults who speak Bengali at home. I started in the first class. I learned the names of animals, then fruit, then vegetables. In the next class, I learned the vowels, which are intricate and often indistinguishable to my ear. In the following class, I learned how to write the vowels. I had regular notebook paper, but rather than forming the letters by starting at the bottom of each line like we do in English, I learned how to write letters by starting at the top. I memorized the 46 characters of the Bengali alphabet. I installed the Bengali keyboard on my phone and translated words from my partner's cousins' Facebook posts. In the next class, when I was 37, I started learning how to put the characters together to sound out words.

I was two weeks away from finishing Bangla school when Donald Trump was elected. The Sunday morning following the election, a security guard greeted me at the gated entrance to the temple. When I entered the classroom, Trump was the subject of my classmates' discussions. They were worried that their parents' visas would be revoked and they would be deported. Their parents held the same visa category as my father-in-law. Many of the students in my class were born in the United States to immigrant parents who started their families after their parent(s) were invited here by large companies looking for uniquely skilled workers. I thought about my spouse and how difficult it was for him to live in India after being raised in the United States. I came home from Bangla school that day and cried for my classmates and their worries about politics, their parents, and their immigration statuses. As immigrants and children of immigrants, this election profoundly affected them.

Christmas

Four days before Christmas in 2016, my spouse and I arrived in Kolkata, India for a trip to fulfill a promise to my partner's grandmother, to bring her grandson to India. My husband's uncle greeted us at the airport and took us to his home. Shortly after we arrived, with an atlas in hand, he asked me where my ancestors were from. He wanted to know how many generations we had been in the United States, and if my family enslaved people. I knew the Hungarian side arrived at Ellis Island after slavery was outlawed, but I admitted I was unsure about my maternal side. We talked about the election. He asked, "What type of country are you from that the person who gets the most votes doesn't win?"

The concept of democracy seemed like a farce. We all agreed the Electoral College is antiquated and doesn't represent the majority. We acknowledged the Electoral College put a white nationalist in office. We also agreed this would have grave effects on world trade and the global economy.

Targets

Just as people of color and Muslims were targeted in the United States, Nahendra Modi's election to Prime Minister of India on May 16, 2014, brought renewed tensions to India. Dabir, an Indian immigrant and board member for *The Texas Orator*, wrote that, unlike his counterpart in the U.S., Modi was elected to other public offices before becoming India's leader. However, like Trump, Modi courts the religious right. Modi was a member of the Rashtriya Swayamsevak Sangh (RSS), which refers to India as Hindustan to underscore the nationalist claims of the Hindu majority (Hedgewar, 2012). RSS's mission statement calls on Hindu men to protect the religious tenets in of the country (Hedgewar, 2012).

In 2014, the American Justice Center filed a lawsuit against Modi for his alleged role in the Gujarat Genocide of 2002. Modi was the Chief Minister of the Indian state of Gujarat at the time and "20,000 Muslim homes and businesses and 360 places of worship were destroyed, and over 150,000 Muslims were displaced" (American Justice Center, 2014, p. 2). The suit alleges:

> The cause of such a massacre is well known as through the actions and inactions of the then Chief Minister of Gujarat Nahendra Modi, the Defendant herein, whose anti-Muslim sentiment, nefarious conduct and outspoken doctrine of maintaining Hinduism as the dominant religion actually initiated and condoned the mass killing and violence that was perpetrated toward the Muslim community. (American Justice Center, 2014, pp. 1–2)

American Justice Center (2014) also contends that the RSS is "a Hindu nationalist party motivated in part by Nazi and fascist ideologies" (American Justice Center, 2014, p. 3).

Barry, a *New York Times* journalist, reported she had to be selective about which Muslim lynchings to discuss because of the sheer volume. In one day, a 15-year-old was stabbed after his skullcap was ripped from his head, and he was called a "beefeater." A police officer was murdered and called an "informer" while outside a mosque. The frequency of these attacks has been connected to Modi's leadership (Barry, 2017).

Dhawan, a writer for *The Economic Times*, covered specific instances of fear resulting from targeting Muslims in India on suspicion of possessing beef. She quoted @AngellicAribam in her story, "I've stopped carrying mutton in my lunchbox nowadays. You never know someone might say I am carrying beef and I might get lynched" (Dhawan, 2017). She states that this is "a fear that is justified in today's times especially when you're a Muslim man" (Dhawan, 2017). Hindus and Sikhs are suspected of being Muslims in the United States and Muslims are being targeted in India. The ideologies of hatred and fear of the "Other" are manifested as parallels in these two nations.

And in the United States Again

CNN Money (2008) named Olathe, Kansas as the 11th best place to live in the U.S., citing the high purchasing power of residents, the beautiful wildflowers, and recreational opportunities. On Wednesday, February 22, 2017, one month and two days after Donald Trump's inauguration, two Indian men who had been educated in American universities and were engineers for Garmin, Alok Madasani and Srinivas Kuchibhotla, went to Austin's Bar and Grill in Olathe, Kansas, after work. A stranger asked if their "status was legal" before opening fire on them with a handgun (Oppenheim, 2018). Ian Grillot tried to help and was also shot (Oppenheim, 2018). Kuchibhotla died of his wounds. The shooter yelled, "get out of my country" as he shot them (Oppenheim, 2018, n.p.).

War on Culture? Ethnicity? Or Religion? Or Race?

Eight days after the inauguration of Donald Trump, a mosque in Victoria, Texas, was set on fire. The evening news showed the solemn white building and orange flames engulfing its roof, much like a crown. I couldn't help but think that three months prior, Riki and I sat in a Hindu Temple and took the seven steps of life together. Jon Wilcox, a journalist for the *Victoria Advocate*, reported that the suspected arsonist "sent a Facebook message eight days before the fire, writing that it's hard to know what Muslims will do 'since Trump is claiming to send them all packing.' Based on his Facebook comment, 'can you pinpoint any mosques that a team can get clear to?' (2018, n.p.)," the prosecutor argued the suspect was targeting multiple mosques.

We watched the television in horror as the mosque burned. I recalled that moment when my partner and I sat next to each other facing the pandit, who shared the same name as my late father-in-law. I thought of the Hindu Worship Center. I thought about the chants, the hats we wore that were specific to Bengali tradition. As much as I knew the difference between Hindu and Muslim faiths, I wondered if the person who set fire to this sacred edifice knew or cared.

WITNESSING THROUGHOUT TIME, SPACE, AND OTHER CONTEXTS

Witnessing Media

In the months following the election, my spouse and I watched television. We felt safe in our home, safer than in other areas of the city, state, and nation, yet we were looking for solace and escape.

Eleven days after Trump was inaugurated, a campaign promise was realized. On January 30, 2017, Trevor Noah began *The Daily Show* with, "Let's get into the start of week two of the Donald Trump Presidency. Protests are happening all around the country as President Trump bans travelers from seven mostly Muslim countries." *The Daily Show* aired clips of police detaining protestors at airports.

"It's official, people. This weekend Trump signed an Executive Order putting his so-called 'Muslim ban' into effect" (The Daily Show, 2017). Noah looked directly into the camera and addressed Trump.

> You banned *everyone* from seven Muslim countries from entering the United States [map appears showing Libya, Sudan, Syria, Yemen, Somalia, Iraq, and Iran highlighted]. Even though you said your ban was to protect America from outside threats, that ban included people with green cards. It even seemed to ban dual citizens of Canada or Britain or any other country you didn't plan to ban. (The Daily Show, 2017, n.p.)

News clips followed, describing families who were separated, physicians and former Iraqi interpreters who were unable to return to the United States (The Daily Show, 2017).

I sighed. I thought about my Muslim friends and co-workers who have not taught their children any language but English, so they would not have a non-

American accent. I thought about Ray. I thought of my husband. Less than a month ago, we flew through the United Arab Emirates, another majority Muslim nation.

Noah introduces Hasan Minhaj. Noah states, "I'm sorry, man. I can't imagine what it is like to have the United States label Muslims as inherently threatening, man" (The Daily Show, 2017, n.p.).

Minhaj responds:

> I'm not surprised. In the past, the United States has had a lot of issues with Muslims. President Carter banned Iranians; Bush built a registry of immigrants from 24 Muslim countries, Obama suspended refugees from Iraq. But Trump is taking this to a whole new level. Shout-outs to all my Republican friends who *promised* me Trump would never do this [emphasis added]. (The Daily Show, 2017, n.p.)

A montage with Lou Dobbs, Marco Rubio, Fred Barnes, and Bill O'Reilly saying that, "Trump wasn't serious" and "[a Muslim ban] wouldn't happen" followed.

The screen cut to Minhaj who said, "We're on day 11, man! That's it! Where do you think this is going to go?" (The Daily Show, 2017, n.p.).

Minhaj described his experience at the airport following Trump's ban:

> White women were turning their scarves into *Hijabs*. Muslims were praying at the airport [cheering and applause from the studio audience]. Think about this, Muslims were praying at the airport. Because of Donald Trump, people were being nice at the airport! Here's the beautiful irony – for years Donald Trump has been terrified at the spread of Islam in America. Well, congratulations, Mr. President. Mission accomplished. [screen shows protests with crowds holding signs 'Resist,' 'You are welcome' with the c as a crescent and a star, 'We are all Muslims now.' 'Refugees welcome,' 'I heart my Muslim neighbors.'] (The Daily Show, 2017)

Watching, we laughed out loud and shook our heads. We were comforted by the protests.

Witnessing Women

Prior to Trump's election, the last protest I went to was in St. Petersburg, Florida in 2005. Ten to 15 people stood on a sidewalk in front of a high-end shopping center and a movie theatre. We stood with signs asking,'"Is this your father's [President H.W. Bush's] war?,' 'Bring our troops home,' 'Where are the WMDs (Weapons of Mass Destruction)?' When I moved out of the Tampa area in 2005, my desire to protest stayed in St. Petersburg. Protesting felt futile. Even John Kerry, the Democratic candidate, gave no timeline for exiting Iraq. I didn't believe there were WMDs in Iraq, but Dick Cheney did and many Americans believed him.

Ten years later, I reflected on these memories. I had been upset about the election of Donald J. Trump and numb for months. My three-week trip to India during that time did nothing to make me feel better about the election or more secure about America's position in the world. Seeing America from across the ocean changes your perspective. Hearing non-Americans rebuke American exceptionalism is hard to take. It feels like your family secret got out. It's a way of confronting your privilege.

I tried to convince my spouse to go to the Women's March with me. It was a futile attempt, but I decided I couldn't be silent any longer. My spouse had his reasons for not going, but I knew I had to put my body out there to show support for myself, my sisters, my friends, and my partner. I came home to report on the march, "There were so many immigrant men there! It felt great to see the other people in this city who feel the way we do!" 'Empowering' was the best way to describe being in a group of 20,000 sympathizers.

He said, "Really?" But he seemed unimpressed. He didn't need or want to go to the march. His body was already called out for being different, for being an immigrant, and for being brown. Every day.

This following year, I protested again, this time against the unfair treatment of immigrants. I envisioned making a sign that said, 'I'm here for the people who are too afraid to be here.' Instead, I woke up late, put a long-sleeved shirt under my 'My Body, My Rights' shirt, and drove 30 minutes to the march.

In that protest, I saw people I knew, colleagues, students, friends, friends of colleagues, and the parents of friends. I didn't realize I had a community in Houston, and I was comforted by seeing them. I felt better because I was with them standing for peace and human rights together. Protesting didn't feel futile. We were building community.

Witnessing through Stories

As does protesting, witnessing has its place. Witnessing is an act that has to be done with love and care to be effective. Witnessing also has to be done in baby steps. In my own life, I've told family members that their comments were racist. By saying something so directly, I was cut off.

Riding along with Border Patrol agents for a research project (Beaupre, Erdely, Mello, & Thomas, 2017), I witnessed two women, two babies, and two toddlers from Guatemala walk across the Texas border, carrying nothing but their purses and babies. The Border Patrol agents spotted them and told them to stop. They stopped. The agents asked them if they were in good health. They nodded their heads, and they began to cry in recognition that their dream of a better life was over. Tears welled up in my own eyes.

My flood of emotions stemmed from thinking about my father-in-law, and his journey to Houston from his home in remote India with $72 in his pocket.

I recounted this story, to family, friends, and acquaintances and asked if these are the "Mexican" "rapists" that we, as people who just so happen to be born in the United States, should fear. They call them "illegals." Rather than telling them that illegal is an adjective and not a noun, I told them, usually tearfully, about what I witnessed at the U.S. – Mexico border. I told them about the contextual implications for my family. Then I rhetorically asked, "Do you ever think about why you and I were 'lucky enough' to be born in the United States and why some people were not?" I thought about how borders were drawn with the blood of indigenous groups. I thought about finding arrowheads on my grandfather's family's farm in West Virginia. I thought about how we're all standing on stolen land.

CONCLUSION

Stories allow space for self-examination and reflexivity. This story, although specific, provides an opportunity for witnessing with several opportunities for the listener's entry. Perhaps the listener doesn't know my spouse but knows me. Perhaps the listener is a parent who wants to provide the best possible life for their child. Perhaps the listener knows my spouse, who is good-natured, light-hearted, and non-threatening.

Autoethnography allows these stories to be told and examined. Oliver's discussion of witnessing assisted in examining these stories. Through these narratives, my spouse and I experience relief and release from the stress of targeted attacks on people of color since Trump announced his candidacy. We watch the news with care to ensure our safety. Media became our safe space: our informant, our solace, our laughter, and our source of tears in the first year of Trump's presidency. I use witnessing as a way to call out the subjugation of individuals, as an action toward all of our best interests.

My partner and I travel often. We have learned that when we put one checked bag in my spouse's name, it inevitably gets searched. We started putting my name on both checked bags, and the pieces of paper from The Security Administration (TSA) stopped appearing in our bags. Although we have nothing to hide; we always put our checked bags in my name.

My family didn't understand why I am so afraid, but I know people who have been attacked verbally and physically on multiple occasions because of their skin color. There is a coordinated attack on people of color in this country. It does not matter if you are Hindu, Muslims, Latinx, Arab, or Persian. What matters is if your skin color is brown.

Trump stimulates these attacks by inciting fear. At 5:37 am on October 22, 2018, just before the polls opened for early voting for the midterm elections, Trump tweeted, "Sadly, it looks like Mexico's Police and Military are unable to stop the Caravan heading to the Southern Border of the United States. Criminals and unknown Middle Easterners are mixed in. I have alerted Border Patrol and Military that this is a National Emergy [sic]. Must change laws!" (Trump, 2018). With each tweet and at each rally, he shares and amplifies reasons to fear people of color.[1]

When I tell my spouse that I feel guilty for keeping my family name and not changing it to reflect our relationship, he says not to worry about it. But I do. For me, it's not just about me being a feminist and not taking my husband's name. If I were to change my name, I would also be taking on the persecution that his name invites.

Perhaps putting our checked bags in my name is the wrong strategy. Perhaps TSA agents need to see that people with last names from South Asia are not inherently suspect. In the meantime, we would just rather not have our luggage searched.

AUTHOR'S NOTE

Just before this chapter went into print, I reread it through the lens of what I'm learning about my whiteness. Whiteness and witnessing are inherently connected. Witnessing is an important step to dismantling white supremacy in ourselves, organizations, and other systems of power and control.

NOTE

1 Editors' note: In fact, this 'caravan' was half the size of original estimates and consisted primarily of women and children, mostly Hondurans, who were attempting to escape gang threats and poverty (Lind, 2018).

REFERENCES

Adams, T. E. (2011). *Narrating the closet: An autoethnography of same-sex attraction.* Walnut Creek, CA: Left Coast Press.

American Justice Center. (2014). American Justice Center, Inc.; Asif; Jane Doe and John Doe v. Nahendra Modi; A national of India and ex Chief Minister of Gujarat, No. 14 CV 7780, 2014 U.S. Dist. Retrieved from http://www.americanjusticecenter.org/wp-content/uploads/2014/09/Modi_Summons__Complaint1.pdf

Barry, E. (2017, June 29). Toll from vigilante mob rises, and India begins to recoil. *The New York Times*. Retrieved from https://www.nytimes.com/2017/06/29/world/asia/india-lynchings-attacks-on-muslims.html

Beaupre, J., Erdely, J., Mello, B., & Thomas, J. (2017, June 8). Border patrol ride along gets real when migrant family appears. *Borderzine.* Retrieved from http://borderzine.com/2017/06/border-patrol-ride-along-gets-real-when-migrant-family-appears/

Boylorn, R. M. (2013). *Sweetwater: Black women and narratives of resilience*. New York, NY: Peter Lang.

Chawla, D. (2014). *Home, uprooted: Oral histories of India's partition.* New York, NY: Fordham University Press.

CNN Money. (2008). *Best places to live: Money's list of America's best small cities.* Retrieved from http://money.cnn.com/magazines/moneymag/bplive/2008/snapshots/PL2052575.html

CNN Staff. (2016, November 9). *Here's the full text of Donald Trump's victory speech.* Retrieved from https://www.cnn.com/2016/11/09/politics/donald-trump-victory-speech/index.html

CNN Staff. (2017, February 16). *Michigan results: Presidential results*. Retrieved from https://www.cnn.com/election/2016/results/states/michigan

Dabir, S., (2017, November 28). What Trump can learn from Prime Minister Modi. *The Texas Orator*. Retrieved from https://thetexasorator.com/2017/11/28/2017-11-28-what-trump-can-learn-from-prime-minister-modi/

Davis, C., & Breede, D. (2015). Holistic ethnography: Embodiment, emotion, contemplation and dialogue in ethnographic fieldwork. *The Journal of Contemplative Inquiry, 2*(1), 77–100.

Dhawan, H. (2018, July 29). The black shadow of the mob on Muslim lives. *The Economic Times.* Retrieved from https://economictimes.indiatimes.com/news/politics-and-nation/the-black-shadow-of-the-mob-on-muslim-lives/articleshow/65183779.cms

Ellis, C., & Bochner, A., (2000). Autoethnography, personal narrative, reflexivity: Researcher as subject. In N. K. Denzin & Y. S. Lincoln (Eds.), *Handbook of qualitative research* (2nd ed., pp. 733–768). Thousand Oaks, CA: Sage Publishing.

Giorgio, G. A. (2013). Reflections on writing through memory in autoethnography. In S. Holman Jones, T. E. Adams, & C. Ellis (Eds.), *Handbook of autoethnography* (pp. 406–424). Walnut Creek, CA: Left Coast Press.

Harris, A. M. (2014). Ghost-child. In J. Wyatt & T. E. Adams (Eds.), *On (writing) families: Autoethnographies of presence and absence, love and loss* (pp. 69–75). Rotterdam, The Netherlands: Sense Publishers.

Hedgewar, K. (2012, October 22). *Vision and mission.* Rashtriya Swayamsevak Sangh. Retrieved from http://rss.org//Encyc/2012/10/22/rss-vision-and-mission.html

Holman Jones, S. (2016). Living bodies of thought: The "critical" in critical autoethnography. *Qualitative Inquiry, 22*(4), 1–10.
Johnson, J. (2015, December 7). Trump calls for 'total and complete shutdown of Muslims entering the United States.' *Washington Post*. Retrieved from https://www.washingtonpost.com/news/post-politics/wp/2015/12/07/donald-trump-calls-for-total-and-complete-shutdown-of-muslims-entering-the-united-states/ ?noredirect=on&utm_term=.88763a76c7fc
Langellier, K., & Peterson, E. (2004). *Storytelling in daily life: Performing narrative*. Philadelphia, PA: Temple University Press.
Larsen, L. J., & Walters, N. P. (2013). Married-couple households by nativity status: 2011: American community survey briefs. *U.S. Census*, 1–6.
Lind, D. (2018, October 25). The migrant caravan, explained. *Vox*. Retrieved from https://www.vox.com/2018/10/24/18010340/caravan-trump-border-honduras-mexico
Madison, D. (1998). Performances, personal narratives, and the politics of possibility. In S. Dailey (Ed.), *The future of performance studies: Visions and revisions* (pp. 276–286). Annandale, VA: National Communication Association.
Morning Joe. (2015). [Online broadcast]. Retrieved from https://www.msnbc.com/morning-joe/watch/trump-we-must-watch-and-study-mosques567563331864? playlist=associated
MSNBC (Producer). (2015, November 16). *Trump: We must watch and study mosques*.
Oliver, K. (2001). *Witnessing: Beyond recognition*. Minneapolis, MN: University of Minnesota Press.
Oppenheim, M. (2018, March 7). Man who shouted 'get out my country' before shooting two Indian immigrants in Kansas bar admits murder: Navy veteran asked if their 'status was legal' before opening fire. *The Independent*. Retrieved from https://www.independent.co.uk/news/world/americas/man-olanthe-shooting-austin-bar-grill-guilty-murder-kansas-indian-immigrants-adam-w-purinton-a8243541.html
Park-Fuller, L. (2000). Performing absence: The staged personal narrative as testimony. *Text and Performance Quarterly, 20*(1), 20–42.
PBS Newshour. (2015, June 6). Watch Donald Trump announce his candidacy for U.S. president. Retrieved from https://www.youtube.com/watch?reload=9&v=SpMJx0-HyOM
Schiller, D. (2016, November 17). Harassment, intimidation reported across nation but Houston fares better than most: Trump's election sparks flurry of intimidation. *Houston Chronicle*. Retrieved from https://www.houstonchronicle.com/news/houston-texas/houston/article/Harassment-intimidation-reported-across-nation-10621625.php
Spry, T. (2016). *Autoethnography and the other: Unsettling power through utopian performatives*. New York, NY: Routledge.
The Daily Show. (2017, January 30). *The daily show with Trevor Noah* [Online Broadcast]. Retrieved from http://www.cc.com/video-clips/bxjc4n/the-daily-show-with-trevor-noah-president-trump-s-muslim-targeted-travel-ban
Trump, D. [@realDonaldTrump]. (2015, December 7). [Tweet]. Just put out. Retrieved from https://twitter.com/realDonaldTrump/status/673982228163072000
Trump, D. [@realDonaldTrump]. (2018, October 22). [Tweet]. Sadly, it looks like. Retrieved from https://twitter.com/realDonaldTrump/status/1054351078328885248?ref_src=twsrc%5Etfw%7Ctwcamp%5Etweetembed&ref_url=https%3A%2F%2Fwww.cnbc.com%2F2018%2F10%2F22%2Ftrump-says-unknown-middle-easterners-are-mixed-in-migrant-caravan.html

Walker, B. (2016, November 17). *Man says 2 men threw something in car to start fire on Katy Freeway*. Retrieved from http://www.click2houston.com/news/man-says-2-men-threw-something-in-car-to-start-fire-on-katy-freeway

Wilcox, J. (2018, January 8). Arson suspect could stand trial by late spring. *Victoria Advocate*. Retrieved from https://www.victoriaadvocate.com/news/local/victoria-man-accused-of-burning-mosque-multimedia/article_48de602a-0496-54ef-a34c-b53b30c4bef9.html

CHRISTINE SALKIN DAVIS AND JONATHAN L. CRANE

DIALOGUE 12

Jon and I pause in the driveway chatting with Elizabeth.

"I didn't ask you this," I say. "What are your hopes and dreams for the future of our country?"

"I want people to have jobs," says Elizabeth, "and food, and a place to live, to be able to support their families, and also have time for recreation activities."

Jon asks, "what's it like to hold the beliefs that you have and live in a county where you know most people voted the other way? Did it affect your relationships with family?"

"Oh, yes!" says Elizabeth. "My brother is a very liberal Democrat. That has caused problems, in talking to him. Both my parents were Republican, and I have another brother and sister who are very conservative Republicans. Now, I actually can say I'm glad I voted for Trump. In my opinion it's worked out well for me, I think it worked out well. I'm not ashamed to say I voted for him now. And yeah, I do tell people I voted for him."

"What's changed to make you more comfortable with your support?" Jon asks.

Elizabeth answers, "after he won it was easier. And, I don't think there've been any disasters with Trump. Like people predicted the end of the world if Trump became president. So I think things are going well and I don't think he's made any terrible disasters like people said there were going to be."

I ask, "so you feel like you've been vindicated?"

Elizabeth nods, "yes, that's a good word to use. Vindicated, yeah. And I'm not afraid to have someone challenge me on why I made my choice, or call me deplorable or stupid, because I feel like I can have a conversation about it now."

I ask, "so, what did it feel like, talking with us about this now? You and I haven't talked about politics since the election. We've stayed away from it. What did this feel like to you?"

"It feels comfortable," Elizabeth says. "When I thought about coming here and talking about politics, I wasn't nervous, I felt comfortable."

DOI:10.1163/9789004436329_024

I sigh in relief.

Later, driving home, I think about her comment and my response of relief in light of the stories told by the contributors to this book, stories of victims of violence and hatred, disunity, and displacement. Are comfort and relief the best we can offer? What is the price of comfort, I wonder?

Blessed are the uncomfortable,
those whose hearts bleed for brothers and sisters in pain and poverty,
who hear these stories and weep,
who see the need and act,
who bend a knee for justice,
take a stand for humanity.
The world cries out.

CHRISTINE SALKIN DAVIS AND JONATHAN L. CRANE

11. CONCLUSION: REAP THE WHIRLWIND

Identity, Intersectionality, and Politics in Trump's Wake

> Truth isn't truth.
>
> – Rudy Giuliani on "Meet the Press with Chuck Todd," August 19, 2018, Morin & Cohen, 2018

> Listen, how much of this shit do we need to listen to, right?
>
> – Trump at Mar-a-Lago private fundraiser on his decision to kill Qasem Soleimani, January 17, 2020, Itkowitz & Fahrenthold, 2020, para. 5

> I'm upper, upper class society
> God's gift to ballroom notoriety
> And I always fill my ballroom
> The event is never small
> All the social papers say I've got the biggest balls of all
>
> – *Big Balls*, Scott, Young, & Young, 1976, track 3

On an overcast day in June 2015, Donald J. Trump formally announced his altogether improbable and ultimately successful run for the office of president of the United States. A fin de siècle, tweet-storming Barnum fit for the sputtering end of the American century, he entered the hustings from the glitzy lobby of his eponymous midtown Manhattan skyscraper. While Trump has long boasted of grand plans to run in prior presidential elections, his 2016 presidential ambitions were taken seriously by very few voters and even fewer members of the commentariat, polling wizards, the academy and seen-it-all pros who road test and direct every facet of modern campaigning. Trump worked especially hard to remove himself from serious consideration as a viable candidate, as, prior to making his 2016 run for the White House, Trump's most notable public initiative was to gaslight the nation and repeatedly attack President Barack Obama as an illegitimate office holder. Trump tirelessly maintained Obama was a Kenyan born Muslim and not a Christian citizen of the United States. For embracing and disseminating

DOI:10.1163/9789004436329_025

easily disproved, racist dirt, Trump was considered by most to be a marginal candidate – one who might attract the ugly, unwanted support of the InfoWars and Pepe loving, alt-right fringe, but a candidate whom the majority of a sensible electorate would find unsuitable for any public office, high or low.[1]

In the company of erstwhile model Melania Trump, our nation's soon-to-be inaugural First Lady of Slovenian extraction, a cruel irony given Donald Trump's disdain for parasitic immigrants, Melania and Donald kicked off a daft tilt for high office as they came down from their magnificent penthouse aerie far above the madding crowd to greet supporters and members of the press. They did so, literally, in a ludicrous, slow motion downhill glide via a gilt escalator, a creepy, barely animated performance of begrudging *noblesse oblige* before a paid crowd of enthusiastic actors posing as true believers (most of those in attendance without press credentials were paid $50.00 per person to herald the mogul and his consort (Palma, 2019, paras. 10–11). As one jaded reporter, Anthony Zurcher of the BBC, remarked at the time, echoing conventional wisdom: "there's a theory that Trump's presidential campaign was a publicity stunt gone awry, a real-life version of The Producers, when an enterprise designed to fail became an accidental success" (Hughes & Newett, 2019, para. 10). Fox News was more circumspect than most news outlets in their take on Trump's debut, asserting that the brash contender would make an "aggressive – and interesting candidate" should he manage to survive the primary gantlet (Trump announces White House bid, 2016, para. 8).

Evoking an uncanny trinity of Moses, Midas and Max Bialystock simultaneously (a Mel Brooks creation, Max is the obese schemer and smarmy gigolo who makes "Springtime for Hitler" a wildly popular showstopper) – a bizarre blend of savior, bunko artiste, and gluttonous robber baron – Trump's pitch brings the scabrous good word and magic touch of an American superstar to the enslaved masses from atop his auric Mt. Sinai. Per the candidate himself, Trump and only Trump, is the sole American capable of making the fallen United States great once more. As the triumphant singularity Trump crowed months later when accepting the nomination as the Presidential candidate of his party at the Philadelphia Republican convention, having vanquished a mammoth slate of experienced Republican opponents, now sad also-rans: "I alone can fix it" (Trump, 2016, para. 86).

Trump's weird restaging of a typical campaign launch at his Midtown Shangri-La and his remarkably egotistical speech at the Republican nominating convention share nothing in common with the ritual obligations and pedestrian niceties American politicians uniformly honor when they publicly announce their desire for high office. Unlike Trump, most other calculating politicians, regardless of party affiliation or divergent policy views, scrupulously attend to the clear prescriptions and iron mandates that constitute the hidebound script for our everyday engagements with communal politics and the shared performance of civic duty. American politicians know better than to get too far above their raisin', rarely failing to honor the cornerstone American credo, enshrined in the Declaration of Independence, that in an egalitarian Republic all men and women are ostensibly created equal. Even if this is nothing more than flimsy chimerical pretense, ideological fairy dust that blinkers the servile, the play for votes and the heart of the electorate requires each of us to honor the pretense that anyone, even a skinny community organizer from the Southside of Chicago, can become President.

As with dated wedding ceremonies and other musty, but still venerable rites, most all of us are capable of repressing private unease with hoary tradition. We know enough to keep our misgivings to ourselves when stale traditions have lasted well beyond their expiry date and, as yet, even among free-thinking progressives and radicals, we have not worked up fitting replacement rituals and new sacraments to bring us together. Not, however, Donald Trump. Unlike most all of us, Trump is not restrained by normative prescription, common expectation, etiquette or ceremonial compact. When everyone else across the wide political spectrum is an observant conservative, ensuring our best, most sensible, collective practices are ready to be passed onto the next generation, as when we quietly usher our kids into the booth when we exercise our right to vote, Trump is an unapologetic, enthusiastic bomb thrower – an eight-fisted grobian with no regard for collateral damage. And, it should be noted, above all his other winning traits, Trump's most ardent defenders esteem his disregard for the sweet guardrails of social convention. A turd bobbing in the punch bowl, Trump's rambunctious camp followers love him most when he makes others wince.

The luxe escalator entry of the real estate tycoon and reality television star may have meant that Trump was done with the everyday protocols of American tradition, but Trump was not campaigning sui generis without models or forerunners. Likely unintentional, as not much ever seems all that well orchestrated or well thought out when Trump steps up to free style at the podium, his grand entrance did double duty as a farcical homage to the opening shots of *Triumph of the Will* (Riefenstahl & Riefenstahl, 1935). Trump's debut campaign appearance and molasses descension to the gold-leaf stump mirrors the opening of the propaganda masterwork sanctifying the 1934 Nazi Party Congress and mad, mythic phantasies of reborn empire.

Triumph commences with aerial shots of der Fuhrer's plane breaking through boiling white clouds high over the homeland and depositing the dear Leader in Nuremberg. Once safe on the ground, the Fuhrer steps boldly unto the tarmac and rides into the city center hailing his subjects from an open motor car as he leads a grand motorcade along cobbled streets packed with throngs of exuberant supporters. The giddy masses revel in the presence of the Leader and embrace the promised glories of the thousand-year Reich. As goose stepping Aryan troops, the hale minions of martial Empire, snake through packed streets, they are greeted with lusty cheers and loud applause. In both the German propaganda film and Trump's Fifth Avenue campaign event, the demi-god of the people comes down from the heavens, an undaunted Apollo, to seize the helm of State, to kindle the hot ardor of grateful subjects and to restore lost luster and greatness to the degenerate swamp of the fetid *Heimat*. Lest this sound too unfair to Trump, one more facile and unwarranted comparison to mad Adolph, remember Trump's keen desire to parade tanks, troops and missiles through the streets of Washington in celebration of America's fearsome might on Independence Day, until warned by the Pentagon that rolling America's most powerful armaments down D.C.'s macadam avenues would shatter the unreinforced pavement of the Capitol (Browne, 2018, para. 1).

No matter the celebrated capacity and rare talents that separate gifted candidates and politicians from the motley pack of average Americans, candidates have always been obliged, with exceedingly rare exceptions, to meet the voters as equals. No longer. At this historic juncture, Trump makes clear that the long-standing directive requiring politicians to humble themselves before the masses is nothing more than a superannuated fiction. Viable candidates for office have most always maintained, at least in public, that what makes them electable is the fact that they have the common touch, and are, when it comes to the core essentials, indistinguishable from Joe and Jane Six Pack. Trump has demonstrated that the successful pol need not present him or herself as one of us. When titan Trump deigns to come down to the lobby of his skyscraping monument to himself, hailing his subjects in the only all access area in the entire building where the hoi polloi are free to wander around and pick up an embroidered red trucker cap, bottle of Trump vino, or other branded trinket, Trump arrives as a cheeky, imperious divine. He comes not to join the company of paid rabble as a rough and ready compatriot, he comes to rule from on high. Knowing his people, as subsequent rallies and the unexpected victory on election night demonstrate, Trump is received as a cocky champion who has to courage to speak his mind no matter the consequences or PC blowback. Like a lysergic evisceration of Whitman's hymn to his own home grown, American magnificence, the siren sound of Trump's "belch'd words" call his electoral majority to "welcome ... every organ and attribute of me" (Whitman, 1892, lines 25, 57).

By nearly all measures of public perception, even by New York City's generous standards for flamboyant conceit, Trump was and is considered a loud, exceptionally vainglorious, self-promotor. In this unprecedented regard, Trump is an unhinged variation of NYC archetype Ralph Kramden, Jackie Gleason's uncouth bus-driving striver, but with the added threat of a mountain of inherited lucre, a monstrous ego and a cold heart with malice and disdain for all. Like raging Kramden who threatened to punch out anyone who found fault with his lunatic ambition ("One of these days, pow! Right in the kisser!"), Trump is powered by a savage self-regard that leads him to lash out at anyone and everyone, even children, like climate crusader Greta Thunberg, whom he deems a foul, wanting critic (Hurdle, 1955–1956).[2]

In case it seems like to a step too far to charge the President with animus toward all and a wanting, barren soul, consider a tweet prompted by Trump's impeachment and the continued attempt by federal prosecutors of the Southern District of New York to obtain Trump's personal and corporate tax records: "All they want to do is investigate to make me hate them even more than I should" (Donald J. Trump, 2019), Or, in the loose cannon, Kramden vernacular: "Bang, zoom, straight to the moon Alice!" (Hurdle, 1955–1956). Of course, Kramden is a tragicomic figure because no matter how outrageous his antics, he has no power to execute his crazy gambits. Thanks to his pitiful social standing, a hard up municipal worker without means, who lives in a sparsely furnished, cold water tenement, Kramden's liberty to wreak havoc is limited to pestering a small circle of long-suffering friends and a forbearing wife. Kramden is nothing but impotent bluster and misogynistic pique. Trump on the other hand, shares the exact same flaws but is a terrifying figure because he has near complete freedom, backed by the august might of his office, accommodating zealots in the GOP who acquiesce to his every caprice, a fully engaged legal team (save for those serving time, indicted, or under investigation), and fabulous wealth, to do and say whatever he desires. He is a captious loudmouth, coddled alpha male, and apex predator.

As Trump does not take any pains to disguise his excitable temperament and a raft of short-comings, public measures indicting the character of the President show little disagreement between those who detest the Commander in Chief and the appreciative responses of his most fervent, hard-core supporters (Garcia, 2019). At a time when polarized people of different political views share very little in common on the ideological horizon, most everyone concurs that Trump is anything but an estimable person. His coarse, narcissistic hubris remains repellent to many, his Q score (a measure of a celebrity's parasocial likeability) is among the most negative recorded for any self-aggrandizing entertainer and his E score (a more recent measure for how notables are regarded by the public) finds American respondents overwhelmingly consider Trump "creepy," "insincere," "arrogant," and "over-exposed." In sum, stable long-term indexes find Trump is someone disgusted opponents "love to hate" (Karni, 2019, paras. 5–6). Zealous acolytes who relish their place onboard the rip-snortin' Trump Train, share the worst views of his critics, and agree that "he's a pompous, arrogant jerk" (Garcia, 2019, para. 10). Despite this, the pivotal rupture between voters who treasure Trump and those who loathe him comes, for those sporting trademarked MAGA trucker caps, with the understanding that Trump is a huge win for the nation, because, given the prohibitive challenges the Union faces, "that's what we [the country] need now" (Garcia, 2019, para. 10). Somehow, we have reached a perilous breach in electoral politics when many American citizens have decided that the most vital asset in an able President is that, and no other phrase in the critical lexicon and pop vernacular will suffice, he must be a complete asshole.

Despite Trump's long history of empty braggadocio, nasty divorces, scurrilous rumors, porn star assignations, audiotaped confessions of serial "pussy" grabbing, "I moved on her like a bitch," idiot PR machinations, including regularly calling New York newspaper reporters under an assumed name to buff the forever smirched Trump image and finagle a mention in the papers, and, finally, a long succession of epic business busts, Trump managed to defeat Hillary Clinton (Transcript: Donald Trump's taped comments about women, 2016, para. 9). Blessed from birth as the second youngest son born to a rapacious, Queens real estate magnate with near unlimited riches to shower on his blessed heirs, Trump was also inordinately fortunate to run against the only candidate in both major parties and furthest reaches of the back bench with the perceived peccadillos anywhere near equal to the steaming midden of character defects possessed by Trump. Nevertheless, even against someone with the checkered mountain of baggage and the perilous negatives of Hillary Clinton, Trump – while he did eke out an Electoral College victory – lost the popular vote by almost three million ballots. Not for nothing is Trump labeled the chaos candidate (see Grossberg, 2018 for a full accounting of Trump's nerve-shattering, discord strategy). He is our dangerous singularity. A fatally flawed human being and an irredeemable candidate who has somehow crossed every red line and still vanquished every foe, Trump's unparalleled ascent has left the disenfranchised majority who did not vote for him mystified, unnerved and dispirited.

Who else in contemporary U.S. history is so clearly unfit for public office and, yet, somehow manages to pull an inside straight and happen upon an unprecedented path to elective victory while maintaining the strong, unwavering support of his dogged following? One last observation on Trump's dissonant bipolar attraction and hot potato repulsion for voters. For the true believers, he is the debauched King David a bedeviled nation needs for a troubled time. As extravagant sinner, Trump is the only president in American history to earn the title of "Chosen One" from a powerful bloc of Evangelical Dominionists (Scott, 2019, para. 6). For the faithful, in spite of, or rather because of, his glaringly obvious foibles, Trump is a golden envoy sent by God to restore the American Republic to greatness. For his Christian disciples, only God has the miraculous means to intervene and take a badly broken vessel like Trump and use him to fulfill the Divine's plan for us and our blessed nation. As Michelle Bachman said about Trump on the radio ministry "Understanding the Times": "he is highly biblical, and … we will in all likelihood never see a more godly, biblical president again in our lifetime" (Cummings, 2019b, para. 4). Going even further, Franklin Graham concurred that God's commanding hand has authored Trump's unlikely rise to the top, but also that those who stand against Trump are likely acting at the behest of "a demonic power" (Wehner, 2019, para. 4). In squaring the Evangelical circle, Trump is a Godsend and those who cannot countenance him or his actions are rebel angels of Satan. As with those voters who cast a ballot for Trump, many Evangelicals see Trump's unparalleled character flaws as unassailable evidence of the power of a magnanimous God to take charge in the affairs of men and turn coprolite into Presidential gold. In this restorative augury, we are still a gleaming City upon a Hill, and God has rendered unto us a Gothamite Boss Tweed cum the archangel Michael in order to make America great once more.

While Trump has now been in office for three years (at the time of this writing), for many American citizens and those from nearby states and abroad keeping a gimlet eye on President Trump and the chaos he engineers, the disbelief that Trump won never fades. For most of us, Trump's win and continued presence as renegade head of state is akin to reliving, in collective, torturous misery, our worst day ever for what feels like a damned eternity. Each morning we awake to greet the day and the realization that Trump is still here and we, the queer, the dispossessed, the poor, the lower classes, people of color, women, and those who ally with each of these overlapping and interlocked constituencies remain the objects of his enmity. Akin to the distressing trauma and epochal aftershocks experienced by the European left, following the election of Margaret Thatcher and the Iron Lady's long tenure in high office, fueling an extended period of intense theorizing to understand and defeat hard-right populism, Trump's election challenges every commonplace we know. As Stuart Hall wrote (1982/2017) upon grappling with the disastrous consequences of Thatcherism and "The Great Moving Right Show": "we are up against the wall of a rampant and virulent gut patriotism" (p. 205). Mutatis mutandis: America First! Trump's victory, as with Thatcher's ruthless efforts to dismantle the welfare state in the name of good people and authoritarian common sense, remains an unstaunched injury leading to obsessive levels of despair, and endless, conjoint self-examination and reflection. How did we get here and what will it take to remove Trump and rebuild in his wake? Infectious Trump Derangement Syndrome is a lived, shared malady. Can we imagine our way to a cure and an end to the Trumpian plague that imperils the health and future of our commonweal and the wider world? Can we recross the Rubicon? Stuff the trickster genie back in the tarnished lamp?

Our ongoing, daily contest to somehow persevere in topsy-turvey Trumpland is akin to reliving a reboot of *Groundhog Day* (Albert & Ramis, 1993) under the combined direction of Bosch, de Sade and Mack Sennett. And, as so many of the entries in this collection make abundantly clear, managing this unreality is painfully grueling for those in the beleaguered resistance. Adapting to Trump's reality, even for those in the administration, as Anonymous notes in *A Warning* (2019), is a nightmare challenge:

> whether you were 'all in' on the president's agenda or not, one reality couldn't be denied – lurching from one spontaneous decision to another was more than a distraction. The day-to-day management of the executive branch was falling apart before our eyes. Trump was all over the place. He was like a twelve-year-old in an air traffic control tower, pushing the buttons of government indiscriminately, indifferent to the planes skidding across the runway and the flights frantically diverting away from the airport. This was not how it was supposed to be. (p. 34)

In light of Anonymous' anguished screed, when even unwoke, hard right functionaries recognize Trump is an abominable bungler, an inept, illiterate moron with the cataclysmic power and fulsome foul will to burn it all down, the American experiment has gone haywire.

To better unpack the forces that led to Trump's left field victory and the severe travails that Trump's election, bombast, and subsequent executive orders and policies have inflicted upon a diverse multitude of the subaltern, it is worth considering Trump's earliest political endeavors to better comprehend his scandalous triumph and continued, seemingly unshakeable popularity with the base voters of the Republican Party. Trump's preposterous success, even when a clear majority of the electorate despises him, is a head-scratching puzzlement. Therefore, to gain a clearer understanding of how such a polarizing, bad subject managed to win the White House, and, how, even though he has been impeached, Trump may somehow shamble on to win again in 2020, it is necessary to return to Trump's earliest political venture. And, as we return to Trump's primal political scene, it is worth keeping in mind that Trump's inconceivable triumph followed Barack Obama's almost as unlikely two-term stint as president. Obama's fast rise to the Oval Office and reelection in the midst of a long, grim recession should have been sufficient evidence that the process whereby American voters select those who govern underwent a radical sea change. Long before Trump abandoned the boardroom set of *The Apprentice* (Petillo, 2004–2015) for the iron throne behind the Resolute Desk in the Oval Office, things changed. And, while the Obama years may seem like a vanished golden age, a halcyon era when hope was something other than an idiot child's pipedream, the historic forces that allowed a neo-liberal activist of color to attain the Presidency are the same epochal currents that ensured we would take one small step forward only to be followed by an unprecedented leap backward. In this fashion, both Obama and Trump are the historic product of the same conjuncture of forces that led legions of voters looking for wholesale change to pull the lever, for a moderate Black politician and, then, just four years later, to reverse course and put a revanchist, bully boy in the Nation's china shop.

In light of Trump's animus toward his celebrated, no drama, predecessor, it is not surprising that Trump's most acclaimed and condemned actions in office entailed those executive orders, new legislation, and administrative actions that countermanded and overturned President Obama's signature achievements. Three brief, comparative examples should suffice. If Obama gave us Dreamers with an executive order ensuring that young children brought illegally to the United States could stay in the country and become lawful citizens, then, in return, Trump engineered the carceral horror of teens, toddlers, and infants forcibly separated from parents and confined indefinitely to dog runs and wire mesh cages. If, in league with the P5 + 1 (the permanent members of the United Nations security council and the European Union), Obama successfully managed to blunt Iran's nuclear ambitions with the 2015 Joint Comprehensive Plan of Action, then a spiteful Trump unilaterally withdrew from the pact in 2018, having long held that the agreement was "the worst deal ever." According to a leaked UK diplomatic memo, the U.S. spurned the other co-signers who represented nearly the entire world, because the Trump "administration is set upon an act of diplomatic vandalism, seemingly for ideological and personality reasons – it was Obama's deal" (New leak claims, 2019, para. 5). Finally, if the Paris Agreement, ratified after long years of intense diplomatic wrangling by almost 200 countries and the European Union, and signed by President Obama in September 2016, demonstrated the warming world had at long last publicly recognized the threat of climate change and the need to respond with aggressive, coordinated measures to reduce greenhouse gas emissions, Trump withdrew the United States from the Agreement and promised to instead put "clean coal" extraction and burning fossil fuels into overdrive. An all-powerful, malefic, yet unaccountably insecure Pharaoh who wants every trace of a popular predecessor struck from public consciousness, Trump aims to raze his retired rival's best work, vanquish memory, and salt the common ground we share with allies and sometime foes alike.

Trump's initial foray into politics began with his short tenure as a Reform party candidate in 2000. The Reform Party has long been home to an eclectic coalition of sometime politicos and wannabe politicians who are not welcome in either of the two dominant parties that currently exercise an iron stranglehold on the path to high elective office in the United States. The Reform Party emerged from Ross Perot's Independent Party, when Perot presented himself to the electorate as a third-party alternative to George H. W. Bush and Bill Clinton in 1992, believing that the two globalists and committed NAFTA supporters would do nothing to preserve good jobs and good wages for the American labor force as they chased the cosmopolitan's dream of a new, world order. When the final ballots were tallied, Perot became the most successful third-party candidate in the modern era. Even as he broke through the Third Party glass ceiling, Perot threw the election to Bill Clinton. Perot gave the election to his Democratic opponent by splitting the vote for a candidate other than Clinton as many disgruntled Republican and right-leaning Independent voters decided to vote for Perot, rather than stick with Bush, the aging, Old Guard, GOP incumbent. Had these voters not strayed from home, Bush would have easily won a second term. While a traditional candidate did win the Presidency in 1992, Perot's unprecedented success demonstrated that the center might not hold for much longer.

It did not help Perot's quixotic and largely self-financed campaign, thanks to the millions Perot earned in international tech support and data processing, when he briefly withdrew from the race in June 1992 following a bizarre, televised harangue aired on *60 Minutes* (Holmes, 1992, para. 1). To the dismay of many viewers, without evidence, a paranoid Perot proclaimed he was the victim of desperate GOP dirty tricks that threatened to soil his reputation, disrupt his daughter's wedding, and menace his family. At the time of the broadcast, Perot's weird rant led many to believe he was unfit for office. In hindsight, Perot's mad ravings foreshadowed the inconceivable possibility that off-the-rails rhetoric and political chaos could be key to seizing the good will and votes of the angry and alienated. Steadfast loyalty to the party platform and factional givens (say a scrupulous disdain for the national debt, a lived commitment to Christian values, limiting the Imperial power of the Executive branch, and a robust commitment to austerity funding) and anything like ideological coherence when campaigning on the stump and shaking hands on the rope line may no longer matter all that much. As pols wage war for votes in the over-amped, supersaturated mediaverse, in our exhausting age of infinite distraction and asignifying noise, winning high office may be best managed by compulsive, moneyed communicators who narrowcast without cease. In the digital age, obsessive devotion to achieving and maintaining 24-7 notoriety and hypnotic celebrity far outstrips any commitment to truth, sound reason, and the stale niceties of measured dialogic exchange.

Perot, past master of the cranky diatribe and trailblazer for the grasping plutocrat in search of public office is Trump's North Star (and a blazing green light for Andrew Yang, Steve Forbes, Mike Bloomberg, Carly Fiorina, Tom Steyer and all the other tycoons and CEOs who presume to be worthy of the State's highest office given the enormous sums they have banked). Perot demonstrated a loose tongue and an endless stream of macho boasts do not alienate voters. Like Trump, Perot too was inordinately proud of his business success and he liked to remind everyone with a microphone and camera just what he had achieved as a canny, business maven. While no enemy of comprehensible speech like Trump, Perot loved to employ colorful aphorisms that, if you did not hail from hard-scrabble east Texas, sounded like bumpkin gobbledygook. Following Perot, media overload, bent proverbs, and malapropisms are to the deliberate give and take of traditional political discourse as a gushing fire hose is to a plant mister for delicate orchids. Or, in the Perot cracker barrel idiom, “Eagles don’t flock, you have to find them one at a time” (Kwong, 2019, para. 6).

Despite his short-term recess and crazed blather that called into question Perot’s judgment and mental health, in harness with a series of gaffes and verbal miscalculations that left him open to charges of racism and homophobia, Perot managed to capture almost 20% of the vote cast for president in the 1992 election. Since Perot’s failed campaign, the Reform Party has run a motley grab bag of losing presidential contenders for every election cycle since 1992. Even though the party is now a ticket mainstay in presidential elections, no Reform Party candidates have come close to Perot’s high-water mark. Perot may not have won or even come all that close to winning, but he did demonstrate that third party candidates can be competitive in national races. Yet, despite Perot’s initial big splash, the Reform Party has been unable to build on his initial success. In part this is because the Reform Party has no consistent slate of political objectives or firm ideological foundation. Having run the premier “America First” candidate of the modern era, right-winger Pat Buchanan, along with consumer crusader Ralph Nader, tech entrepreneur Andre Barnett, and perennial political gadfly Roque “Rocky” De La Fuente at the top of the ticket, in a series of increasingly ill-fated campaigns with ever more limited ballot access across the fifty states, the Reform Party has almost wholly imploded. It is now the political equivalent of the Island of Misfit Toys. The Reform Party is the last stop for irrelevant pols with no mainstream bona fides and no good reason save unbridled ego and a masochistic compulsion to stay in the fight. A room of their own for exiles and jokers, the Reform Party is where tarnished candidates make their final stand. And like aging rockers who commit to farewell tour after farewell tour, they never sign off for good.

Nevertheless, without the efforts of pioneering Reform Party candidates, Trump had no path to the presidency. If Trump is the ‘Chosen One,’ then Perot is his John the Baptist. With Perot as forebear, Trump’s mad vision rested on the real successes of the Perot campaign. And, unlike Perot who in 1992 did not have access to a fifth column of networked social media activists, the consistent attention of 24-7 broadcast, satellite, and new media, or the comradely assistance of foreign actors, internet provocateurs, and the bully pulpits of right-wing and alt-right “news” outlets, Trump and his skeleton crew of outsiders managed to engineer a way to win high office that did not depend on a lifetime of public service, a commitment to lucidity, a sophisticate’s knowledge of the issues, and a solid commitment to win voters retail on the campaign trail and rubber chicken circuit.

Ironically, the Reform Party's inability to maintain a consistent identity, other than as an alternative to sclerotic party and hegemonic politics as usual would become Trump's most important selling point as a candidate in the 2016 election. Trump has never offered consistent policy nostrums and has never committed to a fixed set of guiding precepts. To his benefit, Trump operates without a political, ideological or moral compass. He has been on every side of most every important issue that resonates with voters since has was old enough to enter the voting booth and exercise his franchise as a registered Democrat. Peripatetic Trump left the Democratic Party in 1987 and registered as a Republican supporter, then departed the GOP for the Reform Party, then became an Independent, and, in perhaps his last leap, become a loyal Republican once more. However, this time, in returning to the GOP, he also self-identifies as a "commonsense conservative," "total nationalist," and "law and order candidate" (Baker, 2018, para 13; Diamond, 2016b, para. 2; Nelson, 2016, para 1). In this last self-seeking move, presenting himself as a bare-knuckle fighter with a capital R for his battle standard, Trump has settled on presenting himself as the politician of the last stand. Go to war with Trump fighting for the heart of the heart of the country or shut out the lights.

For those who voted for Trump in 2016 and have supported him ever since, what matters most is the transcendent "I" of Trump. On Trump's turf, there is no we, save for the royal We and no polis or nation comprising a band of ostensible equals. There is nothing greater than the expansive range of Trump's all-encompassing, raging ego. It cannot, for now, be displaced or even altered by a vision of something other than the grasping ambition of the One. Trump's possession of the polis, as the marauding incubus and state coalesce, is regularly and spectacularly instantiated when Trump, as he often does when appearing on stage, literally wraps himself in the Stars and Stripes with a beatific grin on his mug, clinging to Old Glory for dear life. For those who are not convinced of Trump's world-historic majesty, these choreographed displays of full-throated patriotic ardor feel more like a hostage drama than a genuine display of national allegiance. When a ne'er-do-well cloaks himself in the country's flag, we know Dr. Johnson was right in designating false, hyperbolic patriotism as the last refuge of a calculating rogue. Melding with the flag and reconstituting the one-time "big tent" GOP as synonymous with Trump's big stick has recast the quixotic outsider as an amalgamated political immortal. In support of this claim, consider the large number of GOP moderates (this phrase was once not an oxymoron), and Never Trumpers who have elected to quit office or leave the party as the

President has consolidated his unprecedented power. They have no choice but to surrender or quit. The result is, according to *New Republic* writer Matt Ford, "a Republican Party that's whiter, more male, and more aligned with Trumpism, no matter the damage it does to the country as a whole" (2019, para. 3). As head of the GOP and the Union, Trump is angry America's triune Godhead. For the convicted partisan, in frightful consubstantiality, Trump and the party, the State, and the people are now one. And, as Trump has repeatedly made clear, those individuals and groups who refuse to recognize his magisterial authority are themselves, illegitimate. They are suspect, false Americans who should be repatriated to their ancestral wastelands, knocked out with a crowd-sourced sucker punch, popped in the back of the skull for treason, "what we used to do in the old days when we were smart," or locked up ('Spies and Treason', 2019, para. 19). L'état c'est lui.

In his abortive 2000 run, Trump hoped to be partnered on the ticket with Oprah Winfrey as his running mate (Hoffman, 2018, para 5). Imagine that. Trump eventually withdrew from the 2000 primaries and, even though he was no longer a candidate, won the Reform Party primaries in Michigan and California. As a Reform Party Candidate, Trump promised to erase the deficit with a one-time wealth tax and to create a single-payer health care program to replace a broken system that leaves too many low-income Americans without affordable access to medical treatment (Blake, 2017, paras. 7–8; Hirschkorn, 1999, para. 3). Patrick Buchanan, who Trump attacked for his anti-Semitism and suspected high regard for Adolph Hitler, went on to become the Reform Party nominee after Trump quit the race. Trump later apologized for calling Pat a "Hitler lover" who "doesn't like the blacks" and "the gays" (Cummings, 2019a, para. 10). Trump also, way back in 2000, in acid contrast to his present day, unending race baiting, affirmed that "we must recognize bigotry and prejudice and defeat it wherever it appears" (Kornacki, 2018, para. 45). Trump has long since abandoned his commitment to healing the breach between the races. Instead, Trump regularly hates on "shithole" countries and bemoans the fact that too many deplorables desiring to come to the United States do not hail from wholesome countries like heavenly Norway and other five-star nations that are home to homogenous populations of good white folk.

As mind-boggling as the thought of a Trump/Winfrey administration is, a review of Trump's origins as a candidate and campaign strategist demonstrates, if anyone needed additional convincing, that this President has always been a fluid, improvisational player who categorically abjures the third rail limits that are part and parcel of reflective ideological commitment and thoughtful intellectual consistency. Save for a heartfelt apology or measured retraction that suggests a scintilla of thoughtful self-doubt and soul-searching, Trump will say or tweet anything at any time. For Trump and his base, prudence, well-deliberated policy, and intellectual consistency are the hobgoblin of little minds and cream puff constitutions. For this reason, Trump critics and Trump diehards are united in the identifying the source of Trump's appeal and revulsion in the President's unequalled work as a riveting emotional barker who "makes sense" to his constituents and opponents in terms of affect – how he makes his interlocutors feel.

Keep in mind the well-rehearsed interaction that takes place between Trump and the throngs who turn out for his crimson state rallies (as Trump almost exclusively visits those regions of the country that are dead red for his lively, personal appearances). Although his red rallies do provide a rare opportunity for daredevil hecklers to publicly challenge the President and, in the face of a tsunami of hearty boos and the occasional left hook to the face, get tossed on their ear by beefy peace officers, a Trump shindig is, first and foremost, an emotional riot for the fans. When an animated Trump commences a stream of consciousness soliloquy, running through his splenetic showman's patter of making Mexico pay, his "unprecedented" electoral landslide, putting harridan Hillary through the ringer and on and on, audience members respond in lusty huzzahs to each of Trump's deliciously delivered one-note triumphs. As the well-drilled dialogue unfolds, the dynamic exchange between Trump and his stalwart supporters exactly parallels an arena comedy concert featuring studied performers and well informed, whoop-it-up fans who know all the jokes ahead of time, yet still go mad with exuberant joy when the comic sticks the landing and hammers home a roundhouse punch line with deft éclat. So too with Trump's expertly delivered call and response rally rituals. In Trump's electric presence, the pure products of the American heartland go bananas.

No one need bother to listen attentively to just exactly what a stoked mythomaniac has to say; we have all heard it before and before that – Trump has an exceedingly limited number of signature motifs and expressions in his repertoire. Most every communication, whether by 280 character Tweet, at an impromptu chopper talk with the press before the President boards Marine One, or an extemporaneous rally speech, features Trump repeating his catchphrases, playground nicknames, (including, among many others, "Sleepy Joe," "Crazy Nancy," "Lyin' Ted," "Shifty Schiff," "Pocahantas," "Little Marco"), and vitriolic epithets, ad nauseam. Trump never surprises his bright-eyed champions with a novel turn of phrase, unexpected observation or fresh rhetorical spin, unless he breaks new ground with a spelling, syntactical or semantic error, as with one of his infamous late-night tweets, presented here in its entirety: "Despite the constant negative press covfefe" (Andrews, 2017, para. 2).

Trump's turns on the stump are also similarly incoherent, as at a recent meet up in Toledo, Ohio when Trump attacked Democrats as premeditated baby killers who are responsible for "ripping babies right from the mother's womb right up until the mother's womb" (Re, 2020, para. 23). While everyone who spends any time speaking to assemblies or being regularly interviewed will serve up the occasional word salad, Trump takes practiced unintelligibility to unprecedented heights. But, to criticize Trump's linguistic misadventures as the measure of his communication competence is to grossly undervalue Trump's commanding ability to spur his clamoring stadium crowds to ecstatic, affective pandemonium. When Trump asks his people, as he does routinely at most every campaign event he hosts, "is there anything more fun than a Trump rally?" the answer is, to the unmitigated astonishment of the resistance, a resounding and unequivocal no (Cochrane & Haberman, 2018, para. 8). Whatever side you find yourself on, Trump flat kills.

For critics, Trump's compulsive repetition is inarguable evidence of limited intelligence, cognitive decline, and a narcissistic absence of interest in anything other than his own magnetic self. For supporters, hearing Trump return to one of his thematic obsessions is akin to cueing up a favorite tune at maximum volume and entertaining the tactile jolt that comes with once more blasting a charged golden oldie. In this regard, Trump is only unusual because while politicians have always relied on a vital ritual component in their campaign addresses to unite supporters (think of Obama's call and response, stump staple of "Fired Up, Ready To Go" as a campaign appearance comes to a rousing climax), Trump is resolutely committed to sharing reheated triumphs and long-time, festering slights and little else. He is all sour ritual, all the time. Trump cannot or will not communicate anything other than his greatest zingers and takedowns when he arrives center stage. Trump uses language exclusively as an acerbic vehicle of eternal return. When he serves up a pet hobbyhorse, belting out, "lock her up, fake news, enemy of the people, send her back, build the wall, hoax" no one in hearing, other than duplicitous members of the press, is likely disappointed. As well, go after Celine Dion for closing her show with "My Heart Will Go On," or find fault with the Jersey Devil, Bruce Springsteen, for bringing the house down with "Born to Run." Trump gives the people what they want. In so doing, he and his fellow passengers on the Trump Train collectively cement their bond as a great bellicose choir of impassioned nativists airing their shared grievances in a super-sized lemon session.

Trump's public powwows typically conclude with the Rolling Stones "You Can't Always Get What You Want" blaring over the PA as drained supporters stream through the exits. The title of the ballad should give the game away and serve as an ironic riposte to the true nature of the Trump enterprise. The President's most celebrated actions have done very little to relieve the daily struggles of his devoted, core constituency. But again, no one needs a close reading of Trump speeches and musical paratexts to understand the full import of the President's communication. Trump does not uplift, educate or illumine; Trump gives his people the collective opportunity to vent their manifold frustrations and dance cathartically all over their shared troubles as they collectively abuse the villainous scum tearing America apart. We're OK, you suck.

In his peculiar fashion, Trump functions like a one-of-a-kind emotional support animal who brings comfort and joy to the aggrieved by snarling at and attacking favored scapegoats and revolting enemies (see Stevenson, 2014 for his scarifying description of Alabama deputies posting attack dogs at the courtroom door to drive away black supporters desiring to attend open, public trials, pp. 176–181). Unlike the typical politician, who tries –regardless of party affiliation – to send off assembled constituents with some scintilla of glad tidings and a bracing measure of hope, Trump inspires his army with consoling obloquy, a weeping pound of flesh, and the rich communal bounty of shared, seething resentment.

In many mainstream religious services, it is typical practice at a signal moment in the sacred ceremony for congregants to rise en masse at the direction of the cleric and put out an open hand and wish their neighbors God's sweet favor, peace and love. This vital performance of fellow feeling is regularly parodied at Trump convocations when Trump brings the proceedings to a halt and points out the treasonous men and women of the press at the back of the hall. Usually corralled behind flimsy barricades, as Trump heaps scorn upon them, the inflamed crowd jeers the messengers of darkness with unglued abandon. Occasionally the press are hit with more than a wave of insults, as, following Trump's lead, quisling reporters and camera operators are spit on or slugged for having the profane temerity to defile a Trump event with their presence (Iati & Bever, 2019; Trump supporter attacks, 2019). Trump also relishes the opportunity to lambaste protesters with comments about their sad appearance and a call for the crowd to meet out a little Trump justice, as Trump did at a rally in Cedar Rapids, Iowa, when he implored his people to "knock the crap out of them, would you? Seriously, ok? Just knock the hell …. I promise you, I will pay for the legal fees. I promise" (McCaskill, 2016, para. 3). At a rally in St. Louis, just 10 miles from rough justice and Ferguson, MO, Trump pouted that our sad sack nation has lost its killer instinct when he cried "no one wants to hurt each other anymore" (MacGuill, 2015, paras. 15 & 32). And so on. Under Trump's direction, we are once more a nation of boisterous scrappers who won't back down when crossed.

Trump may not be able to articulate anything of nuance and complexity, but he is supremely effective in eliciting and channeling the outrage and anger his supporters feel as they try to make their way in a world gone wrong. The largest body of Trump supporters are the struggling men and women, without a college education, who are overwhelmingly white, with modest or declining incomes (at best), and limited employment prospects. Trump and his campaign call them "the forgotten Americans" and, Trump professes to adore them and their hapless imperfections, as when he told reporters during his Nevada primary victory speech that he "loves the poorly educated. (Hafner, 2016, para. 2). Gathered together with Trump main stage, his supporters are free to revel with abandon as, fetters off, they collectively release poisoned reserves of bitter acrimony and celebrate the symbolic reclamation of America.

Even as we recognize that many in the Trump base are struggling not because they are poorly educated, but rather, they are undereducated and unprepared to find solid footing in a dynamic and rapidly changing economy, it is Trump who, for now, seems best able to recognize their plight and in response serve up comforting (but empty) something burgers that suggest vital action, but could mean anything, e.g. "drain the swamp," "make our farmers great again," "we don't have victories anymore," with seeming, absolute conviction and no attempt to hide his complete disdain for those who disagree with him. In the eyes of himself and his roiling throngs, Trump stands alone and defiant as a bold leader with the intestinal fortitude to speak from the gut. Trump tells it like it is; no double talk or mealy-mouthed, PC platitudes for the man who proudly proclaims "I have a gut, and my gut tells me more sometimes than anybody else's brain can tell me" (Zhang, 2019, para. 1). And so, at the end of the American century, we have arrived at the place where, in lieu of Lincoln's team of rivals or other carefully curated, pantheon of gifted guides and sages, we are held in thrall to our winning leader's infallible digestive tract and its inevitable end product.

In the interviews we conducted with chary friends and neighbors who voted for Trump, you can hear, even as they are expressed with the usual disclaimers and carefully delineated reservations about Trump's willful intemperance, character deficits and sharp elbows, how Trump is heralded as the apotheosis of authority and decisive leadership. A hard-driving, supremely confident magnate, he will run the country like a business. In this updated trope for a nation in precarious decline, Trump is a gifted turnaround wizard and, as Tom Wolfe put it in *The Bonfire of the Vanities* (1987), a "Master of the Universe." Ditch the toque blanche and think Gordon Ramsay in pin stripes and long red tie, here to impose tough reforms, rock the status quo, and whip things back into right, apple pie order. Brought in by disgusted voters who recognize the need to for a convulsive shake-up, radical change does not come without cost or spillover damage. When the ship of state is in danger of going down, it is absurd to expect a tough salt who can right a foundering vessel to be a prim observer of Victorian social convention. Sure, his followers and our interviewees readily admit, he sometimes goes too far, giving his ungoverned motor mouth too much rein, but catalytic Trump is a salutary respite from picayune, linguistic fastidiousness and the straitjacket of cowardly, mewling courtesy. Circumlocutory politesse is for feckless, weak-kneed losers, not Trump. He is, in stark comparison to every dissembling politician, overly concerned with cultivating an image as a sober, fair minded respecter of democratic difference – the ultimate straight shooter.

Conversely, for those who take strong exception to Trump's crude tongue and wayward behavior, he is an irredeemable bully. One of the consistent observations that runs through each of the essays collected in this volume, is that regardless of the skin color, gender, nation of origin, sexual orientation, religious conviction, in fact, regardless of any vital marker of difference, that is today's target of his vitriol, Trump's reckless authority is predicated on his unchecked and unprincipled eagerness to lash out and give the back of his hand to the millions here and abroad he deems worthless wastrels. For those not enamored by Trump's outlaw mode of self-presentation, he is not a wild and wooly, pugilistic Godsend. He is a vicious blowhard who cannot advance his own inchoate aims and policy ambitions without savagely deprecating those citizens and foreigners he considers incorrigibly Other. To be clear, the essays in this collection are not refined, bloodless musings written in the soft comfort of our nicely appointed, book-lined dens; these are the assembled cries of people in need of a lifeline. These are the voices of people, genuinely, realistically, and plaintively afraid for their lives. Don't read these essays the way academic work is typically appraised, hear them for what they are – a call to 911 for immediate, emergency assistance.

Trump's consistently abrasive and alarming abuse of countless others is singularly off-putting for those with no seat in even the furthest reaches of the GOP big tent. Whether threatening violence himself or encouraging others to start clobbering rally interlopers, pantomiming spastic disability, using derogatory slurs with illiberal abandon (knowing full well any punk schoolboy who spoke in the same fashion would merit a long stint in detention), celebrating sexual assault, coining spiteful nicknames for opponents, providing cover for white supremacists, castigating people of color and their "shitholes," trashing dead war heroes and their heartbroken Gold Star survivors, falling in love with murderous despots, adopting a foreign accent to mock non-native adversaries, and on and on, is more than just the game imposture of a modern day Peck's "bad" boy. There is no generous heart and keen intelligence hidden under a crude mask of brassy machismo and throwback racial animus. Forget the misleading, sleight of hand directive offered by far too many Trump apologists. It is dangerous and bootless to take him seriously but not literally. There is no daylight or wiggle room between the black words and animating spirit of a pitiless scourge. A man who pardons convicted war criminals against strong pushback from his active military commanders and Pentagon, is himself a killer (Cox, 2019).

With a super majority of Senators failing to remove him from office in the impeachment trial of early 2020, it is Trump's forever campaign of unceasing Othering that may lead to his eventual undoing. Many scholars, political scientists, and commentators concur with Nobel Laureate Paul Krugman who argues that "what distinguished Trump voters [from other members of the electorate] wasn't financial hardship but "attitudes related to race and ethnicity" (Krugman, 2018, para. 10). In making the case that Trump won by appealing to desperate white tribalism, Krugman references the work of political scientists John Sides, Michael Tesler, and Lynn Vavreck who argue in *Identity Crisis: The 2016 Presidential Campaign and the Battle for the Meaning of America* (2018) that it was not economic issues that led so many of the disenfranchised to pull the lever for Trump. Instead, Trump voters relied on identity factionalism to provide clear direction at the polling place. During hard times of crisis, as with the extraordinary misery endured by most Americans of busted means in the wake of the Great Recession, voters go nativist and turn fiercely partisan when the good times end. Not surprisingly, Trump ruthlessly exploited people's pain during the campaign and has not abandoned this divisive strategy since taking the oath of office. Trump's obsession with blaming Others for the people's nightmare and his relentless attacks on treasonous pols who sold out the nation, as with his "chronic and debilitating case of Obama envy," is alarmingly exemplified in his red meat, "American Carnage" Inaugural Address (Robinson, 2019, para. 1). Showcasing the base humiliation of the nation as well-paying jobs depart for foreign shores, factories are shuttered, wars are lost, America's young warriors are killed and crippled for naught and, worst of all, "the wealth of the middle class has been ripped from their homes and then redistributed across the entire world," Trump paints a vivid picture of absolute degradation and disgraceful privation (Trump Inaugural Address, 2017, para. 33). We have been played for suckers. We are dead-meat dopes, according to Trump and his speechwriters expertly channeling the President's apocalyptic and sectarian vision. Scourged, naked and bleeding, with nothing left for alien Others and double-crossing apparatchiks to fleece, the good folk of the country have been reduced to weeping carcasses of picked-over carrion.

Making a parallel case for how voters go about selecting those candidates who merit their support, attention, money and votes, scholars Christopher Achen and Larry Bartels, the authors of *Democracy for Realists: Why Elections do Not Produce Responsive Government* (2016) contend, à la Sides et al., that voting behavior is, at base, a question of identity. Typically too busy and unprepared to sift through mountains of complex data prior to casting a ballot, voters rely on their longstanding core identities and self-interest to figure out what and whom to vote for on election day. Achen affirms "there's a variety of identities people have that are more or less salient and can be made more or less salient politically. For many people, the principles become part of the identity and are important moving parts of the way they think about politics. But our claim is that identities are more fundamental, the principles come later rather than the other way around" (Illing, 2017, para. 56).[3] Trump leverages white, working class identity by obsessively blaming Others for whatever ills his forsaken voters, victims all, have suffered in a tumultuous period of increasing inequality and murderous global competition.

And, while Trump could surely not articulate identity-driven, white resentment as the power train that drives his dire rhetoric, he, by virtue of his own feral Manichean worldview, knows the inflammatory impetus of hate when our united enemies take us for saps. Trump, like Nixon before him, has been kicked around, but, unlike a resigned quitter, Trump knows how to man up and counter punch when the going gets rough. For Trump, every slight must be returned with overwhelming force. Or, as the President himself tweets, paying homage to his one-time consigliere Roy Cohn: "when someone attacks me, I always attack back … except 100x more. This has nothing to do with a tirade but rather, a way of life!" (Trump, 2012).[4] Red in tooth and claw, Trump will rock you.

Never before has the United States been led by a cracked fabulist whose choleric bile could have been ghosted by Conan the Barbarian. Trump before Trump, the Barbarian butcher enthuses: "Crush your enemies, see them driven before you and hear the lamentations of their women" (Feitshans, De Laurentiis, De Laurentiis & Miluis, 1982). In the Queen's English, Trump's home borough, or the barbaric Cimmerian, any and all adversaries deserve nothing less than our worst. And, even though Trump maintains the Bible is his favorite book, given Christ's cardinal injunction to love one's neighbor as one's self and to offer up the other cheek when we are received with harsh malice, it is impossible to reconcile Trump's repeated claims of his abiding love for Jesus with attacking one's adversaries with 100 fold the original force first deployed. Historically our most effective leaders have called upon the nation to embrace our better angels in trying times, to remember the supernal ties that bind, and to exercise force sparingly and judiciously when all other options are foreclosed, but not Trump. The itchy, trigger finger of the big Trump hand is always dancing over the red button, and, as he tweeted to the world and to North Korea's Kim Jong Un (prior to falling in love with Rocket Man), "it is a much bigger & more powerful one than his, and my Button works!" (Trump, 2018). Under this administration, the mystic chords of memory have gone quiet and just mercy is dead.

As every entry in this volume persuasively argues, Trump and his administration, allied with a significant body of true believers, have pushed the majority of the country to the brink. Those who do not support the scorched earth policies and caustic rhetoric of the President are in deep despair. Trump has set us one against the other, leading too many to abandon the possibility of a workable national entente, even among the members of our extended families and blood kin who do not share a similar political orientation. And, if a holiday dinner or wedding reception among our riven families is a no go, what hope do we have for those vastly more complex alliances required to address the pressing problems that face our local communities, the nation and the planet?

Yet, despite Trump's many self-proclaimed, triumphant conquests, "one of the most successful presidencies ever" (Trump, 2019), as even his clear wins are short term Pyrrhic victories at best (save for the tremendous number of lifetime, Federal judiciary appointments that have been rammed through the Senate), as he and we careen from crisis to crisis and lunatic tweetstorm to tweetstorm, the country is locked in a vertigo-inducing 24-7 spin cycle that feels like being in a spiraling plane plummeting out of the sky. Nevertheless, despite our shared malaise and dread foreboding, Trump has provided the means required to remove him from office. Yes, he has forged an adamantine nexus with his immovable base. As he bragged prior to the election, Trump is probably free to plug some poor schmuck on Fifth Avenue without risking the loss of even one voter from his dead-set voting bloc. In response to Trump's inflammatory boast that he could get away with a public murder in broad daylight, CNN focus group respondents said they would need to know why Trump shot someone before they elected not to vote for him (Diamond, 2016a, para. 2). The Trump Train will steam on and few, if any, hardcore confederates will take their leave no matter what bloody crime or tort Trump commits. Yet, Trump's relentless Othering has also energized and bonded the plurality of heterogeneous voters who collectively find him a puerile abomination. And here, he has done something that no one, not Hillary or any of the dozen plus Republican primary candidates could achieve. In nurturing his cult, Trump has also secured a steadfast company of Others who too 'shall not be moved.' In his reckless abandon, making decency and wisdom uncommon virtues at the top, Trump has managed to fashion the disparate many into a motley congregation of staunch allies with a common cause and laser focus. In this reversal, think, for instance of Michael Bloomberg's billion dollar commitment to support any nominee running against Trump in the 2020 presidential election. Think as well of Rick Wilson, GOP strategist and hard-right sectarian, who argues in *Running against the Devil: A Plot to Save America from Trump – and Democrats from Themselves* (2020), that the key to defeating Trump is recognizing that "it almost doesn't matter what the alternative is, as long as it's not another flavor of evil … this is a country over party thing" (Obeidallah, 2020, para. 31). Yes, our differences matter, but measured against the possibility of another four years of Trump in office, the divides that cleave us are of little import. When some of us are caged because we are dark-skinned asylum seekers, when some of us merit the worst for claiming the same rights accorded the hale and heterosexual, when non-binary means non-human, when health care is a perk to which only the rich are entitled, we all have reason to rise up. Save for aggrieved supremacists and dead-enders who long ago gave up the notion of common cause with people unlike themselves, we have everything to lose.

In this signal turn, Trump has, unintentionally to be sure, advanced one of the primary home truths developed by intersectional theorists and activists. We are, indeed, all connected. Not because we exactly share the same assortment of traits and demographic characteristics, but because we are never wholly and exhaustively defined by any fixed constellation of features, genes, and experiences. Elect to focus on race and you miss the constitutive role of gender in the construction of identity. Highlight sexual orientation and you overlook the defining impact that regional mores and local culture play in the performance of our loving selves. Any single quality or even a wildly extravagant, extensive bundle of demographic denominators will necessarily fall well short of capturing the full, forever mutating, kaleidoscopic richness that is each of us, separately and together. There is always an impossible, forever changing surplus when it comes to the exact calibration of personal and genetic effects that shape the instantiation and expression of our individual and collective identities.

We are bound to another, not because all of us are gay, not because all of us are persons of color, not because all of us worship an Abrahamic deity, not because all of us are financially insecure, not because all of us are in poor health, not because all of us have run afoul of the law and spent time behind bars, but because, at this critical conjuncture, as one body, we reject, the way our churning guts bring up a hunk of bad meat, Trump's bloody cleaver and the politics of dismemberment. We rebuke the singularly dangerous man who aims to sow division and discord and batter every one of us who values difference into mute submission. We repudiate the man and the punitive ethos that will lead to pain for any and all who fail to pass through the needle's eye of the Trumpian straight and narrow.

Here a personal detour must suffice to demonstrate a small-scale version of how Trump's American vendetta, his project to define who is and who is not a welcome American, just might lead to his dismissal. Several years back, I was walking down Michigan Avenue with a gay colleague and friend. We were attending NCA in Chicago. As we strolled down the Magnificent Mile, a high end, pick-up truck slowed to a crawl and the passengers and driver started screaming. We narrowly missed getting pelted with empty beer cans as our assailants yelled something like "pencil-necked faggots, go home." After reflexively ducking the missiles, my first reaction was to get ready for a tussle because I work out hard nearly every day and there is no way anyone can tell me I have a skinny, pencil neck. Now, I am also straight, but the gay slam didn't register. It was the beer cans and pencil neck slander that got on the fighting side of me. In this same regard, when Trump devotes so much of himself to assailing and besmirching others, the particular genesis of his brickbats and calumnies no longer registers and all that counts is the recognition that Trump is treacherous, deranged threat. Like an improvised explosive device in a busy thoroughfare, it is time to defuse the bomb and secure the public weal. That could be you, your aunt, your neighbor, your barista, your doctor, your favorite poet, your trash collector, or Adam Schiff who Trump has elected to denigrate because his queer anatomy disgusts him.

Trump fashions himself the spirit and Savior of the age. This is hyperbolic poppycock. The nation is, and always has been, a messy, unruly collection of Others. The greatest lesson of American history is not that some do not belong here, it is that apart from a tiny handful of white, protestant Northern European brahmins, every unwelcome refugee, every indigenous exile driven from their land, every swarthy group of foreigners, every shanghaied and shackled person of color has, at some sad moment in time been pitilessly attacked for being an unwelcome pox on the nation. Eventually, at least for some of these laudable outlanders, aboriginals and trespassers (for too many others, violent marginalization continues unabated), it dawns on "established" citizens that the manifold gifts of these so-called interlopers are exactly what make the American nation and the unfinished American project great. E Pluribus Unum. Thanks to our President we know the appropriate intersectional response to nationwide intimidation: Attack one of us and you attack us all. That's us, being best and doing the right thing.

We have better stories to tell than Trump. Unlike our President and his bitter, tall tale spew, we maintain the public good is what's best for all, not the favored coterie of the providential few. Our stories are infinitely more hopeful, more inclusive, more authoritative, not authoritarian, more forthright, more enlightened, more generous of spirit, more truthful, more compelling, empirically grounded, uniformly leavened with open-minded grace, and infinitely more representative of our democratic ideals and aspirations. Well-wrought and fearlessly disseminated, our stories can bring us together to dispatch a mutual menace. Tell them. Now.

NOTES

1 For those not well-versed in the coded ciphers and stars of the alt-right, Pepe the frog is an insidious internet meme that has been appropriated by white supremacists. Unlike the swastika or other immediately recognizable symbols of hate, the rumpled, green amphibian Pepe is not universally synonymous with racially fueled, hate speech. Brownshirt posses who meet up on 4 and 8 Chan, troll farmers, and lone wolf, digital racists, who glory in larding the internet with hateful venom, know better.

Alex Jones is the crackpot host of an eponymously titled radio show and the website InfoWars. Alex is most (in)famous for his assiduously asserted claim that the Sandy Hook Elementary School massacre was a hoax. Jones was sued by Sandy Hook parents for defamation in the Texas Courts (as Jones is based in Austin, TX).

For an insider's guide to the furthest reaches of the influential and dangerous alt-right margins, see *The New Right: A Journey to the Fringe of American Politics* (2019) by Michael Malice. No author's project is better synced with a consummate surname than Malice.

[2] As is now the rule, when Trump violates a norm, ovine others are sure to follow. Stephen Mnuchin, Trump's Secretary of The Treasury, piled on when he attacked the fifteen year old Ms. Thunberg at Davos 2020 for her lack of college training in economics. Ms. Thunberg was an invited guest and speaker at the annual conclave of world plutocrats as this year's assembly was devoted to addressing climate change.

[3] Taking a reverse tack, and arguing that these authors and the school of thought they represent have oversold the claim that American racial solidarity and communal loyalties, not economic crisis, lead to Trump's impossible win, see Cooper (2019) and Maitland (2018).

[4] In aligning himself with natural born killers, it does not come as a great shock to find that the obese, seventy-three year old Trump has retweeted an image of his handsome face and iconic cotton candy hairdo atop the body of a ripped and oiled Rocky Balboa in boxing trunks, gloves and heavyweight champion's belt. There was no indication he did so in jest. Ave Donald.

REFERENCES

Achen, C. H., & Bartels, L. (2016). *Democracy for realists: Why elections do not produce responsive government*. Princeton, NJ: Princeton University Press.

Albert, T. (Producer), & Ramis, H. (Director). (1993). *Groundhog day* [Motion picture]. United States: Columbia Pictures.

Andrews, T. M. (2017, May 31). Trump targets 'negative press covfefe' in garbled midnight tweet that becomes worldwide joke. *The Washington Post*. Retrieved from https://www.washingtonpost.com/news/morning-mix/wp/2017/05/31/president-trump-tweets-despite-the-constant-negative-press-covfefe-twitter-explodes/

Anonymous. (2019). *A warning*. New York, NY: Twelve.

Baker, P. (2018, October 23). 'Use that word!': Trump embraces the 'Nationalist' label. *The New York Times*. Retrieved from https://www.nytimes.com/2018/10/23/us/politics/nationalist-president-trump.html

Blake, A. (2017, May 5). Trump's forbidden love: Single-payer healthcare. *The Washington Post*. Retrieved from https://www.washingtonpost.com/news/the-fix/wp/2017/05/05/trumps-forbidden-love-singe-payer-health-care/

Browne, R. (2018. March 11). Exclusive: Trump getting a parade but tanks won't roll down Pennsylvania Avenue. *CNN*. Retrieved from https://www.cnn.com/2018/03/09/politics/pentagon-memo-trump-military-parade/index.html

Carlson Brooke, S. (Director). (2018, August 19). Interview with Rudolph Giuliani [Television series episode]. In J. H. Reiss (Executive Producer), *Meet the press with Chuck Todd*. New York, NY: NBC.

Cochrane, E., & Haberman, M. (2018, May 10). Trump host fiery rally on heels of whirlwind week. *The New York Times*. Retrieved from https://www.nytimes.com/2018/03/10/us/politics/trump-rally-pittsburgh.html

Cooper, R. (2019, August 26). Why did you vote? [Review of the book Identity crisis: The 2016 presidential campaign and the battle for the meaning of America, by J. Sides, M. Vester & L. Vavreck]. *The Nation*. Retrieved from https://www.thenation.com/article/archive/identity-crisis-and-the-roots-of-2016-book-review/

Cox, M. (2019, November 19). Trump issued pardons in soldiers' war crimes cases. What now? *Military.com*. Retrieved from https://www.military.com/daily-news/2019/11/19/trump-issued-pardons-soldiers-war-crimes-cases-what-now.html

Cummings, W. (2019a, January 14). Trump tweets op-ed by Pat Buchanan, who he derided as a 'Hitler lover.' *USA Today*. Retrieved from https://www.usatoday.com/story/news/politics/onpolitics/2019/01/14/trump-quotes-pat-buchanan/2568197002/

Cummings, W. (2019b, April 17). We'll likely never see a more 'godly President Donald Trump,' Michelle Bachman says. *USA Today*. Retrieved from https://www.usatoday.com/story/news/politics/onpolitics/2019/04/17/michele-bachmann-trump-most-godly-biblical-president/3495256002/

Diamond, J. (2016a, January 24). Trump: I could 'shoot somebody and I wouldn't lose voters.' *CNN*. Retrieved from https://twitter.com/realdonaldtrump/status/1204379706235203586?lang=en

Diamond, J. (2016b, February 16). Trump: 'I'm a commonsense conservative.' *CNN*. Retrieved from https://www.cnn.com/2016/02/16/politics/donald-trump-commonsense-conservative/index.html

Feitshans, B., De Laurentiis, R., & De Laurentiis, D. (Producers), & Milius, J. (Director). *Conan the barbarian* [Motion picture]. USA: Universal.

Ford, M. (2019, August 5). The incredible shrinking GOP. *The New Republic*. Retrieved from https://newrepublic.com/article/154646/shrinking-republican-party-house-representatives-congress-retirements-will-hurd

Garcia, G. (2019, October 11). Trump supporters stand by their man: 'He's a pompous arrogant jerk,' says one. 'That's what we need now.' *San Antonio News*. Retrieved from https://www.expressnews.com/news/news_columnists/gilbert_garcia/article/Local-Trump-supporters-remain-on-board-14515082.php

Grossberg, L. (2018). *Under the cover of chaos: Trump and the battle for the American right*. London: Pluto Press.

Hafner, J. (2016, February 24). Donald Trump loves the 'poorly educated' – and they love him. *USA Today*. Retrieved from https://www.usatoday.com/story/news/politics/onpolitics/2016/02/24/donald-trump-nevada-poorly-educated/80860078/

Hall, S. (2017). The empire strikes back. In S. Davison, D. Featherstone, M. Rustin, & B. Schwarz (Eds.), *Selected political writings: The great moving right show and other essays* (pp. 200–207). Durham, NC: Duke University Press. (Original work published 1982)

Hirschkorn, P. (1999, November 9.) Trump proposes massive one-time tax on the rich. *CNN*. Retrieved from https://www.cnn.com/ALLPOLITICS/stories/1999/11/09/trump.rich/index.html

Hoffman, A. (2018, January 8). Donald Trump wanted Oprah Winfrey to be his running mate for years. *Time*. Retrieved from https://time.com/5092937/oprah-winfrey-golden-globes-donald-trump-running-mate/

Holmes, S. (1992, October 28). The 1992 campaign: Behind the scenes: '60 Minutes' producer differs with Perot account. *The New York Times*. Retrieved from https://www.nytimes.com/1992/10/28/us/1992-campaign-behind-scenes-60-minutes-producer-differs-with-perot-account.html

Hughes, R., & Newett, J. (2019, June 16). The day Trump ran for president (and what people predicted. *The BBC News*. Retrieved from https://www.bbc.com/news/world-us-canada-48595411

Hurdle, J. (Producer). (1955–1956). *The honeymooners* [Television series]. New York, NY: CBS.

Iati, M., & Bever, L. (2019, June 19). A Trump supporter was arrested after smacking a reporter's phone. 'MAGA,' a GOP lawmaker responded. *The Washington Post*. Retrieved from https://www.washingtonpost.com/politics/2019/06/19/trump-supporter-arrested-after- smacking-reporters-phone-maga-gop-lawmaker-responded/

Illing, S. (2017, June 24). Two eminent political scientists: The problem with democracy is voters. *Vox*. Retrieved from https://www.vox.com/policy-and-politics/2017/6/1/15515820/donald-trump-democracy-brexit-2016-election-europ

Itkowitz, C., & Fahrenthold, D. A. (2020, January 18). Trump privately told new details about Soleimani airstrike at Mar-a-Lago fundraiser. *The Washington Post*. Retrieved from https://www.washingtonpost.com/politics/trump-privately-detailed-the-soleimani-airstrike-to-donors-at-mar-a-lago-fundraiser/2020/01/18/ab0c2414-3a03-11ea-bb7b-265f4554af6d_story.html

Karni, A. (2019, April 1). Trump lives by ratings. He won't like this one. *The New York Times*. Retrieved from https://www.nytimes.com/2019/04/01/us/politics/trump-e-score-rating.html

Kornacki, S. (2018, October 2). When Trump ran against Trump-ism: The 1990s and the birth of political tribalism. *NBC News*. Retrieved from https://www.nbcnews.com/think/opinion/when-trump-ran-against-trump-ism-story-2000-election-ncna915651

Krugman, P. (2018, November 19). The new economy and the Trump rump. *The New York Times*. Retrieved from https://www.nytimes.com/2018/11/19/opinion/economy-trump-red-blue-states.html

Kwong, J. (2019, July 9). Ross Perot quotes: Most famous lines from former third-party presidential candidate. *Newsweek*. Retrieved from https://www.newsweek.com/ross-perot-famous-quotes-1448287

MacGuill, D. (2015, August 11). Did Trump encourage violence at his rallies. *Snopes.com*. Retrieved from https://www.snopes.com/fact-check/donald-trump-incitement-violence/

Maitland, D. (2018, February 19). [Review of the book Identity crisis: The 2016 presidential campaign and the battle for the meaning of America, by J. Sides, M. Vester & L. Vavreck]. *New York Journal of Books*. Retrieved from https://www.nyjournalofbooks.com/book-review/identity-crisis

Malice, M. (2019). *The new right: A journey to the fringe of American politics*. New York, NY: All Points Books.

McCaskill, N. D. (2016, February 2). Trump urges crowd to 'knock the crap out of' of anyone with tomatoes. *Politico*. Retrieved from https://www.politico.com/blogs/iowa-caucus-2016-live-updates/2016/02/donald-trump-iowa-rally-tomatoes-218546

Morin, R., & Cohen, D. (2018, August 19). Giuliani: 'Truth isn't truth.' *Politico*. Retrieved from https://www.politico.com/story/2018/08/19/giuliani-truth-todd-trump-788161

Nelson, L. (2016, July 11). Trump: 'I am the law and order candidate'. *Politico*. Retrieved from https://www.politico.com/story/2016/07/trump-law-order-candidate-225372

New leak claims Trump scrapped Iran nuclear deal 'to spite Obama.' (2019, July 14). *BBC News*. Retrieved from https://www.bbc.com/news/uk-48978484

Obeidallah, D. (2020, January 20). Former GOP Strategist Rick Wilson: "F**king hating" Trump is the key to winning in 2020. *Salon*. Retrieved from https://www.salon.com/2020/01/16/rick-wilson/

Palma, B. (2019, June 20). Did Trump Campaign offer actors $50 to cheer him at Prez announcement. Retrieved from https://www.snopes.com/fact-check/trump-campaign-actors-announcement/

Petillo, J. (Producer). (2004–2015). *The apprentice* [Television series]. New York, NY: NBC.
Re, G. (2020, January 9). Trump, at Ohio rally, says Democrats would have leaked Soleimani plans. *Fox News*. Retrieved from https://www.foxnews.com/politics/trump-toledo-ohio-rally-iran-impeachment
Riefenstahl, L. (Producer), & Riefenstahl, L. (Director). (1935). *Triumph of the will* [Motion picture]. Germany: Bavaria Film.
Robinson, E. (2019, August 20). Trump's Obama envy getting worse. *Salt Lake Tribune*. Retrieved from https://www.sltrib.com/opinion/commentary/2019/08/27/eugene-robinson-trumps/
Scott, B., Young, A., & Young, M. (1976). Big balls [Recorded by AC/DC]. On *Dirty deeds done dirt cheap* [CD]. New York, NY: Atlantic Records.
Scott, E, (2019, December 18). Comparing Trump to Jesus, and why some evangelicals believe Trump is God's chosen one. *The Washington Post*. Retrieved from https://www.washingtonpost.com/politics/2019/11/25/why-evangelicals-like-rick-perry-believe-that-trump-is-gods-chosen-one/
Sides, J., Tesler, M., & Vavreck, L. (2018). *Identity crisis: The 2016 presidential campaign and the battle for the meaning of America*. Princeton, NJ: Princeton University Presss.
'Spies and treason': Read a transcript of Trump's remarks related to the whistleblower. (2019, September 16). *The New York Times*. Retrieved from https://www.nytimes.com/2019/09/26/us/politics/trump-treason-spies-whistle-blower.html
Stevenson, B. (2014). *Just mercy: A story of justice and redemption*. New York, NY: Spiegel & Grau.
Transcript: Donald Trump's taped comments about women. (2016, October 8). *New York Times* Retrieved from https://www.nytimes.com/2016/10/08/us/donald-trump-tape-transcript.html
Trump announces White House bid, joins crowded GOP field. (2016, June 16). *Fox News*. Retrieved from https://www.foxnews.com/politics/trump-announces-white-house-bid-joins-crowded-gop-field
Trump, D. J. [@RealDonaldTrump]. (2012, November 11). When someone attacks me [Tweet]. Retrieved from https://twitter.com/realdonaldtrump/status/267626951097868289
Trump, D. J. (2016, July 19). *Donald J. Trump Republican Nomination acceptance speech*. Retrieved from https://assets.donaldjtrump.com/DJT_Acceptance_Speech.pdf
Trump, D. J. [@RealDonaldTrump]. (2018, January 2). *North Korean leader Kim Jong Un just stated that 'The nuclear button is always on my desk'* [Tweet]. Retrieved from https://twitter.com/realdonaldtrump/status/948355557022420992?lang=en
Trump, D. J. [@RealDonaldTrump] 2019, December 10). *To impeach a President who has proven through results* [Tweet]. Retrieved from https://twitter.com/realdonaldtrump/status/1204379706235203586?lang=en
Trump, D. J. [@RealDonaldTrump]. (2019, December 28). *So sad to see that New York City and State are falling apart* [Tweet]. Retrieved from https://twitter.com/realdonaldtrump/status/1211032731012018182?lang=en
Trump inaugural address. (2017, January 20). *Whitehouse.gov*. Retrieved from https://www.whitehouse.gov/briefings-statements/the-inaugural-address/
Trump supporter attacks BBC cameraman at rally. (2019, February 12). *BBC*. Retrieved from https://www.bbc.com/news/world-us-canada-47208909
Wehner, P. (2019, November 25). Are Trumps critics demonically possessed? *The Atlantic*. Retrieved from https://www.theatlantic.com/ideas/archive/2019/11/to-trumps-evangelicals-everyone-else-is-a-sinner/602569/

Whitman, W. (1892). *Song of myself*. Retrieved from https://www.poetryfoundation.org/poems/45477/song-of-myself-1892-version

Wilson, R. (2020). *Running against the devil: A plot to save America from Trump – and Democrats from themselves*. New York, NY: Crown Forum.

Wolfe, T. (1987). *The bonfire of the vanities*. New York, NY: Farrar, Straus & Giroux.

Zhang, S. (2019, January 13). Unthinkable: Trump's most trusted advisor is his own gut. *The Atlantic*. Retrieved from https://www.theatlantic.com/politics/archive/2019/01/trump-follows-his-gut/580084/

CHRISTINE SALKIN DAVIS AND JONATHAN L. CRANE

DISCUSSION QUESTIONS

1. To what extent is Trump responsible for:
   a) Acts of violence perpetrated by his followers?
   b) The increase in racial and hate crimes since his election?
   c) The fear Black people, people of color, and people from marginalized groups have?
   d) Why/how?
2. To what extent are his supporters responsible for:
   a) The racist and hateful language by Trump?
   b) Trump's seeming support of white supremacists?
   c) The racial and hate crimes/rhetoric by other Trump supporters?
   d) The fear Black people, people of color, and marginalized groups have?
   e) This administration's policies that harm Black people, people of color, LGBTIQ people, refugees, etc.?
3. To what extent are we all, as Americans, responsible for:
   a) Systemic racism?
   b) Acts of violence, racial and hate crimes, racial/hate rhetoric in the U.S.?
   c) This administration's policies that harm Black people, people of color, LGBTIQ people, refugees, etc.?
4. In what ways, if any, has the election of Donald Trump affected relationships among your family and friends? How does, as so many of our authors maintain, the political become the personal and vice versa?
5. The tone of many of the interviews and accounts contained in this collection are deeply negative and troubling. At the same time, the accounts and descriptions of Trump voters are much more positive about the consequences of the election. On balance, which of these bipolar accounts best captures our collective experience of life in the Trump era?
6. All our respondents agree that it has become exceedingly difficult to hold a calm, collected conversation with people who vote differently than ourselves. As a matter of interpersonal communication, how do we talk through our divisive political identities?

DOI:10.1163/9789004436329_026

7. How do our identities shape our political commitments?
8. How do our political commitments shape our identities?
9. Many of the authors and interviewees maintain that the election of Trump was a response to the two-term tenure of President Barack Obama. Do you feel that is the case? And, if the policies and communication style of a President influence who the voters pick as a successor, what sort of politician is likely to follow Trump in 2020 or 2024?
10. How should leaders communicate with the people in the age of social media?
11. Should Presidents tweet? If yes, how should Presidents best employ Twitter?
12. This volume presents all sorts of competing visions for a better democracy. What are the policy aims and ambitions best suited for a more equitable Union?

NOTES ON CONTRIBUTORS

Naved Bakali is an Assistant Professor of Education at the American University in Dubai. Naved also serves as a non-resident Research Fellow with Trends Research and Advisory; he is a Senior Fellow at Yaqeen Institute for Islamic Research; and a Research Affiliate with the Canadian Network for Research on Terrorism, Security and Society. He has published extensively in the fields of Islamophobia Studies, critical approaches to countering violent extremism, and Muslim youth identity in the post 9/11 context. He is the author of *Islamophobia: Understanding Anti-Muslim Racism through the Lived Experiences of Muslim Youth*, published by Sense.

Amy Burt is an Associate Professor of Rhetoric in the Department of Communication at Georgia College in Milledgeville. Her research interests involve community-based performance, narrative, faith, and identity. She has directed, acted, and sang in a variety of venues throughout middle Georgia. Her writings can be found in *Text and Performance Quarterly, Liminalities,* and *Women in Language.* She was honored to be awarded the Southern States Communication Association Performance Studies Scholar of the Year in 2016.

Jonathan L. Crane, PhD (1991), University of Illinois, Urbana-Champaign, is Associate Professor of Communication Studies at UNC Charlotte. He studies culture, media and communication and is co-author of *End of Life Communication: Stories from the Dead Zone* (Routledge, 2019).

Kimberly Dark is a writer, professor and raconteur, working to reveal the hidden architecture of everyday life so that we can reclaim our power as social creators. She's the author of *Fat, Pretty and Soon to be Old* (AK Press, 2019), *The Daddies* (Brill | Sense, 2018) and *Love and Errors* (Puna Press, 2018). Her essays, stories and poetry are widely published in academic and popular online publications alike. Dark teaches Sociology at Cal State San Marcos and Writing/Arts at Cal State Summer Arts.

Christine Salkin Davis, PhD (University of South Florida, 2005), is Professor in the Communication Studies Department at the University of North Carolina at Charlotte. She studies end of life communication in the contexts of family, culture, and power. She is author of *Death: The Beginning of a Relationship* (Hampton Press, 2010) and co-author of *Talking through Death: Communicating about Death in Interpersonal, Mediated, and Cultural Contexts* (Routledge, 2018); and *End of Life Communication: Stories from the Dead Zone* (Routledge, 2019).

Ana X. de la Serna is Assistant Professor at Cal State Dominguez Hills. Ana obtained her PhD in Communication from the University of Kentucky and her Master's degree from Tec de Monterrey in Mexico City. Prior to her doctoral studies, Ana worked as a photojournalist and in media relations. Ana's research interests are in intercultural communication and health contexts. In this particular case, she presents the experience of international graduate students as they navigate the transition to the Trump presidency. This experience came with very specific challenges and uncertainty.

Jennifer L. Erdely, PhD, is an Associate Professor of Communication in the Brailsford College of Arts and Sciences and Prairie View A&M University where she teaches classes in performance studies, ethnography, activism, and documentary criticism and methods. She has a PhD in Communication Studies from Louisiana State University. As a scholar who employs qualitative methods, Dr. Erdely centers the individual, their body, and their stories as the basis of her work. Lived experiences serve as a framework for understanding phenomena of the human experience. Specifically, her published research has employed ethnographic and autoethnographic methods. Through a method of ethnographic touring, she has explored storytelling, fandom, trauma, altruism, and pilgrimage. Her upcoming project utilizes performance, ethnographic, and autoethnographic inquiry to explore narratives of chronic pain, empathy, and decision-making.

Diane Forbes Berthoud (PhD, Howard University) is an Assistant Vice Chancellor at the University of California, San Diego, affiliate faculty of George Washington University, and faculty emeritus for the RISE Urban Leadership Institute in California. Diane's research focuses on gendered, raced, and intersectional processes of organizing, with particular attention to the experiences of Black women and other women of color. She has presented her work at national and international conferences and published in academic journals such as *Management Communication Quarterly and the Journal of International and Intercultural Communication.* Her most recent work appears in the International Leadership Association book series,

Women and Leadership: Research, Theory, and Practice, and *Race, Work, & Leadership: New Perspectives on the Black Experience* (2019), published by Harvard University Press.

Stacy Holman Jones is a Professor in the Centre for Theatre and Performance. Her research focuses broadly on performance as a socially, culturally, and politically resistive and transformative activity. Over the course of a 20-year career, she has developed an international reputation for leading the development of performance, feminist and cultural studies research, gender and sexualities studies and innovative and critical arts-based methodologies. Her performance-based and narrative research spans cultural critique and social inclusion, education and resilience building, and enhancing health and well-being among minoritarian cultures and communities. She is recognized for a collaborative and impact-focused research program that integrates theory and creative practice as a means of critique and transforming lives, relationships, ways of living, and communities.

Billy Huff is a lecturer in the Department of Communication at University of Illinois Urbana-Champaign. He is also a researcher with the Unit for Institutional Change and Social Justice at the University of the Free State in Bloemfontein South Africa.

Sonia R. Ivancic is an Assistant Professor at the University of South Florida. She specializes in Organizational and Health Communication and explores the politics and possibilities of creating social change. Dr. Ivancic asks questions about how we organize around embodied difference and analyzes discourses about work, identity, health, food, and the body.

Robyn R. Jardine is a licensed marriage and family therapist supervisor, licensed professional counselor, AAMFT Approved Supervisor, and owns Life Solutions Counseling and Family Therapy. As a social justice therapist, her scholarship focuses on approaches for dismantling oppressive social systems/structures, and illuminating the intersectionality of race, gender, sexuality, and social equality. Her current work is focused on the generational impact of white supremacy and the responsibility of white/Caucasian Americans using their privilege to systemically change and create equitable living systems. She has applied these concepts in a variety of clinical and higher education settings regarding race relationships, inclusion/diversity, student success/

retention for marginalized and underrepresented students, effective parenting practices, family/intimate partner violence, and Safe Conversations.

Eun Young Lee (Bowling Green State University, PhD) is Assistant Professor in the Department of Communication at Central Washington University. Her scholarship lies in intersections between Critical Intercultural Communication and Rhetorical Studies. Her research interests include the rhetoricity of place and space, representations of culture on mass media and in popular culture, postcolonialism, and politics in globalization. Currently, she is working on immigration discourses and media representations of (im) migrants primarily focusing on the US contexts.

Hadia Mubarak iis an Assistant Professor of Religion at Queens University of Charlotte. She previously taught Religious Studies at Guilford College, Davidson College and UNCC. As a former fellow at the Research Institute in the Humanities (2017–2018) at New York University Abu Dhabi (NYUAD), she wrote her forthcoming book with Oxford University Press on women and gender in modern Qur'anic commentaries. Mubarak completed her PhD in Islamic Studies from Georgetown University, where she specialized in modern and classical Qur'anic exegesis, modern Islamic movements, and gender reform in the modern Muslim world. Mubarak lives with her husband and two children in Charlotte, NC.

Kristen E. Okamoto is an Assistant Professor of Health Communication at Clemson University in the Department of Communication. She specializes in the use of ethnographic methods to understand the role of cultural discourses in shaping the ways we think about, and react to, the vulnerable body. Okamoto's prior work has examined diverse sites of engagement including food auctions, running groups, and group fitness classes. Adopting a narrative approach, Dr. Okamoto is interested in asking how and in under what conditions counter-narratives can serve to reimagine or articulate alternative possibilities.

Bethany Simmons is a licensed marriage and family therapist, licensed professional counselor, AAMFT Approved Supervisor, an Associate Professor, Program Director and former Director of Clinical Training at California Lutheran University's M.S. Counseling Psychology-MFT Program. Her current scholarship applies systemic/cybernetic theory to training and supervision, as well as broader social/political/cultural contexts to understand and address issues around social responsibility, power, privilege, cultural diversity and mental health practices, particularly with oppressed, marginalized and vulnerable populations. Her clinical work spans diverse settings working with underserved and marginalized populations including adult and juvenile inpatient psychiatric hospitals, intensive outpatient programs and private practice.

Jillian A. Tullis, PhD, is Associate Professor in the Department of Communication Studies at the University of San Diego. Her teaching and research interests focus on health communication, specifically communication about dying and death in and outside of healthcare settings. Tullis' scholarship uses qualitative methods to study such topics as hospice team communication, tumor boards, spirituality, dying, death, quality of life, and a "good death." Jillian has a well-loved Velcro dog at home named Rouxbee who is a constant source of much needed levity.

INDEX